Bless the Lord, O My Soul

365 DEVOTIONS *for* PRAYER *&* WORSHIP

Our Daily Bread

Our Daily Bread Publishing™

Bless the Lord, O My Soul: 365 Devotions for Prayer and Worship
© 2020 by Our Daily Bread Ministries

Requests for permission to quote from this book should be directed to: Permissions
Department, Our Daily Bread Publishing, PO Box 3566, Grand Rapids, MI 49501, or
contact us by email at permissionsdept@odb.org.

Scripture quotations, unless otherwise indicated, are taken from the Holy Bible, New
International Version®, NIV®. Copyright © 1973, 1978, 1984, 2011 by Biblica, Inc.™
Used by permission of Zondervan. All rights reserved worldwide. www.zondervan.com.

Scripture quotations marked ESV are from The Holy Bible, English Standard Version®
(ESV®), copyright © 2001 by Crossway, a publishing ministry of Good News Publishers.
Used by permission. All rights reserved.

Scripture quotations marked KJV are from the King James Version.

Scripture quotations marked NKJV are from the New King James Version.® Copyright
© 1982 by Thomas Nelson. Used by permission. All rights reserved.

Scripture quotations marked NLT are taken from the Holy Bible, New Living Translation,
copyright ©1996, 2004, 2015 by Tyndale House Foundation. Used by permission of Tyndale
House Publishers, Inc., Carol Stream, Illinois 60188. All rights reserved.

Cover design: Michelle Lenger
Interior design: Hillspring Books, Inc., Jessica Ess

ISBN: 978-1-64070-031-4

Printed in China

21 22 23 24 25 26 27 / 8 7 6 5 4 3 2

Introduction

"Heads up" is a funny little term when you think about it. If you are at sports event and someone yells, "Heads up!" that could be a problem. Perhaps an errant ball is coming your way, and the best thing for you to do is to duck and cover, not look up and risk getting smacked in the face.

But if we understand that the term is not to be taken literally but that it means to be alert, it makes sense to be "heads up" about things. To be aware of what is going on around us and to be engaged in our situation.

Can we say as well that it's important to be "heads up" about matters of faith? In other words, should we be alert and active mentally and spiritually? Of course we should, and what is the best way to do that? Well, by looking up.

If we are truly "heads up" about our relationship with God, we will engage in God-directed activities such as praying to our Father, who is "up" in heaven. We will lift our hearts up to God and worship Him. We will raise our praises to God in honor of His greatness and His great gift of salvation to us through Jesus.

Our complicated world seems intent on putting roadblocks in the way of our dedication to our faith. If we begin to listen to the many voices around us that distract us from godliness and our day-to-day relationship with the Lord, we will find ourselves mired in a worldview that will keep us from looking to Jesus—from looking up, as it were.

That's one reason this new volume of devotionals from Our Daily Bread Publishing can be so vital. It can help us to lift our eyes above this world—to be "heads up" in our daily walk. Imagine the joy of continually *praying* (1 Thessalonians 15:17) and of living in a way that keeps us *worshiping* God (Psalm 96:9).

We hope the selections in this book, gleaned from both the classic *Our Daily Bread* writers of days past (Henry Bosch, Herb Vander Lugt, Paul Van Gorder, Richard DeHaan, and others) and from the writers of today (James Banks, Anne Cetas, Bill Crowder, Xochitl Dixon, and others) will lift your hearts—will help you keep "heads up"—as you daily find ways to say, "Bless the Lord, O my soul."

Dave Branon
Compiler

New Year, New Priorities

Read Ecclesiastes 9:4–12

Whatever your hand finds to do, do it with all your might.
Ecclesiastes 9:10

I've always wanted to learn how to play the cello. But I've never found the time to enroll in a class. Or, perhaps more accurately, I haven't made the time for it. I had thought that in heaven I could probably master that instrument anyway. In the meantime, I wanted to focus on using my time in the particular ways God has called me to serve Him now.

Life is short, and we often feel the pressure to make the most of our time on Earth before it slips away. But what does that really mean?

As King Solomon contemplated the meaning of life, he offered two recommendations. First, we're to live in the most meaningful way we can, which includes fully enjoying the good things God allows us to experience in life, such as food and drink (Ecclesiastes 9:7), clothing and perfume (v. 8 nlt), marriage (v. 9), and all of God's good gifts, which might include learning how to play the cello!

His second recommendation was diligent work (v. 10). Life is full of opportunities, and there is always more work to be done. We're to take advantage of the opportunities God gives us, seeking His wisdom on how to prioritize work and play in a way that uses our gifting to serve Him.

Life is a wonderful gift from the Lord. We honor Him when we take pleasure both in His daily blessings and in meaningful service.

Poh Fang Chia

We can both enjoy God's blessings and be a blessing to others.

From Nothing

Read Genesis 1:1–13

In the beginning God created the heavens and the earth. *Genesis 1:1*

Nothing. Absolutely nothing. No light. No sky. No land. It's incomprehensible to our finite thinking—the barren nothingness that existed before Genesis 1:1.

Then suddenly, through the work of the Almighty, God supplanted nothingness with "the heavens and the earth." The divine hand reached through the void and produced a place, a world, a universe. Through the magnificent convergence of the workings of the Godhead—with the Son enacting the will of the Father as the Agent of creation, and the Holy Spirit as the hovering Presence—nothing became something. History began its long march toward today.

The first verse of Genesis provides us with sufficient concepts to contemplate for a lifetime. That introductory statement speaks of enough glory, enough majesty, enough awe to leave us speechless before God. Just as today we would have no life, no breath, no existence without His sustaining action, neither would we have the cosmos without His mighty act at the moment of creation.

In awe we wonder what went on before "the beginning." With breathless praise we marvel at the words "God created the heavens and the earth." We read—and we stand in adoration. "Nothing" has never been so fascinating!

Dave Branon

Nature is but a name for an effect whose cause is God.

Why Pray?

Read Nehemiah 1:4–11; 2:1–8

Jesus told his disciples a parable to show them
that they should always pray and not give up. *Luke 18:1*

A new Christian asked me why the Bible places so much emphasis on prayer. He said that if God knows our feelings and needs, why does He want us to express our gratitude and make requests?

In answering this question, let's begin by recognizing the fact that God does place great value on prayer. The Bible repeatedly exhorts us to seek the Lord's face in supplication and intercession. You see, God is our heavenly Father, and He takes delight in our coming to Him just as parents rejoice when their children feel free to talk to them. Then too, we read that Jesus and His disciples prayed often. In the Old Testament, Nehemiah called upon God at stated times.

The Scriptures teach us that God is honored when His people pray. Since He knew all about our petitions before time began, He worked them into the fabric of the universe just as He did when He foresaw our sins and mistakes and overruled them for our good. I've never stopped my car on a railroad track in front of a speeding train just because I figured I wouldn't die until my time. But that would be about as sensible as saying, "I won't pray because what's to be will be."

As we make prayer an important part of our lives, we'll see the Lord work, and we'll never again ask the question, "Why pray?"

Herb Vander Lugt

Prayer does not change God's purpose, it releases it.

Eating as Worship

Read Genesis 2:8–17

If you find honey, eat just enough. *Proverbs 25:16*

When you walk into the bookstore and see a table filled with books on dieting, you know it must be January. After several weeks of overeating all kinds of holiday foods, people in many cultures turn their attention to not eating.

Food plays an important role in Scripture. God uses it not only to bless us but also to teach us. Our misuse of food keeps us from knowing God in ways He wants to be known.

In the Old Testament, God gave instructions to Adam as to what to eat and what not to eat (Genesis 2:16–17). Later He gave the Israelites manna to convince them that He was God and to test them to find out if they believed Him (Exodus 16:12; Deuteronomy 8:16). In the New Testament, the apostle Paul stated the proper attitude for everything we do, including eating: "Whether you eat or drink, . . . do it all for the glory of God" (1 Corinthians 10:31).

When we think of food as a friend that comforts us or an enemy that makes us fat, we miss the wonder of receiving with gratitude a splendid gift from God. Obsessive eating or not eating indicates that we are focused on the gift rather than on the Giver, which is a form of idolatry.

When eating becomes a true act of worship, we will no longer worship food.

Julie Ackerman Link

When food becomes our god,
our appetite for the Bread of Life is diminished.

Just Like My Father

Read 1 Peter 5:8–12

It is written: "Be holy, because I am holy." *1 Peter 1:16*

My father's dusty, heeled-over, cowboy boots rest on the floor of my study, daily reminders of the kind of man he was.

Among other things, he raised and trained cutting horses—equine athletes that move like quicksilver. I loved to watch him at work, marveling that he could stay astride.

As a boy, growing up, I wanted to be just like him. I'm in my eighties, and his boots are still too large for me to fill.

My father's in heaven now, but I have another Father to emulate. I want to be just like Him—filled with His goodness, fragrant with His love. I'm not there and never will be in this life; His boots are much too large for me to fill.

But the apostle Peter said this: "The God of all grace, who called you to his eternal glory in Christ . . . will himself restore you and make you strong, firm and steadfast" (1 Peter 5:10). He has the wisdom and power to do that, you know (v. 11).

Our lack of likeness to our heavenly Father will not last forever. God has called us to share the beauty of character that is His. In this life we reflect Him poorly, but in heaven our sin and sorrow will be no more and we'll reflect Him more fully! This is the "true grace of God" (v. 12).

David Roper

Through the cross, believers are made perfect in His sight.

Who Gets the Thanks?

Read 1 Chronicles 29:1–20

Everything comes from you. *1 Chronicles 29:14*

According to *USA Today*, a Costa Mesa, California, resident found on her doorstep a package that contained a car key and a note. The note quoted Bible verses and ended with the words, "This is a gift for you because I love you." It was signed, "An angel of the Lord." In her driveway the woman found a newer model Ford. It was just what she needed to replace her unreliable, twenty-year-old car. A neighbor child asked, "Did God just drop the car down from heaven?" The woman's answer was not reported, but she did hang a poster on her garage that said, "THANK YOU, GOD." Putting up that sign didn't mean the woman actually thought the car had fallen out of the sky without touching human hands. But notice that her sign did not say, "THANK YOU, MY ANONYMOUS FRIEND." She was acknowledging that all things ultimately come from God.

David recognized this truth as he and his people celebrated the enormous offering that had been given for the construction of the temple. They could have merely congratulated one another. They could have slapped one another on the back and exchanged mutual praise for the other's generosity. But they didn't. David showed his wisdom and maturity as Israel's leader by thanking the Lord for all blessings.

He recognized that every time a gift comes from human hands, it's the Lord who deserves the praise.

Mart DeHaan

Don't let the abundance of God's gifts cause you to forget the Giver.

A Forever Service

Read Revelation 22:1–7

He who was seated on the throne said, "I am making
everything new! Then he said, "Write this down,
for these words are trustworthy and true." *Revelation 21:5*

Two young brothers sat on the front row in church every Sunday, observing their dad as he led the worship service. One night after sending the boys to bed, the dad overheard one of his boys crying. He asked him what was wrong, but the boy was hesitant to answer. Finally, he confessed, "Daddy, the Bible says we're going to worship God in heaven forever. That's an awfully long time!" Because he pictured heaven as one long worship time with his dad up front leading, heaven sounded pretty boring to him!

While I sometimes wish we had more information about what heaven will be like, we know this for sure: *boring* can't possibly be the right word to describe it. We will see beauty like we've never seen before, including "a pure "river of the water of life, as clear as crystal" (Revelation 22:1). We will experience "the glory of God," which will illuminate heaven (21:23; 22:5). And we will enjoy a life without pain or sorrow (21:4).

Yes, we will definitely worship in heaven. People "from every tribe and language and people and nation" (5:9) will rejoice in praising Jesus, the worthy Lamb who died for us and rose again (5:12).

We will bask in the glory of the Lord's presence—forever. But not for one second will we be bored!

Anne Cetas

The pleasures of earth cannot be compared to the joys of heaven.

Gates of Worship

Read Psalm 100

Sing to the LORD a new song. *Psalm 98:1*

When you enter some of the greatest cities in the world, you can encounter famous gates such as the Brandenburg Gate (Berlin), the Jaffa Gate (Jerusalem), and the gates at Downing Street (London). Whether the gates were built for defensive or ceremonial purposes, they all represent the difference between being outside or inside certain areas of the city. Some are open; some are closed to all but a few.

The gates into the presence of God are always open. The familiar song of Psalm 100 is an invitation for the Israelites to enter into the presence of God through the temple gates. They were told to "shout for joy" and "come before him with joyful songs" (vv. 1–2). Shouting for joy was an appropriate expression when greeting a monarch in the ancient world. All the earth was to sing joyfully about God! The reason for this joyful noise was that God had given them their identity (v. 3). They entered the gates with praise and thanksgiving because of God's goodness and His steadfast and enduring love which continues through all generations (vv. 4–5). Even when they forgot their identity and wandered away from Him, God remained faithful and still invited them to enter His presence.

The gates into God's presence are still open, inviting us to come and worship.

Marvin Williams

The gates into the presence of God are always open.

Worthy of Our Praise

Read Hebrews 1:1–10

For in [Christ] all things were created. *Colossians 1:16*

When we fully grasp the truth of Colossians 1:16, what gratitude wells up in our hearts! What praise should flow from our lips! Jesus Christ is the Creator and Sustainer of the universe, and all good gifts come through Him. That is the clear testimony of Scripture.

Composer Joseph Haydn was present at the Vienna Music Hall where his oratorio *The Creation* was being performed. Weakened by age, the great composer sat in a wheelchair. As the majestic work moved along, the audience was caught up with tremendous emotion. When the passage "And there was light!" was reached, the chorus and orchestra burst forth in such power that the crowd could no longer restrain their enthusiasm. The grandeur of the music and the presence of the composer himself brought that vast assembly to its feet in spontaneous applause. Haydn struggled to get out of his wheelchair. Finally up, he motioned for silence. The enraptured crowd heard him call out with what strength he could muster, hand pointed toward heaven, "No, no, not from me, but from thence comes all!" Having given the glory and praise to the Creator, he fell back into his chair exhausted.

In a sacrilegious society marked by ingratitude, little recognition is given to Jesus as the One who sustains "all things by his powerful word" (Hebrews 1:3). We who are saved by His sacrifice for us, though, realize His greatness.

Let's praise Him. He is worthy!

Paul Van Gorder

The humble Carpenter of Nazareth
was also the mighty Architect of the universe.

A Hidden Ministry

Read 2 Corinthians 1:8–11

On him we have set our hope that he will continue to deliver us, as you help us by your prayers. *2 Corinthians 1:10–11*

A big academic project was weighing on me, and I was fretting over whether I could complete it by the deadline. In the midst of my anxious thoughts, I received three notes of encouragement from friends who were cheering me on. Each one said, "God brought you to mind today when I was praying." I felt humbled and encouraged that these friends would contact me without knowing what I was going through, and I believed God had used them as His messengers of love.

The apostle Paul knew the power of prayer when he wrote to the people in the church of Corinth. He said he trusted that God would continue to deliver them from peril "as you help us by your prayers" (2 Corinthians 1:10–11). And when God answered their prayers, He would be glorified as the people gave Him thanks for the "answer to the prayers of many" (v. 11).

My friends and Paul's supporters were engaging in the ministry of intercession, which Oswald Chambers calls "a hidden ministry that brings forth fruit through which the Father is glorified." As we focus our minds and hearts on Jesus, we find Him shaping us, including how we pray. He enables us to give the gift of true intercession to friends, family members, and even strangers.

Has God put someone on your heart and mind for whom you can pray?

Amy Boucher Pye

God hears the prayers of His people.

Worship Only God

Read Deuteronomy 5:1–7

You shall have no other gods before me. *Exodus 20:3*

British statesman W. E. Gladstone (1809–98) visited Christ Church College and spoke optimistically about the betterment of English society during his lifetime. His outlook was so positive that a student challenged him: "Sir, are there no adverse signs?" Gladstone reflected, "Yes, there is one thing that frightens me— the fear that God seems to be dying out of the minds of men."

Obeying the first commandment would prevent this from happening. Yet man attempts to make gods out of money, material possessions, pleasure, knowledge, people, and in so doing forgets the true God. But no created thing can ever fill the place in our heart God intends for himself.

A child was asked, "How many gods are there?" "Only one," he replied. "How do you know?" "Because," he said, "God fills heaven and earth, so there's room for only one."

Our worship of God becomes focused when we receive Jesus as our personal Savior, for He is God in the flesh (John 1:14). But why does God command us to love and worship Him alone? Because in Him we live and move and have our being (Acts 17:28), and from Him we receive eternal life (Colossians 1:13–18). He has every right to say, "No other gods!" because He alone is the living and true God, who created us and redeemed us.

Dennis DeHaan

Only God who fills the universe can fill the human heart.

From Wailing to Worship

Read Psalm 30

You turned my wailing into dancing; you removed my sackcloth and clothed me with joy. Psalm 30:11

Kim began battling breast cancer in 2013. Four days after her treatment ended, doctors diagnosed her with a progressive lung disease and gave her three to five years to live. She grieved, sobbing prayers as she processed her emotions before God. By the time I met Kim in 2015, she had surrendered her situation to Him and radiated contagious joy and peace. Though some days are still hard, God continues to transform her heart-wrenching suffering into a beautiful testimony of hope-filled praise as she encourages others.

Even when we're in dire circumstances, God can turn our wailing into dancing. Though His healing won't always look or feel like we'd hoped or expected, we can be confident in God's ways (Psalm 30:1–3). No matter how tear-stained our path may be, we have countless reasons to praise Him (v. 4). We can rejoice in God, as He secures our confident faith (vv. 5–7). We can cry out for His mercy (vv. 8–10), celebrating the hope He's brought to many weeping worshipers. Only God can transform wails of despair into vibrant joy that doesn't depend on circumstances (vv. 11–12).

As our merciful God comforts us in our sorrow, He envelops us in peace and empowers us to extend compassion toward others and ourselves. Our loving and faithful Lord can and does turn our wailing into worship that can lead to heart-deep trust, praise, and maybe even joyful dancing.

Xochitl Dixon

True worship of Christ changes admiration into adoration.

Thank You, Father

Read Philippians 4

We always thank God, the Father of our Lord Jesus Christ,
when we pray for you. *Colossians 1:3*

To have a grateful heart in every circumstance is not easy, for life
is filled with reverses, hardships, and perplexities. Yet no situation
is hopeless as long as we trust in God; whatever happens to us has
been screened through His wise providence; no hardship is totally
without some blessing.

I read about a saintly old preacher whose pastoral prayer was a
source of great inspiration to the members of his congregation. Sunday after Sunday he would begin his supplication with praise and
thanksgiving to God. Downhearted worshipers were often lifted
by his positive spirit. One Lord's Day, however, it seemed as if there
was nothing that anyone could be happy about. The weather was
cold and damp, only a handful of parishioners came to the service,
and gloom pervaded the atmosphere. The few who did show up that
morning wondered, what can the pastor be grateful for on a day
like this? At the beginning of the service the minister stood up and
folded his hands in his usual manner. Then he began, "Thank You,
Father, that every Lord's Day morning is not like this one!"

Even when our hearts are tossed about on the dark sea of pain
and sorrow, God is still there. If we place our lives in His hand, we
know that He will not forsake us. In everything He wants to hear us
say, "Thank you, Father!"

Dennis DeHaan

If you can't be grateful for what you receive,
be grateful for what you escape.

No Blankets for Betty

Read Psalm 150

I will extol the LORD at all times;
his praise will always be on my lips. *Psalm 34:1*

A Scottish minister of another era preached in a rather straight-forward way. In his congregation was a woman who was warm-hearted and full of love for the Savior. She couldn't help but say out loud, "Praise the Lord," and "Amen," when anything particularly helpful was said by her pastor. This bothered the minister because of his stoic personality.

The minister stopped by one winter's day to see her. "Betty," he said, "I'll make a bargain with you. When you call out 'Praise the Lord' just when I get to the best part of my sermon, it upsets my thoughts, so if you will stop doing that all this next year, I'll give you a woolen blanket!" Betty said she could use the blanket, so she promised to give it a try. She did her best to earn the blankets, and Sunday after Sunday she kept quiet.

One Lord's Day another preacher delivered the sermon—a man bubbling over with the zeal of the Lord. As he preached on forgive-ness of sin, Betty's vision of the blankets began to fade, while the joys of her salvation grew brighter. At last the enraptured woman could stand it no longer. Jumping up she cried, "Blanket or no blan-ket, HALLELUJAH!"

Are you so joyful in Jesus, so confident of what He has done for you that you are full of praise and joy to the point of "running over"?

Henry Bosch

The secret of perpetual revival is the constant offering
of thanksgiving in every circumstance.

Love of Another Kind

Read John 15:9–17

My command is this: Love each other as I have loved you. *John 15:12*

One of my favorite churches started several years ago as a ministry to ex-prisoners who were transitioning back into society. Now the church flourishes with people from all walks of life. I love that church because it reminds me of what I picture heaven will be like—filled with different kinds of people, all redeemed sinners, all bound together by the love of Jesus.

Sometimes, though, I wonder if church seems more like an exclusive club than a safe haven for forgiven sinners. As people naturally gravitate into groups of "a certain kind" and cluster around those they feel comfortable with, it leaves others feeling marginalized. But that's not what Jesus had in mind when He told His disciples to "love each other as I have loved you" (John 15:12). His church was to be an extension of His love mutually shared with all.

If hurting, rejected people can find loving refuge, comfort, and forgiveness in Jesus, they should expect no less from the church. So let's exhibit the love of Jesus to everyone we encounter—especially those who are not like us. All around us are people Jesus wants to love through us. What a joy it is when people unite to worship together in love—a slice of heaven we can enjoy here on earth!

Joe Stowell

Share Christ's love with another.

"If You Are Willing"

Read Matthew 8:1–4

A man with leprosy came and knelt before him and said,
"Lord, if you are willing, you can make me clean." *Matthew 8:2*

Molly wanted her dad's help, but she was afraid to ask. She knew that when he was working on his computer, he didn't want to be interrupted. *He might get upset at me,* she thought, so she didn't ask him.

We need not have such fears when we come to Jesus. In Matthew 8:1–4, we read about a leper who didn't hesitate to interrupt Jesus with his needs. His disease made him desperate—he had been ostracized from society and was in emotional distress. Jesus was busy with "great multitudes," but the leper made his way through the crowd to talk with Jesus.

Matthew's gospel says that the leper came and "knelt before him" (v. 2). He approached Jesus in worship, with trust in His power, and with humility, acknowledging that the choice to help belonged to Jesus. He said, "Lord, if you are willing, you can make me clean" (v. 2). In compassion, Jesus touched him (leprosy had made him "untouchable" by the standards of Jewish law), and he was cleansed immediately.

Like the leper, we don't need to hesitate to approach Jesus with our desire for His help. As we go to Him in humility and worship, we can trust that He will make the best choices for us.

Anne Cetas

Let us therefore come boldly to the throne of grace,
that we may obtain mercy. —Hebrews 4:16 (nkjv)

Praying Like Jesus

Read Luke 22:39-44

*Father, if you are willing, take this cup from me;
yet not my will, but yours be done. Luke 22:42*

Every coin has two sides. The front is called "heads" and, from early Roman times, usually depicts a country's head of state. The back is called "tails," a term possibly originating from the British ten pence depicting the raised tail of a heraldic lion.

Like a coin, Christ's prayer in the garden of Gethsemane possesses two sides. In the deepest hours of His life, on the night before He died on a cross, Jesus prayed, "Father, if you are willing, take this cup from me; yet not my will, but yours be done" (Luke 22:42). When Christ says, "take this cup," that's the raw honesty of prayer. He reveals His personal desire, "This is what I want."

Then Jesus turns the coin, praying "not my will." That's the side of abandon. Abandoning ourselves to God begins when we simply say, "But what do You want, God?"

This two-sided prayer is also included in Matthew 26 and Mark 14 and is mentioned in John 18. Jesus prayed both sides of prayer: take this cup (what I want, God), yet not My will (what do You want, God?), pivoting between them.

Two sides of Jesus. Two sides of prayer.

Elisa Morgan

"Your will be done" is the key to every prayer.

God's Radiant Beauty

Read Romans 1:18–25

For since the creation of the world God's invisible qualities—his eternal power and divine nature— have been clearly seen. Romans 1:20

Lord Howe Island is a small paradise of white sands and crystal waters off Australia's east coast. When I visited some years ago, I was struck by its beauty. Here, one could swim with turtles and with fish like the shimmering trevally, while moon wrasses drifted nearby, flashing their neon colors like a billboard. In its lagoon I found coral reefs full of bright orange clownfish and yellow-striped butterfly fish that rushed to kiss my hand. Overwhelmed by such splendor, I couldn't help but worship God.

The apostle Paul gives the reason for my response. Creation at its best reveals something of God's nature (Romans 1:20). The wonders of Lord Howe Island were giving me a glimpse of His own power and beauty.

When the prophet Ezekiel encountered God, he was shown a radiant Being seated on a blue throne surrounded by glorious colors (Ezekiel 1:25–28). The apostle John saw something similar: God sparkling like precious stones, encircled by an emerald rainbow (Revelation 4:2–3). When God reveals himself, He is found to be not only good and powerful but beautiful too. Creation reflects this beauty the way a piece of art reflects its artist.

Nature often gets worshiped instead of God (Romans 1:25). What a tragedy! Instead, may earth's crystal waters and shimmering creatures point us to the One standing behind them who is more powerful and beautiful than anything in this world.

Sheridan Voysey

The beauty of creation reflects the beauty of our Creator.

His Excellent Name

Read Psalm 8

LORD, our Lord, how majestic is your name in all the earth!
You have set your glory in the heavens. *Psalm 8:1*

A friend of mine had a good reputation as an upholsterer. A craftsman who believed in doing every job right, he created items that were so superior that they were known far beyond our area. He upholstered furniture for the state capitol, for top hotels, and for some of the wealthiest people in our state. Because of the quality of his work, he made a name for himself.

God's excellent name is also known because of His workmanship. In Psalm 8, the writer said, in effect, "Look to the heavens. See the majesty of God reflected in the planets and the stars. Look at the marvels of the sea and the wonders of the animal world—amazing and wonderful creations from God's hand that live together in an awe-inspiring balance and beauty. And look at man—crowned with glory and honor, made a little lower than the angels, and given authority over all creation" (vv. 5–6).

Let's praise God! He's the One who spoke the heavens into being by the word of His power. He's the One who keeps the stars and planets spinning on their unseen courses. Let's magnify Him, the One who gives us the mysteries of the oceans, the rugged beauty of the mountains, and the intricate marvels of plant and animal life. Let's exalt Him, the One who made us and crowned us with glory and honor.

"LORD, our Lord, how majestic is your name in all the earth!" All praise be unto you!

David Egner

God's work of creating is done;
our work of praising has just begun.

Worshiping with Questions

Read Psalm 13

But I trust in your unfailing love;
my heart rejoices in your salvation. *Psalm 13:5*

It's not uncommon during a long (or short!) trip for someone in a group of travelers to ask, "Are we there yet?" or "How much longer?" Who hasn't heard these universal queries coming from the lips of children and adults eager to arrive at their destination? But people of all ages are also prone to ask similar questions when wearied because of life challenges that never seem to cease.

Such was the case with David in Psalm 13. Four times in two verses (vv. 1–2), David—who felt forgotten, forsaken, and defeated—lamented "How long?" In verse two, he asks, "How long must I wrestle with my thoughts?" Psalms that include lament, like this one, implicitly give us permission to worshipfully come to the Lord with questions of our own. After all, what better person to talk to during prolonged times of stress and strain than God? We can bring our struggles with illness, grief, the waywardness of a loved one, and relational difficulties to Him.

Worship need not stop when we have questions. The sovereign God of heaven welcomes us to bring our worry-filled questions to Him. And perhaps, like David, in due time our questions will be transformed into petitions and expressions of trust and praise to the Lord (vv. 3–6).

Arthur Jackson

Take your questions to God.

Clean Hands

Read Psalm 24

Who may ascend the mountain of the LORD?
Who may stand in his holy place?
The one who has clean hands and a pure heart. *Psalm 24:3–4*

It seems that wherever you go these days, you see signs encouraging people to wash their hands. With the constant threat of germs and viruses spreading disease throughout the general public, health officials continually remind us that unwashed hands form the single greatest agent for the spread of germs. So, in addition to the signs calling for vigilant handwashing, public places will often provide hand sanitizers to help take care of germs and bacteria.

David also spoke of the importance of "clean hands," but for a dramatically different reason. He said that clean hands are one key to being able to enter into God's presence for worship: "Who may ascend the mountain of the Lord? Who may stand in his holy place?" he asked. And the answer? "The one who has clean hands and a pure heart" (Psalm 24:3–4). Here "clean hands" is not a reference to personal hygiene but a metaphor for our spiritual condition—being cleansed from sin (1 John 1:9). It speaks of a life committed to what is right and godly—enabling us to stand blameless before our Lord in the privilege of worship.

As His life is lived out in our lives, He can help us to do what's right so that our hands are clean and our hearts are ready to give worship to our great God.

Bill Crowder

The road to worship begins with gratefulness
for the cleansing of God.

Hymns of Praise

Read Psalm 149:1-9

Praise the LORD. Sing to the LORD a new song,
his praise in the assembly of his faithful people. *Psalm 149:1*

Music is one of those good things in life we take for granted. Good music is a blessing from the Lord. It's a soothing tonic for troubled hearts. It motivates us to live for Christ. And through it we lift our hearts in praise to the Lord. Without music, we would be greatly deprived.

An old Jewish legend says that after God had created the world He called the angels to himself and asked them what they thought of it. One of them said, "The only thing lacking is the sound of praise to the Creator." So God created music, and it was heard in the whisper of the wind and in the song of the birds. He also gave man the gift of song. And throughout all the ages, music has blessed multitudes of people. Yes, we should be grateful for the gift of music.

With a new appreciation for the expression music gives to our souls, let us join voices with fellow believers and lift our hearts in hymns of praise whenever we have the privilege. It's honoring to the Lord. It's edifying to our brothers and sisters in Christ. And it brings us joy.

As we join with other Christians in singing—whether at church or in some other setting of praise, let's do so with a renewed appreciation of music. Sing to the Lord a new song!

Richard DeHaan

No music so pleases God as the heartfelt singing of His saints.

When God Intervenes

Read Numbers 23:13-23

"Do not touch my anointed ones;
do my prophets no harm." *Psalm 105:15*

In a poem titled "This Child Is Beloved," Omawumi Efueye, known affectionately as Pastor O, writes about his parents' attempts to end the pregnancy that would result in his birth. After several unusual events that prevented them from aborting him, they decided to welcome their child instead. The knowledge of God's preservation of his life motivated Omawumi to give up a lucrative career in favor of fulltime ministry. Today, he faithfully pastors a London church.

Like Pastor O, the Israelites experienced God's intervention at a vulnerable time in their history. While traveling through the wilderness, they came within sight of King Balak of Moab. Terrified of their conquests and their vast population, Balak engaged a seer named Balaam to place a curse on the unsuspecting travelers (Numbers 22:2–6).

But something amazing happened. Whenever Balaam opened his mouth to curse, a blessing issued instead. "I have received a command to bless; he has blessed, and I cannot change it," he declared. "No misfortune is seen in Jacob, no misery observed in Israel. The LORD their God is with them; . . . God brought them out of Egypt" (Numbers 23:20–22). God preserved the Israelites from a battle they didn't even know was raging!

Whether we see it or not, God still watches over His people today. May we worship in gratitude and awe the One who calls us blessed.

Remi Oyedele

Worship is a heart overflowing with praise to God.

The Final Opening Ceremony

Read Revelation 15

All nations will come and worship before you,
for your righteous acts have been revealed. *Revelation 15:4*

Some words used to describe the opening ceremony of Olympic Games are *awesome*, *breathtaking*, and *extravagant*. One commentator observed of a recent Games said, "This shows what happens when you give an artist an unlimited budget."

When I heard this, I thought, *That's what God did at creation! He held nothing back. The resulting universe is stunning in beauty, staggering in complexity, extravagant in all regards.*

An Olympic Games opening ceremony is often perfect in its precision; but if just one drummer or dancer had decided to alter the artist's vision, the whole ceremony could have been flawed.

That's what happened shortly after creation. Unlike the Olympic producer, God allowed free choice, and His work of art was marred by Adam and Eve's idea of a better way. In Isaiah's words, "each of us has turned to our own way" (53:6).

God's solution to our waywardness was unimaginable: The Artist paid the price to recreate what we ruined. One day, there will be another opening ceremony, and everyone in heaven and on earth will bow at the name of Jesus (Philippians 2:10). And those from every nation who have accepted God's plan in Christ will worship together in the flawless New Jerusalem (Revelation 15:4).

Julie Ackerman Link

We have all eternity to praise God—begin today.

"Semp" Prayer

Read Ephesians 3:14–21

> I kneel before the Father. . . . I pray that out of
> his glorious riches he may strengthen you with power
> through his Spirit in your inner being. *Ephesians 3:14, 16*

A friend sent me an email that concluded with a list of prayer requests. She said, "Spiritually, I am confused, so pray for understanding. Emotionally, I am very weak, so pray for strength. Mentally, I am worried, so pray for peace. Physically, I am tired, so pray for rest."

When I saw her later, I told her, "I've been SEMP praying for you." She looked confused, so I told her I was praying for her spiritual, emotional, mental, and physical well-being.

Scripture illustrates God's care in each of these areas.

Spiritual: Jesus prayed for His disciples: "Sanctify them by the truth; your word is truth" (John 17:17). Truth leads to spiritual understanding, eliminating confusion.

Emotional: Often the psalmists asked God for relief from distress (4:1; 18:6; 107:6–7). He brings hope.

Mental: Insight and wisdom are promised for those who cry out to God (Proverbs 2:3–6; James 1:5–7). Through prayer and reading His Word, the peace of God can be found.

Physical: Peter had a physical need—release from jail. His friends prayed—and he got out (Acts 12:1–11). In God's care we find security and rest (Psalm 16:9).

Are you struggling? Ask God for spiritual, emotional, mental, and physical assistance.

Dave Branon

Turn your cares into prayers.

A Heart for Prayer

Read Psalm 27:7–14

My heart says of you, "Seek his face!"
Your face, LORD, I will seek. *Psalm 27:8*

While traveling on an airplane with her four- and two-year-old daughters, a young mom worked at keeping them busy so they wouldn't disturb others. When the pilot's voice came over the intercom for an announcement, Catherine, the younger girl, paused from her activities and put her head down. When the pilot finished, she whispered, "Amen." Perhaps because there had been a recent natural disaster, she thought the pilot was praying.

Like that little girl, I want a heart that turns my thoughts toward prayer quickly. I think it would be fair to say that the psalmist David had that kind of heart. We get hints of that in Psalm 27 as he speaks of facing difficult foes (v. 2). He said, "Your face, LORD, I will seek" (v. 8). Some say that David was remembering the time he was fleeing from Saul (1 Samuel 21:10) or from his son Absalom (2 Samuel 15:13–14) when he wrote this psalm. Prayer and dependence on God were in the forefront of David's thinking, and he found Him to be his sanctuary (Psalm 27:4–5).

We need a sanctuary as well. Perhaps reading or praying this psalm and others could help us to develop that closeness to our Father-God. As God becomes our sanctuary, we'll more readily turn our hearts toward Him in prayer.

Anne Cetas

In prayer, God can still our hearts and quiet our minds.

Oceans of Praise

Read Psalm 104:24–30

How many are your works, LORD!
In wisdom you made them all. *Psalm 104:24*

Whenever I see the ocean (which is not often enough), I am awed by its sheer volume and beauty and power. Great ships loaded with oil or food or merchandise make long journeys across its vast surface. Fishing vessels, working near the shore or hundreds of miles at sea, harvest its rich provisions: lobster and crab, tuna and swordfish. Beneath its churning surface is a storehouse of wealth of all kinds, some still undiscovered.

The author of Psalm 104, recounting the works of God in a lofty hymn of praise, used the "sea, vast and spacious" as an example of God's creative power and wisdom (vv. 24–25). The Lord rules over the sea that is "teeming with creatures beyond number—living things both large and small" that inhabit the oceans (v. 25). The psalmist referred in poetic terms to the ocean as the playground of Leviathan, a giant sea monster that God "formed to frolic there" (v. 26).

The surging ocean, both life-sustaining and dangerous, points us to the greatness of our God. He is awesome in His works, unlimited in His provision, and generous in His bestowal of all kinds of life.

Lord, truly your works are magnificent! As I think of them, I join the psalmist in praising you.

David Egner

All creation sings God's praise.

The Victory Is the Lord's

Read Obadiah 1:15–21

The kingdom will be the Lord's. *Obadiah 1:21*

Obadiah is the first of the prophets to mention the "day of the Lord" (1:15) and the kingdom that is eventually to be established. We need as never before to turn to these prophecies if we are to understand the events of this present day and know the "signs of the times." Verse 15 speaks of the coming day of tribulation at the close of this age, which will precede the glorious return of Christ to set up His kingdom.

Anyone who studies the Scriptures must recognize that there are dark days ahead. The nations are in confusion. Unprecedented convolutions in nature—floods, hurricanes, famines, and wars—are constantly making the headlines. Violence seems to be the order of the day.

Obadiah speaks of these things that are to come, but then he utters a cry of hope in the darkness. All will not be lost, for the Lord will return to take things over, and upon Mount Zion shall be deliverance. This little book closes with the words, "the kingdom will be the Lord's" (v. 21).

No matter how dark things grow, the Lord is still on the throne, and will—in His own good time—step into the picture and usher in that blessed day when it can be said, "The kingdom of the world has become the kingdom of our Lord and of his Messiah, and he will reign for ever and ever" (Revelation 11:15).

For the believer, the future is bright. Praise God!

Mart DeHaan

The truth of the Lord's second coming runs
through all the Scripture like a silver cord of hope!

Seeing God

Read Exodus 34:1–9

The LORD is slow to anger, abounding in love and forgiving sin and rebellion. Yet he does not leave the guilty unpunished. *Numbers 14:18*

Caricature artists set up their easels in public places and draw pictures of people who are willing to pay a modest price for a humorous image of themselves. Their drawings amuse us because they exaggerate one or more of our physical features in a way that is recognizable but funny.

Caricatures of God, on the other hand, are not funny. Exaggerating one of His attributes presents a distorted view that people easily dismiss. Like a caricature, a distorted view of God is not taken seriously. Those who see God portrayed only as an angry and demanding judge are easily lured away by someone who emphasizes mercy. Those who see God as a kindhearted grandfather will reject that image when they need justice. Those who see God as an intellectual idea rather than a living, loving being eventually find other ideas more appealing. Those who see God as a best friend often leave Him behind when they find human friends who are more to their liking.

God declares himself to be merciful and gracious, but also just in punishing the guilty (Exodus 34:6–7).

As we put our faith into action, we need to avoid portraying God as having only our favorite attributes. We must worship all of God, not just what we like.

Julie Ackerman Link

God is God alone.

How Wesley Learned to Praise

Read Psalm 150

I will give thanks to you, LORD, with all my heart;
I will tell of all your wonderful deeds. *Psalm 9:1*

John Wesley was about twenty-one years of age when he went to Oxford University. He came from a Christian home, and he was gifted with a keen mind and good looks. Yet in those days he was a bit snobbish and sarcastic. One night, however, something happened that set in motion a change in Wesley's heart.

While speaking with the man who had been hired to carry his luggage, Wesley discovered that the porter had only one coat and lived in such impoverished conditions that he didn't even have a bed. Yet he was an unusually happy person, filled with gratitude to God. In his immaturity, Wesley thoughtlessly joked about the man's misfortunes. "And what else do you thank God for?" he said with a touch of sarcasm. The porter smiled, and in the spirit of meekness replied with joy, "I thank Him that He has given me my life and being, a heart to love Him, and above all a constant desire to serve Him!"

Deeply moved, Wesley recognized that this man knew the meaning of true thankfulness. Many years later, in 1791, John Wesley lay on his deathbed at the age of eighty-eight. Those who gathered around him realized how well he had learned the lesson of praising God in every circumstance. Despite Wesley's extreme weakness, he began singing the hymn, "I'll Praise My Maker While I've Breath."

Like that porter, we must learn to praise God in everything.

Henry Bosch

A heart in tune with God can sing melodies
of praise in the darkest night.

Praying the Distance

Read Luke 18:1-8

*Devote yourselves to prayer,
being watchful and thankful.* Colossians 4:2

Christians assemble at church to worship God. They concentrate their thoughts on Him, ascribe honor to Him, acknowledge His greatness, and express their love for Him. Sometimes, however, the atmosphere of reverence that should accompany their worship is hindered by the chatter that precedes the service.

In his book *Living Under the Smile of God*, Roger Palms wrote, "Every church has two people, one who can't hear and one who can't whisper, and they always sit next to each other. One Sunday morning during the prelude, two women were busily engaged in conversation, oblivious to those around them whom they were disturbing. The organist, noticing them, gradually increased the volume of the hymn she was playing until the music was resounding through the sanctuary. The women, to compensate, increased their own volume until they were shouting into each other's ears. Then at the height of the crescendo the organist paused and changed the stops. In the sudden silence that followed, the entire church body heard one woman shouting to the other, 'I fry mine in butter!' "

Now, I wouldn't recommend that your church musicians try this. But the point is made. Believers who want to prepare for worship are sometimes disturbed by others. So, let's determine that when the first chords of the music begin, we will turn our attention toward God. That's how we can have a heart that's ready to worship.

James Banks

A heart aflame with worship
begins with the kindling of song and prayer.

A World of Provision

Read Psalm 104:10–18, 24–26

There is the sea, vast and spacious, teeming with creatures beyond
number—living things both large and small. *Psalm 104:25*

It's 2 a.m. when Nadia, a farmer of sea cucumbers, walks into a
roped-off pen in the ocean shallows near her Madagascar village to
harvest her "crop." The early hour doesn't bother her. "Life was very
hard before I started farming," she says. "I didn't have any source
of income." Now, as a member of a marine-protection program
called Velondriake, meaning "to live with the sea," Nadia sees her
income growing and stabilizing. "We thank God that this project
appeared," she adds.

It appeared in large part because God's creation provided what
their project needs—a natural supply of sea life. In praise of our
providing God, the psalmist wrote, "He makes grass grow for the
cattle, and plants for people to cultivate" (Psalm 104:14). As well,
"there is the sea . . . teeming with creatures beyond number—living
things both large and small" (v. 25).

It's a wonder, indeed, how God's wondrous creation also provides
for us. The humble sea cucumber, for example, helps form a healthy
marine food chain. Careful harvesting of sea cucumbers, in turn,
grants Nadia and her neighbors a living wage.

Nothing is random in God's creation. He uses it all for His glory
and our good. Thus, "I will sing to the LORD all my life," says the
psalmist (v. 33). We too can praise Him today as we ponder all that
He provides.

Patricia Raybon

The beauty of God's creation gives us reason to sing God's praises.

25,000 Gifts a Day

Read Psalm 104:20–35

He is not served by human hands, as if he needed anything. Rather, he himself gives everyone life and breath and everything else. Acts 17:25

What do you do eighteen times a minute, 1,080 times an hour, and about 25,000 times a day, yet rarely notice? You breathe. If you are forty years old, you've already taken more than 365 million breaths of air. And each of those breaths was a measured gift of life from the hand of God!

Our lungs are among the most important parts of our body. They furnish our blood with oxygen, and they carry away carbon dioxide and water. A few moments without breathing, and we would lose consciousness. A minute or two longer without oxygen could prove fatal.

To whom are we indebted for the blessing of respiration? Job said that in the Lord's hand is "the life of every creature and the breath of all mankind" (Job 12:10). The Lord gives those 25,000 gifts per day so can honor Him with the life they sustain.

A dear, aged Christian woman was near death. Her children had gathered around her bedside, and the minister had come to pay a final visit. Realizing that she would soon go to be with the Lord, he asked her which portion of Scripture she'd like him to read. She said, "Make your own selection, pastor, but let it be of praise!" She wanted her parting testimony to agree with the admonition of the psalmist who said, "Let everything that has breath praise the LORD. Praise the LORD" (Psalm 150:6).

That's an attitude all of us should possess!

Henry Bosch

Don't save your breath when it is time to breathe a prayer of thanks.

Choose Life

Read Deuteronomy 30:11–20

Choose life, so that you and your children may live and that you may
love the LORD your God, listen to his voice. *Deuteronomy 30:19–20*

What is God's will for my life? The question haunted me when I was
growing up. What if I couldn't find it? What if I didn't recognize it?
God's will seemed like a needle in a haystack. Hidden. Obscured by
look-alikes. Outnumbered by counterfeits.

But my view of God's will was wrong because my view of God
was wrong. God takes no pleasure in seeing us lost, wandering,
searching. He wants us to know His will. He makes it clear, and He
makes it simple. He doesn't even make it multiple-choice. He gives
just two choices: "life and prosperity" or "death and destruction"
(Deuteronomy 30:15). In case the best choice isn't obvious, He even
says which one to choose: "Choose life" (v. 19). To choose life is to
choose God himself and obey His Word.

When Moses addressed the Israelites for the last time, he pleaded
with them to make the right choice by observing "all the words of
this law. . . . They are your life" (32:46–47). God's will for us is
life. His Word is life. And Jesus is the Word. God may not give a
prescription for every decision, but He gave us a perfect example to
follow—Jesus. The right choice may not be easy, but when the Word
is our guide and worship is our goal, God will grant us the wisdom
to make life-affirming choices.

Julie Ackerman Link

The evidence of God's guidance can be seen more clearly
by looking back than by looking forward.

Priceless Worship

Read Mark 12:38–44

*They all gave out of their wealth; but she, out of her poverty,
put in everything—all she had to live on.* Mark 12:44

I use writing to worship and serve God, even more so now that health issues often limit my mobility. So, when an acquaintance said he found no value in what I wrote, I became discouraged. I doubted the significance of my small offerings to God.

Through prayer, study of Scripture, and encouragement from my husband, family, and friends, the Lord affirmed that only He—not the opinions of other people—could determine our motives as a worshiper and the worth of our offerings to Him. I asked the Giver of all gifts to continue helping me develop skills and provide opportunities to share the resources He gives me.

Jesus contradicted our standards of merit regarding our giving (Mark 12:41–44). While the rich tossed large amounts of money into the temple treasury, a poor widow put in coins "worth only a few cents" (v. 42). The Lord declared her gift greater than the rest (v. 43), though her contribution seemed insignificant to those around her (v. 44).

Although the widow's story focuses on financial offerings, every act of giving can be an expression of worship and loving obedience. Like the widow, we honor God with intentional, generous, and sacrificial gifts given from whatever He's already given us. When we present God the best of our time, talents, or treasure with hearts motivated by love, we are lavishing Him with offerings of priceless worship.

Xochitl Dixon

Sacrificial offerings motivated by our love for God
will always be priceless expressions of worship.

Our Triune God

Read Matthew 3:13–17

He appeared in the flesh, was vindicated by the Spirit, . . .
taken up in glory. *1 Timothy 3:16*

In an interview, a young woman said that she converted to another faith system because she found the Christian doctrine of the Trinity too complicated. What she failed to realize is the system she turned to—with its solitary, distant concept of God—is inadequate. We need the triune God, who became one of us to show His love and to provide salvation. He understands our trials because He himself experienced them.

The Bible teaches that the Father is God (John 6:27), the Son is God (John 1:1, 18), and the Holy Spirit is God (Acts 5:3, 4). Each is distinct, but they are so united that not one of them could exist without the others. The Father, the Son, and the Holy Spirit were all present at Jesus's baptism (Matthew 3:16,17).

Most of us are not as concerned about the deep theology of the Trinity as we are about its practical meaning in a world of sin, pain, sorrow, and death. Yet it is because God is triune that He could come to earth in the person of Jesus to provide salvation for us (John 3:16) and to be our sympathetic helper (Hebrews 4:14–16). It is because God is triune that the Holy Spirit can live in us and make our bodies the temples of God (1 Corinthians 6:19).

Let's reaffirm our faith in our triune God and praise the Father, Son, and Holy Spirit.

Herb Vander Lugt

The triune God reveals himself not to confuse us
but to convict, cleanse, and comfort us.

Hidden Away

Read Psalm 119:9–16

I have hidden your word in my heart
that I might not sin against you. *Psalm 119:11*

By the time I was born, my great-grandfather, Abram Z. Hess, had already lost his sight. He was known for the beautiful wooden objects he had carved on a lathe—and also as someone who could quote many verses of Scripture. He and his friend Eli would often share Scripture verses back and forth. A bit of a competitive spirit resulted in their admission that Eli could cite more references while my grandfather could recite more verses.

Today, the family often remembers Abram as "Blind Grandpa." His practice of memorizing Scripture became a lifeline for him when he lost his physical sight. But why is it important that we memorize the Word of God?

Psalm 119 gives us instruction on how to follow God by hiding His Word in our hearts. First, in this way, we arm ourselves when temptation comes (v.11; Ephesians 6:17). Then, as we meditate on His Word, we come to know Him better. Finally, when we have His words etched in our minds, we are better able to hear His voice when He instructs and guides us. We use those phrases of Scripture as we talk with Him, worship Him, and teach or witness to others (Colossians 3:16).

The Word of God is "living and powerful" (Hebrews 4:12 NKJV). Hide its precious words away "in [your] heart" (Psalm 119:11) where they will always be with you.

Cindy Hess Kasper

When God's Word is hidden in our heart,
His ways will become our ways.

Pure Worship

Read Mark 11:15-18

"Is it not written: 'My house will be called a house of prayer for all nations'? But you have made it 'a den of robbers.'" *Mark 11:17*

Jose pastored a church known for its programs and theatrical productions. They were well done, yet he worried the church's busyness had slipped into a business. Was the church growing for the right reasons or because of its activities? Jose wanted to find out, so he canceled all extra church events for one year. His congregation would focus on being a living temple where people worshiped God.

Jose's decision seems extreme, until you notice what Jesus did when He entered the temple's outer courts. The holy space that should have been full of simple prayers had become a flurry of worship business. "Get your doves here! Lily white, as God requires!" Jesus overturned the merchant's tables and stopped those who bought their merchandise. Furious at what they were doing, He quoted Isaiah 56 and Jeremiah 7: "'My house will be called a house of prayer for all nations.' But you have made it 'a den of robbers' " (Mark 11:17). The court of the gentiles, the place for outsiders to worship God, had been turned into a mundane marketplace for making money.

There's nothing wrong with business or staying busy. But that's not the point of church. We're the living temple of God, and our main task is to worship Jesus. We likely won't need to flip over any tables as Jesus did, but He may be calling us to do something equally drastic.

Mike Wittmer

A good indicator of our spiritual temperature
is our eagerness to worship.

Waiting . . .

Read Psalm 130

Be joyful in hope, patient in affliction,
faithful in prayer. *Romans 12:12*

Day after day for years Harry shared with the Lord his concern
for his son-in-law John who had turned away from God. But then
Harry died. A few months later, John turned back to God. When
his mother-in-law Marsha told him that Harry had been praying for
him every day, John replied, "I waited too long." But Marsha joyfully shared: "The Lord is still answering the prayers Harry prayed
during his earthly life."

Harry's story is an encouragement to us who pray and wait. He
continued "faithful in prayer" and waited patiently (Romans 12:12).

The author of Psalm 130 experienced waiting in prayer. He said,
"I wait for the Lord, my whole being waits" (v. 5). He found hope
in God because he knew that "with the LORD is unfailing love and
with Him is full redemption" (v. 7).

Author Samuel Enyia wrote about God's timing: "God does not
depend on our time. Our time is chronological and linear but God . . .
is timeless. He will act at the fullness of His time. Our prayer . . .
may not necessarily rush God into action, but . . . places us before
Him in fellowship."

What a privilege we have to fellowship with God in prayer and to
wait for the answer in the fullness of His time.

Anne Cetas

God may delay our request,
but He will never disappoint our trust.

Turning Pain into Praise

Read 2 Corinthians 1:7–11

No temptation has overtaken you except what is common
to mankind. And God is faithful; he will not let you be tempted
beyond what you can bear. But when you are tempted, he will
also provide a way out so that you can endure it. *1 Corinthians 10:13*

After years of a remarkable and fruitful ministry in India, Amy Carmichael became a bedridden sufferer. As the courageous founder and dynamic heart of the Dohnavour Fellowship, she had been instrumental in rescuing hundreds of girls and boys from a terrible life of sexual servitude. All the while she carried on that rescue operation of bringing young people into spiritual freedom through faith in Jesus Christ, she was writing books, and especially poems, which continue to bless readers around the world.

Then arthritis made Amy a pain-wracked woman, unable to get around. Did she bemoan her affliction or question God? No. Amy was still the guiding inspiration of Dohnavour, and she still kept on writing. Her meditations, letters, and poems are full of praise to God and encouragement to her fellow pilgrims.

When affliction strikes us, how do we react? Are we embittered, or do we trustfully appropriate God's sustaining grace? (1 Corinthians 10:13). And do we prayerfully encourage those around us by our Spirit-enabled cheerfulness, our courage, and our confidence in God?

As we rely on the Lord, He can help us to turn pain into praise.

Vernon Grounds

When you're up to your neck in hot water,
be like a teapot and start to sing.

Let Down Your Hair

Read John 12:1–8

Mary took about a pint of pure nard, an expensive perfume;
she poured it on Jesus' feet and wiped his feet with her hair. John 12:3

Shortly before Jesus was crucified, a woman named Mary poured a bottle of expensive perfume on His feet. Then, in what may have been an even more daring act, she wiped His feet with her hair (John 12:3). Not only did Mary sacrifice what may have been her life's savings but she also sacrificed her reputation. In first-century Middle Eastern culture, respectable women never let down their hair in public. But true worship is not concerned about what others think of us (2 Samuel 6:21–22). To worship Jesus, Mary was willing to be thought of as immodest, perhaps even immoral.

Some of us may feel pressured to be perfect when we go to church so that people will think well of us. Metaphorically speaking, we work hard to make sure we have every hair in place. But a healthy church is a place where we can let down our hair and not hide our flaws behind a façade of perfection. In church, we should be able to reveal our weaknesses to find strength rather than conceal our faults to appear strong.

Worship doesn't involve behaving as if nothing is wrong; it's making sure everything is right—right with God and with one another. When our greatest fear is letting down our hair, perhaps our greatest sin is keeping it up.

Julie Ackerman Link

Our worship is right when we are right with God.

Help by Praying

Read 2 Corinthians 1:8–11

You help us by your prayers. Then many will give
thanks on our behalf for the gracious favor granted us
in answer to the prayers of many. *2 Corinthians 1:11*

When I was a young boy, we lived in a house without running water. Instead, we had a pump attached to our kitchen sink. If we used the pump frequently, the water from our well poured out at the first stroke. But when it hadn't been used for several hours, the water level subsided, and we would pump a long time without results. Then we would prime it by pouring water into it, and our efforts would be rewarded.

So it is with prayer. We must constantly be on speaking terms with God through confession of sin and fellowship with the Lord. Then the desire to pray and the words to say will always be fresh, no matter how insignificant the problems we bring to Him. If, however, we neglect prayer, it will become more difficult for us to talk with the Lord, for the water level will recede. The best way to "prime the pump" is to keep it in constant use.

British writer Samuel Chadwick said this: "To pray as God would have us pray is the greatest achievement on earth. Such a prayer life costs. In these days, there is no time to pray; but without time, and a lot of it, we shall never learn to pray."

Jesus wants your fellowship and your praise; He waits to have you bring your requests to Him. Therefore, let's heed the biblical exhortation to "pray continually" (1 Thessalonians 5:17).

David Egner

You can expect God to intervene
when you have taken time to intercede.

Wrong Worship

Read Acts 19:23–41

There is danger . . . that our trade will lose its good name. *Acts 19:27*

If you really want to get folks upset, threaten their economy.

A bad economic picture gets politicians voted out of office, and the threat of a downturn nearly got the apostle Paul kicked out of Ephesus.

Here's what happened. Paul came to town and started "arguing persuasively about the kingdom of God" (Acts 19:8). For more than two years he shared the gospel, and many began following Jesus.

Because Paul was so successful in getting people to see that there is only one true God, many Ephesians stopped worshiping the goddess Diana. This was bad news for the local silversmiths, who made their living creating and selling Diana statuettes. If enough people stopped believing in her, business would dry up. A commotion and an uproar broke out when the craftsmen figured this out.

This Ephesus incident can remind us to evaluate our reasons for worshiping God. The silversmiths wanted to protect their worship as a way of protecting their prosperity, but may that never be said of us. We should never let our worship of God become an avenue to good fortune.

We worship God because of His love for us and because of who He is, not because loving Him can help our bottom line. Let's worship God the right way.

Dave Branon

Don't worship God to gain His benefits—you already have them.

Emergency Prayers

Read Daniel 6:1-10

> When Daniel learned that the decree had been published,
> he went home to his upstairs room.... Three times a day
> he got down on his knees and prayed. *Daniel 6:10*

When we pray about something because we are in "hot water," so to speak, we have good company. When Peter walked on the water and began to sink, he cried out to Jesus, "Lord, save me!" (Matthew14:30). Jonah is to be commended for praying inside the belly of the fish, even though he was in that "tight spot" because of his own disobedience (Jonah 2:1). The Lord answered both Peter and Jonah. But whether things are going against us or going for us should make no difference. Prayer should be such a natural part of our lives that we engage in it no matter the situation.

Daniel 6:1–10 illustrates this truth. The enemies of Daniel had gone to Darius, king of Babylon, and encouraged him to sign a document which, according to the law of the Medes and Persians, could not be changed. The decree stated that for thirty days anyone who asked a petition of any god or man other than the king himself would be thrown into a den of lions. Daniel knew this, but "three times a day he got down on his knees and prayed, giving thanks to his God, just as he had done before." Those last six words tell it all. Daniel's emergency praying reflected his consistent devotion to the Lord.

Our heavenly Father takes great delight in our thankful prayers. Whatever our circumstances, therefore, let's make prayer a vital part of our life. Have you talked with God today?

Richard DeHaan

If you want to know how to pray in hard times,
practice praying in easy times.

Going to the Top

Read Philippians 4:1–9

I urge, then, first of all, that petitions, prayers, intercession
and thanksgiving be made for all people. *1 Timothy 2:1*

Prayer is much more than a quieting of the mind. To be sure, it does
have positive psychological effects, but something of greater significance is happening when we engage in this spiritual exercise. We
are appealing to the highest authority in the universe for help—the
sovereign Creator and Sustainer of all things. We are "going directly
to the top" with every problem that we have.

An amusing little story captures this thought. A rather egotistical
supervisor, jealous of his position in the company, called one of his
employees into his office. "Smith," he said gravely, "I'm told that
you've been praying for a raise. I want you to know that I will not
tolerate anyone going over my head!"

Sometimes we are walled in by circumstances that cannot be
changed, no matter what we do. Often people are part of the situation, and this makes it seem more hopeless than ever. Though
"locked in," we have one recourse that is always effective. We can
bring everything to the Lord with supplication and thanksgiving.
He will give us His peace, which transcends all understanding and
which stabilizes our hearts and minds through Christ Jesus (Philippians 4:6–7).

What a privilege to go to the top with all our concerns and burdens! We know that God is in a position to do something about
them. He may change our circumstances or the people involved—
but more than likely, He will change us.

Dennis DeHaan

Through prayer, the finite man
can tap the power of the infinite God.

Blessings of the Dew

Read Hosea 14

"I will be like the dew to Israel; he will blossom like a lily." *Hosea 14:5*

The Word of God is compared to water (Ephesians 5:26). In the cool atmosphere of prayer and meditation, our fevered spirits may find refreshment from the Scriptures. Someone has said: "The dew is nature's provision for renewing the face of the earth. It falls at night; and in the early morning the grass of the meadow and the flowers of the field are refreshed and moistened by it. Without it the vegetation would die. Just as nature is bathed by the dew, so in a similar fashion the Lord renews the strength of His people."

Spiritual dew comes from lingering in Jesus's presence. Its unique blessings fall only when our old natures have been quieted by prayer and meditation. Wait patiently, therefore, before the Lord until you feel saturated with His presence. Then you will be able to go forth to your daily duties with the conscious, invigorating joy of the Holy Spirit's blessing.

An elderly Christian woman was asked the source of her power. "Well," she replied, "at the beginning of the day I take out my hymnbook and sing a few songs of praise to the Lord. Then I get my Bible and let the Lord speak to me. Finally, when I am tired of reading and I cannot sing any more, I just sit still awhile and let the Lord love me!"

Do you want to experience the blessings of the "dews of grace?" Then follow her challenging example!

Henry Bosch

They that wait upon men often dissipate their energies,
but they that "wait upon the Lord" renew their strength!

Fully Known

Read Jeremiah 1:1–8

Before I formed you in the womb I knew you,
before you were born I set you apart;
I appointed you as a prophet to the nations. *Jeremiah 1:5*

"You shouldn't be here right now. Someone up there was looking out for you," the tow truck driver told my mother after he had pulled her car from the edge of a steep mountain ravine and studied the tire tracks leading up to the wreck. Mom was pregnant with me at the time. As I grew, she often recounted the story of how God saved both our lives that day, and she assured me that God valued me even before I was born.

None of us escape our omniscient (all-knowing) Creator's notice. More than 2,500 years ago He told the prophet Jeremiah, "Before I formed you in the womb I knew you" (Jeremiah 1:5). God knows us more intimately than any person ever could and is able to give our lives purpose and meaning unlike any other. He not only formed us through His wisdom and power but He also sustains every moment of our existence—including the personal details that occur every moment without our awareness: from the beating of our hearts to the intricate functioning of our brains. Reflecting on how our heavenly Father holds together every aspect of our existence, David exclaimed, "How precious to me are your thoughts, God!" (Psalm 139:17).

God is closer to us than our last breath. He made us, knows us, and loves us, and He's ever worthy of our worship and praise.

James Banks

God alone is worthy of our worship.

Leading by Praying

Read Colossians 1:3–14

Since the day we heard about you,
we have not stopped praying for you. *Colossians 1:9*

People who have had an arm in a cast for a lengthy period of time can tell you what happens when the plaster is finally removed. The muscles of the arm have atrophied; that is, they have shrunk and become weak because they have not been used. A lack of effort and exercise has greatly diminished their power.

That's precisely what happens to a church when its leaders don't pray—its ministry becomes powerless and ineffective. E. M. Bounds emphasized the need for a ministry of prayer within the church when he wrote, "Church leaders are to be men whose lives are made and molded by prayer, whose heart and life are made up of prayer. These are the men—the only men—God can use in the furtherance of His kingdom and the implanting of His message in the hearts of men."

If you have accepted a position of leadership in your church, be it pastor, elder, Sunday school teacher, or whatever, learn from Paul, a leader in the early church. Pray for your local assembly, for its people, for its outreach, and for God's direction for its future. Your life should be permeated by prayer so your leadership will have confidence, compassion, and effectiveness. The church will be strong only as its leaders exercise the power of prayer.

David Egner

A prayerless Christian is a powerless Christian.

God Is Good

Read Psalm 100

*Enter his gates with thanksgiving and his courts with praise;
give thanks to him and praise his name. Psalm 100:4*

I stopped at the home of a Christian man who was confined to his bed because of a severe back ailment. He and his wife were dedicated servants of the Lord. Lying flat on his back and in discomfort, he told me the doctors had been unable to clearly diagnose his malady and had given him little encouragement.

When I said something about this being a rather disheartening situation, he replied, "I'm not going to let this get me down spiritually. I'm almost seventy years old and have always enjoyed the best of health. When I think of all the Lord has done for me, I feel I would have nothing to complain about, even if I never walk again. God has been so good!" These words of gratitude touched my heart, and I found myself repeating, "Yes, God is good."

Psalm 100 is a wonderful song of praise and thanksgiving. It was sung by worshipers as they entered the outer court of the temple to bring their thank offerings to the Lord. They expressed their joy in knowing the one true God—both their great Creator and their loving Shepherd. Verse five sums up their reasons for gladness of heart, "For the Lord is good and his love endures forever; his faithfulness continues through all generations."

Yes, God is good! Every believer should daily remind himself of this glorious truth. Those who do so will be enabled to sing praise even in the darkest night.

Herb Vander Lugt

Because of His infinite care and kindness,
God alone is worthy of the name "Good." —Beecher

Don't Miss the Chance

Read Psalm 19:1–4

The heavens declare the glory of God;
the skies proclaim the work of his hands. *Psalm 19:1*

"Don't ever miss the chance to show your babies the moon!" she said. Before our midweek prayer service began, a group of us talked about the previous night's harvest moon. The full moon was striking, as it seemed to sit on the horizon. Mrs. Webb was the elder voice in our conversation, a gray-haired lover of God's grand creation. She knew that my wife and I had two children in our home at the time, and she wanted to help me train them in a way worth going. Don't ever miss the chance to show your babies the moon!

Mrs. Webb would've made a good psalmist. Her brand of attentiveness is reflected in David's description of the heavenly bodies that "have no speech. . . . Yet their voice goes out into all the earth, their words to the ends of the world" (Psalm 19:3–4). Neither the psalmist nor Mrs. Webb had any intention of worshiping the moon or the stars but rather the creative hands behind them. The heavens and skies reveal nothing less than the glory of God (v. 1).

We too can encourage those in our circles—from babies and teenagers to spouses and neighbors—to stop, look, and listen for declarations and proclamations of God's glory are all around us. Drawing attention to the work of His hands in turn leads to worshiping the awesome God behind the whole show. Don't ever miss the chance.

John Blase

If we stop, look, and listen,
we'll see creation declaring God's glory.

The Fairest

Read Revelation 5:8–14

Worthy is the Lamb, who was slain. *Revelation 5:12*

When I first became a Christian and started attending church at age nineteen, I immediately fell in love with singing the great hymns of the faith. My heart overflowed with joy and thanksgiving as we sang of God's love for us in Christ. Soon one of my favorite hymns (from the late 1600s) became "Fairest Lord Jesus!" I love the simplicity of the melody and the awesomeness of the One exalted in these words:

> Fair is the sunshine, fairer still the moonlight,
> and all the twinkling starry host: Jesus shines brighter,
> Jesus shines purer than all the angels heaven can boast.
> Beautiful Savior!
> Lord of the nations!
> Son of God and Son of Man!
> Glory and honor, praise, adoration and forevermore be Thine!

God's Son, whom we sing about in this song, came to this earth, lived a perfect life, and gave himself for us on the cross (Luke 23:33). He arose from the grave (Luke 24:6) and is now seated at God's right hand (Hebrews 1:3). One day we'll join in worship with thousands upon thousands and say: "To him who sits on the throne and to the Lamb be praise and honor and glory and power, for ever and ever!" (Revelation 5:13). Maybe we'll sing "Fairest Lord Jesus!" too.

Until then, let's allow Jesus to be "the fairest" above all in our personal lives by seeking wisdom from His Word and following in His ways.

Anne Cetas

We can never praise Jesus too much.

That's Awesome

Read Psalm 66

Come and see what God has done,
his awesome deeds for mankind. *Psalm 66:5*

The word *awesome* is tossed around a lot these days. Talk about cars, movies, songs, or food—and somebody will say, "That's awesome!"

But if we call earth-side stuff "awesome" and then call God "awesome," we diminish how truly awesome He is. A friend of mine has a rule in her house—the word *awesome* is reserved only for God.

Trivializing God is no trivial matter. He is far more than a companion who will fit into our "buddy system" or a divine ATM responding to our impulses. Until we are stunned by the awesomeness of God, we will be way too impressed with ourselves and lose the joy of the privilege of belonging to an awesome God.

A look at the Psalms puts it all in perspective. One psalmist declares, "For the Lord Most High is awesome; the great King over all the earth" (Psalm 47:2). And another psalm commands: "Say to God, 'How awesome are your deeds!' . . . Come and see what God has done, his awesome deeds for mankind" (Psalm 66:3, 5).

What could be more awesome than the love that compelled Jesus to go to the cross for us? Put Him in His proper place as the only One who is truly awesome, and praise God for His awesome work in your life!

Joe Stowell

If you're too impressed with yourself,
take a closer look at God's awesomeness.

Heard by God

Read 1 Samuel 1:9–20

Hannah was praying in her heart; . . .
her voice was not heard. *1 Samuel 1:13*

After reading several children's books with my daughter, I told her that I was going to read a grown-up book for a while and then we would look at books together again. I opened the cover and began to read in silence. A few minutes later, she looked at me doubtfully and said, "Mommy, you aren't really reading." She assumed that since I wasn't speaking, I wasn't processing the words.

Like reading, prayer can be silent. Hannah, who longed for a child of her own, visited the temple and "was praying in her heart." Her lips were moving, but "her voice was not heard" (1 Samuel 1:13). Eli the priest saw but misunderstood what was happening. She explained, "I was pouring out my soul to the LORD" (v. 15). God heard Hannah's silent prayer request and gave her a son (v. 20).

Since God searches our hearts and minds (Jeremiah 17:10), He sees and hears every prayer—even the ones that never escape our lips. His all-knowing nature makes it possible for us to pray with full confidence that He will hear and answer (Matthew 6:8, 32). Because of this, we can continually praise God, ask Him for help, and thank Him for blessings—even when no one else can hear us.

Jennifer Benson Schuldt

God fills our heart with peace when we pour out our heart to Him.

Expect a Blessing

Read Isaiah 2:1–5

I rejoiced with those who said to me,
"Let us go to the house of the LORD." *Psalm 122:1*

I overheard a conversation recently between two men who attend the same church. One said, "I get a blessing from our pastor's messages almost every Sunday, and when I don't, I'm usually to blame because of my own unspiritual attitude."

Often, when someone leaves church grumbling and complaining about something in the service, the fault is with the complainer. Someone has said that leaving a worship service with little or no edification is like going into a huge retail store and coming out with a thirty-nine-cent item. Literally hundreds of thousands of dollars' worth of merchandise are available to a shopper, but he will take away with him only what he has predetermined to get.

When we enter the sanctuary of a Bible-teaching church expecting a blessing, we are taking the first step toward receiving one. If we participate with a genuine desire to hear God speaking to us through the Scriptures, we will surely come away with our hearts filled. We will walk away blessed and encouraged.

Let's enter our worship center in the spirit of the psalmist, who declared, "I rejoiced with those who said to me, 'Let us go to the house of LORD' " (122:1). The songs of praise, the fellowship of believers, and the preaching of the Word will bless our soul and send us rejoicing into the new week.

Richard DeHaan

If you want to be spiritually fed,
go to church with a good appetite.

Let Us Praise!

Read Psalm 67

May the nations be glad and sing for joy,
for you rule the peoples with equity and guide
the nations of the earth. *Psalm 67:4*

When the alarm on Shelley's phone goes off every day at 3:16 in the afternoon, she takes a praise break. She thanks God and acknowledges His goodness. Although she communicates with God throughout the day, Shelley loves to take this break because it helps her celebrate her intimate relationship with Him.

Inspired by her joyful devotion, I decided to set a specific time each day to thank Christ for His sacrifice on the cross and to pray for those who have yet to be saved. I wonder what it would be like if all believers in Jesus stopped to praise Him in their own way and pray for others every day.

The image of a beautiful wave of worship rolling to the ends of the earth resounds in the words of Psalm 67. The psalmist pleads for God's grace, proclaiming his desire to make His name great in all the nations (vv. 1–2). He sings, "May the peoples praise you, God; may all the peoples praise you" (v. 3). He celebrates His sovereign rule and faithful guidance (v. 4). As a living testimony of God's great love and abundant blessings, the psalmist leads God's people into jubilant praise (vv. 5–6).

God's continued faithfulness toward His beloved children inspires us to acknowledge Him. As we do, others can join us in trusting Him, revering Him, following Him, and acclaiming Him as Lord.

Xochitl Dixon

Worship is a heart overflowing with praise to God.

God's Answers

Read Daniel 9:20–27

While I was still in prayer, Gabriel . . . came to me. Daniel 9:21

Daniel poured out his heart to God (Daniel 9:3). He had read Jeremiah and rediscovered God's promise that Israel's captivity in Babylon would last seventy years. So, in an effort to represent his people before God, Daniel fasted and prayed. He pleaded with God not to delay in rescuing His people (v. 19).

When we pray, there are things we can know and other things we cannot. For instance, we have the assurance that God will hear our prayer if we know Him as our heavenly Father through faith in Jesus, and we know that His answer will come according to His will. But we don't know when the answer will come or what it will be.

For Daniel, the answer to his prayer came in miraculous fashion, and it came immediately. While he was praying, the angel Gabriel arrived to provide the answer. But the nature of the answer was as surprising as the quick reply. While Daniel asked God about "seventy years," the answer was about a prophetic "seventy weeks of years." Daniel asked God for an answer about the here and now, but God's answer had to do with events thousands of years into the future.

Focused as we are with our immediate situation, we may be shocked by God's answer. Yet we can know that the answer will be for His glory.

Dave Branon

God's answers to our prayers may exceed our expectations.

New Song

Read Psalm 40:1–10

He put a new song in my mouth,
a hymn of praise to our God. *Psalm 40:3*

The song of the humpback whale is one of the strangest in nature. When the sound is reproduced and sped up electronically, it resembles the chirping of a songbird. At its natural tempo it is a weird combination of high- and low-pitched groanings. In deep water these sounds echo between the surface and the bottom, creating an eerie effect. Those who have studied the humpback whale say that their songs are also noteworthy because these giants of the deep are continually changing them. Over a period of time the whale actually sings a whole new song.

This reminded me of today's Scripture. There's a sense in which the Christian should be improvising new music around the fresh mercies of God. Sometimes we sing the "same old song." Most certainly, we must never be moved from the old landmarks. We must never let go of the fundamentals of our faith. But as the psalmist tells us, there's another side to this. The works of God's deliverance are many. His thoughts, which are available to us, are greater than can be numbered (Psalm 40:5).

So then, why is our testimony of God's saving grace expressed in the same way year after year? A fresh experience of the mercies of the cross and of Christ's resurrection power should fill our minds and hearts with new songs continually. Sure, the story is old. Thank God for that. But the verses of our praise should be endlessly new.

Mart DeHaan

God's work in our lives puts a new song on our lips.

Spurgeon's Heating Plant

Read 2 Thessalonians 2:13–17; 3:1–2

Brothers and sisters, pray for us that the message of the Lord may
spread rapidly and be honored, just as it was with you. *2 Thessalonians 3:1*

The great British preacher Charles H. Spurgeon (1834–1892) once
declared with emphasis, "Among all the formative influences that go
to make up a man honored of God in the ministry, I know of none
more mighty than . . . the intercession of his parishioners. Without
it he will most likely be a failure!"

Why was Spurgeon so zealous in seeking the help of others to
present his needs before the Throne? Because he had proved the
worth of prayer in his own ministry. Some years before he made
that statement, five young college students came to hear Spurgeon
preach. The students were greeted by a man who said, "Gentlemen,
would you like to see the heating plant of this church?" They were
not particularly eager to do so, for it was a very warm day in July,
but not wanting to offend the stranger, they consented. They were
taken down a stairway, a door was quietly opened, and their guide
whispered, "There is our heating apparatus."

They saw before them 700 people bowed in prayer, seeking a
blessing on the service that was soon to begin in the tabernacle
above. Softly closing the door, their unknown guide then introduced himself. It was none other than Spurgeon. With such an
army of prayer warriors undergirding his ministry, is it any wonder
that he presented God's Word with such power and effectiveness?

Imagine if every church had a "heating plant" like Spurgeon's!

Henry Bosch

There will be more power in the pulpit
when there is more prayer in the pew!

Words in Space

Read Ephesians 3:8–13

In [Christ] we may approach God with freedom
and confidence. *Ephesians 3:12*

True confession: When I found out that astronaut Rex Walheim would be taking a copy of *Our Daily Bread* with him into space for the last mission of the shuttle *Atlantis*, I looked ahead to find out which devotionals I had written that he would be reading. The idea of having my words read in outer space seemed, well, pretty amazing for this small-town kid.

No sooner had I satisfied my curiosity, however, than I had another thought. Why do I consider this such a big deal? My words are heard in heavenly places whenever I pray. What has happened to me that I take for granted the concept that the God who created the universe listens to my words? In Christ, I can approach God with freedom and confidence (Ephesians 3:12). Why be more awestruck at having a human read what I have written than having Almighty God hear what I pray?

If that idea isn't enough to rouse me from complacency, there's this: The Lord is using the church to make known His wisdom to the "rulers and authorities in heavenly realms" (v. 10). Imagine. God not only hears our prayers, but He uses us earthlings to teach heavenly beings the plan of redemption He has accomplished through Christ. Now, that's a big deal!

Julie Ackerman Link

God is always available to hear the prayer of His child.

Strengthened in Song

Read Psalm 59:1, 14–17

I will sing of your strength, in the morning I will sing of
your love; for you are my fortress. *Psalm 59:16*

When French villagers helped Jewish refugees hide from the Nazis
during World War II, some sang songs in the dense forest surrounding their town—letting the refugees know it was safe to come out
from hiding. These brave townspeople of Le Chambon-sur-Lignon
had answered the call of local pastor André Trocmé and his wife,
Magda, to offer wartime refuge to Jews on their windswept plateau
known as "La Montagne Protestante." Their musical signal became
just one feature of the villagers' bravery that helped save up to 3,000
Jews from almost certain death.

In another dangerous time, David sang when his enemy Saul
sent nighttime assassins to his house. His use of music wasn't a
signal; rather, it was his song of gratitude to God his refuge. David
rejoiced, "I will sing of your strength, in the morning I will sing of
your love; for you are my fortress, my refuge in times of trouble"
(Psalm 59:16).

Such singing isn't "whistling in the dark" during danger. Instead,
David's singing conveyed his trust in almighty God. "You, God, are
my fortress, my God on whom I can rely" (v. 17).

David's praise, and the villagers' singing in Le Chambon, offer
an invitation to bless God today with our singing, making melody
to Him despite the worries of life. His loving presence will respond,
strengthening our hearts.

Patricia Raybon

Our praise to God can strengthen our hearts
as it transforms our worry into worship.

Raise Praise

Read Psalm 48

Like your name, O God, your praise reaches to the ends of the earth; your right hand is filled with righteousness. *Psalm 48:10*

You can generally tell where a map was drawn by what lies in its middle. We tend to think our home is the center of the world, so we put a dot in the middle and sketch out from there. Nearby towns might be fifty miles to the north or half a day's drive to the south, but all are described in relation to where we are. The Psalms draw their "map" from God's earthly home in the Old Testament, so the center of biblical geography is Jerusalem.

Psalm 48 is one of many psalms that praise Jerusalem. This "city of our God, his holy mountain" is "beautiful in its loftiness, the joy of the whole earth" (vv. 1–2). Because "God is in her citadels," He "makes her secure forever" (vv. 3, 8). God's fame begins in Jerusalem's temple and spreads outward to "the ends of the earth" (vv. 9–10).

Unless you're reading this in Jerusalem, your home is not in the center of the biblical world. Yet your region matters immensely, because God will not rest until His praise reaches "to the ends of the earth" (v. 10). Would you like to be part of the way God reaches His goal? Worship each week with God's people, and openly live each day for His glory. God's fame extends "to the ends of the earth" when we devote all that we are and have to Him.

Mike Wittmer

Our worship should not be confined to times and places;
it should be the spirit of our lives.

Amazing Skill

Read Psalm 139:7–16

I praise you because I am fearfully and wonderfully made; your works are wonderful, I know that full well. *Psalm 139:14*

The leader of our college singing group directed the group and accompanied us on the piano at the same time, skillfully balancing those responsibilities. At the close of one concert, he looked particularly weary, so I asked him if he was okay. He responded, "I've never had to do that before." Then he explained. "The piano was so out of tune that I had to play the whole concert in two different keys—my left hand playing in one key and my right hand in another!" I was blown away by the startling skill he displayed, and I was amazed at the One who creates humans to be capable of such things.

King David expressed an even greater sense of wonder when he wrote, "Thank you for making me so wonderfully complex! Your workmanship is marvelous—how well I know it" (Psalm 139:14 NLT). Whether in people's abilities or nature's marvels, the wonders of creation point us to the majesty of our Creator.

One day, when we're in God's presence, people from every generation will worship Him with the words, "You are worthy, our Lord and God, to receive glory and honor and power, for you created all things, and by your will they were created and have their being" (Revelation 4:11). The amazing skills God gives us and the great beauty God has created are ample reason to worship Him.

Bill Crowder

Only God is worthy of our adoration and devotion.

The Mood Mender

Read Psalm 94:2, 16–23

When anxiety was great within me,
your consolation brought me joy. *Psalm 94:19*

As I waited at the train station for my weekly commute, negative thoughts crowded my mind like commuters lining up to board a train—stress over debt, unkind remarks said to me, helplessness in the face of a recent injustice done to a family member. By the time the train arrived, I was in a terrible mood.

On the train, another thought came to mind: write a note to God, giving Him my lament. Soon after I finished pouring out my complaints in my journal, I pulled out my phone and listened to the praise songs in my library. Before I knew it, my bad mood had completely changed.

Little did I know that I was following a pattern set by the writer of Psalm 94. The psalmist first poured out his complaints: "Rise up, Judge of the earth; pay back to the proud what they deserve. . . . Who will rise up for me against the wicked? Who will take a stand for me against evildoers?" (Psalm 94:2, 16.) He didn't hold anything back as he talked to God about injustice done to widows and orphans. Once he'd made his lament to God, the psalm transitioned into praise: "But the LORD has become my fortress, and my God the rock in whom I take refuge" (v. 22).

God invites us to take our laments to Him. He can turn our fear, sadness, and helplessness into praise.

Linda Washington

Praise has the power to lighten our heaviest burden.

A Joyful Heart

Read 2 Chronicles 7:1–10

Shout for joy to the LORD, all the earth. *Psalm 100:1*

My granddaughter's favorite tune is one of John Philip Sousa's marches. Sousa, known as "The March King," was a US composer in the late nineteenth century. Moriah isn't in a marching band; she's only twenty months old. She just loves the tune and can even hum a few notes. She associates it with joyful times. When our family gets together, we often hum this song along with claps and other boisterous noises, and the grandchildren dance or parade in circles to the beat. It always ends in dizzy children and lots of laughter.

Our joyful noise reminds me of the psalm that implores us to "worship the LORD with gladness" (Psalm 100:2). When King Solomon dedicated the temple, the Israelites celebrated with praises (2 Chronicles 7:5–6). Psalm 100 may have been one of the songs they sang. The psalm declares: "Shout for joy to the LORD, all the earth. Worship the LORD with gladness; come before him with joyful songs. . . . Enter his gates with thanksgiving and his courts with praise; give thanks to him and praise his name" (vv. 1–2, 4). Why? "For the LORD is good and his love endures forever"! (v. 5).

Our good God loves us! In grateful response, let's "shout for joy to the LORD"! (Psalm 100:1).

Alyson Kieda

Praise is the overflow of a joyful heart.

The Antidote of Praise

Read Psalm 42:1–5

Why, my soul, are you downcast? Why so disturbed within me?
Put your hope in God, for I will yet praise him,
my Savior and my God. *Psalm 42:11*

The writer of Psalm 42 is at the point of despondency. After taking spiritual inventory, however, he recognizes the folly of dwelling on his unfavorable circumstances when he should be concentrating on the bright reality that he is the object of the Lord's loving care. He ends his review of the situation with a testimony of faith as he presents the solution to his problems: "Hope in God; for I will yet praise him!"

We can look to the future with confidence, for we have this assuring promise: "No good thing does he withhold from those whose walk is blameless" (Psalm 84:11). If we shake off our fear and depression by giving thanks for our afflictions, our hearts will be lifted.

The apostle Paul frequently experienced great difficulties, but he reacted to the woes of life as did the psalmist: "Rejoice always. . . . Give thanks in all circumstances; for this is God's will for you in Christ Jesus" (1 Thessalonians 5:16, 18).

Yes, we must "hope in God" even when difficulties loom large on our horizon. By glorying in tribulation, we find peace of mind; for praise is still the great biblical antidote for tough times!

Henry Bosch

Those who praise the Lord in spite of their trials
change burdens into blessings!

Prayer Marathon

Read 1 Thessalonians 5:16–28

Pray continually. *1 Thessalonians 5:17*

Do you struggle to maintain a consistent prayer life? Many of us do. We know that prayer is important, but it can also be downright difficult. We have moments of deep communion with God, and then we have times when it feels like we're just going through the motions. Why do we struggle so in our prayers?

The life of faith is a marathon. The ups, the downs, and the plateaus in our prayer life are reflections of this race. And just as in a marathon we need to keep running, so we keep praying. The point is: Don't give up!

That is God's encouragement too. The apostle Paul said, "pray continually" (1 Thessalonians 5:17), "keep on praying" (Romans 12:12 NLT), and "devote yourselves to prayer" (Colossians 4:2). All of these statements carry the idea of remaining steadfast and continuing in the work of prayer.

And because God, our heavenly Father, is a personal being, we can develop a time of close communion with Him, just as we do with our close human relationships. A. W. Tozer writes that as we learn to pray, our prayer life can grow "from the initial most casual brush to the fullest, most intimate communion of which the human soul is capable." And that's what we really want—deep communication with God. It happens when we keep praying.

Poh Fang Chia

There is never a day when we don't need to pray.

Praising through Problems

Read Job 1:13-22

He replied, "You are talking like a foolish woman.
Shall we accept good from God, and not trouble? In all this,
Job did not sin in what he said. *Job 2:10*

"It's cancer." I wanted to be strong when Mom said those words to me. But I burst into tears. You never want to hear those words even one time. But this was Mom's third bout with cancer. After a routine mammogram and biopsy, Mom learned that she had a malignant tumor under her arm.

Though Mom was the one with bad news, she had to comfort me. Her response was eye-opening for me: "I know God is always good to me. He's always faithful." Even as she faced a difficult surgery, followed up by radiation treatments, Mom was assured of God's presence and faithfulness.

How like Job. Job lost his children, his wealth, and his health. But after hearing the news, Job 1:20 tells us "he fell to the ground in worship." When advised to curse God, he said, "Shall we accept good from God, and not trouble?" (2:10). What a radical initial response. Though Job later complained, ultimately he accepted that God had never changed. Job knew that God was still with him and that He still cared.

For most of us, praise is not our first response to difficulties. Sometimes the pain of our circumstances is so overwhelming, we lash out in fear or anger. But watching Mom's response reminded me that God is still present, still good. He will help us through hard times.

Linda Washington

Even at our lowest point, we can lift our eyes to the Lord.

Praying for the Opposition

Read John 19:1–5

Love your enemies and pray for those
who persecute you. *Matthew 5:44*

When I was a freshman in Bible college, I began to be bolder about speaking up for the Lord. Not surprisingly, my new habit created friction with some. Attending a social event with my former high school friends bore this out. One young woman to whom I had witnessed earlier laughed at my concern about where she would spend eternity. Ed, a friend who knew of my faith, said jokingly, "Three cheers for the old rugged cross!" I felt put down and rejected.

But later that evening I was filled with an unexplainable love. Recalling our Lord's command to "Love your enemies and pray for those who persecute you" (Matthew 5:44), I prayed for Ed who had mocked the cross of Christ. With my eyes filled with tears, I asked the Lord to save him.

About a year later, I got a letter from Ed saying he wanted to get together. When we finally met, he shared how he had wept over his own sinfulness and had invited Jesus Christ to be his Savior and Lord. Later, to my surprise I heard that Ed had become a missionary to Brazil. The lesson I learned from that experience is that prayer is the best response to spiritual opposition. What critic of your faith might need your prayers today?

Dennis Fisher

People may mock our message
but they are helpless against our prayers.

A Lifter

Read Galatians 6:1–10

Carry each other's burdens, and in this way
you will fulfill the law of Christ. *Galatians 6:2*

A man had just written a very harsh letter to someone who had injured him. The mailbox into which he was going to drop the letter had the instructions on the door: "Lift up." As he paused to read it, those words jolted him. The Spirit of God convinced him that his letter certainly would not "lift up" anybody, but it would have been more appropriate if the sign had read "Pull down."

No doubt you can think of fellow Christians who are going through trials and are carrying heavy burdens. Perhaps someone near and dear to you is weighed down. Are you a "lifter"? Paul said if we are to fulfill Christ's law, the law of love, we must get under the load and assist them.

We have a friend who is confined to her bed in a convalescent home. Much of her day is occupied in "lifting" others. Between times of prayer for those in need, she calls others who would welcome a word of cheer. She also sends cards of sympathy, encouragement, and happy greetings.

The body of Christ (the church) is made up of particular members, and "there should be no division in the body, but . . . its parts should have equal concern for each other" (1 Corinthians 12:25) and make it a point to "lift up." We should participate in spiritual friendships that lift the weight of trouble and woe. How about it, are we lifters?

Paul Van Gorder

Your own burdens lighten as you lift others' burdens!

God Hears

Read Romans 12:9–21

Be joyful in hope, patient in affliction,
faithful in prayer. *Romans 12:12*

Diane listened as the others in the group asked for prayers for their family members and friends facing challenges or illness. She had a family member who had been struggling with an addiction for years. But Diane kept her request silent. She couldn't bear to see the looks on people's faces or hear the questions or advice that often followed whenever she spoke the words aloud. She felt that this request was usually better left unspoken. Others simply didn't understand how her loved one could be a believer in Jesus and still struggle daily.

Although Diane didn't share her request with that group, she did have a few trusted friends she asked to pray with her. Together they asked God to set her loved one free from the very real bondage of addiction that he might experience freedom in Christ—and that God would give Diane the peace and patience she needed. As she prayed, she found comfort and strength from her relationship with Him.

Many of us have earnest, persistent prayers that seem to go unanswered. But we can be assured that God does care and He does hear all our requests. He urges us to continue to walk closely with Him, being "joyful in hope, patient in affliction, faithful in prayer" (Romans 12:12). We can lean on Him.

Alyson Kieda

Let us draw near to God with a sincere heart
and with the full assurance that faith brings. —Hebrews 10:22

But Prayer

Read Acts 12:5–17

The church was earnestly praying to God for [Peter]. *Acts 12:5*

When I was a pastor, I often visited residents in rest homes. I'll never forget one dear elderly lady I met. She was blind and had been bedridden for seven years, yet she remained sweet and radiant. One day she told me about a dream she had. She was in a beautiful garden where the grass was a luxuriant carpet beneath her and the fragrance of flowers filled the air.

She dropped to her knees, entranced by the scene. As her thoughts were drawn heavenward, she felt the need to pray for her own pastor, for me, and for others. When she awakened, however, she discovered that she was still in her hospital bed. With a smile she said to me, "You know, Pastor, at first I was a bit disappointed. But in a sense the dream was true. This old bed has been a garden of prayer these seven years!" Prayer had made her room a holy place of meditation and blessing.

Prayer also made a difference when Peter was in prison (Acts 12). It isn't always easy to pray, for real intercession takes self-discipline. Many of us lapse into saying fine-sounding words without truly praying. God often drives us to our knees through the press of circumstances, where we are to "look to the LORD and his strength; seek his face always" (1 Chronicles 16:11).

Herb Vander Lugt

God and prayer go together;
to neglect one is to neglect the other.

The Altogether Lovely One

Read Song of Songs 5:9–16

His mouth is sweetness itself; he is altogether lovely. This is my beloved, this is my friend, daughters of Jerusalem. Song of Songs 5:16

One of the most beautiful books of the Old Testament is the Song of Solomon, which describes the relationship between two people who are deeply in love. While this is its primary interpretation, many Bible teachers also see in the book a picture of Christ, the Bridegroom, and His bride, the church. How fitting, therefore, are the words of Song of Songs 5:16, in which the bride declares that her beloved is "altogether lovely." To the believer, that is a perfect description of the sinless Son of God.

Charles H. Spurgeon penned the following thought-provoking sentence about Jesus: "Not one feature in His glorious person attracts attention at the expense of others; but He is perfectly and altogether lovely." Continuing, Spurgeon exclaimed, "Oh, Jesus! Thy power, Thy grace, Thy justice, Thy tenderness, Thy truth, Thy majesty, and Thine immutability make up such a man, or rather such a God-man, as neither heaven nor earth hath seen elsewhere. . . . Thou art music without discord; Thou art many, and yet not divided; Thou art all things, and yet not diverse. As all the colors blend in one resplendent rainbow, so all the glories of heaven and earth meet in Thee and unite so wondrously, that there is none like Thee in all things; nay, if all the virtues of the most excellent were bound in one bundle, they could not rival Thee."

Jesus is worthy of our deepest love and highest praise! We too would say of our Savior, "He is altogether lovely."

Richard DeHaan

Jesus Christ is light to the eye,
honey to the taste, and music to the ear.

Gleaning the Fields

Read Ruth 2:1–12

And Ruth the Moabite said to Naomi, "Let me go to the fields and pick up the leftover grain behind anyone in whose eyes I find favor. Naomi said to her, "Go ahead, my daughter. *Ruth 2:2*

A Tanzanian friend has a vision for redeeming a piece of desolate land in the capital city of Dodoma. Recognizing the needs of some local widows, Ruth wants to transform these dusty acres into a place to keep chickens and grow crops. Her vision to provide for those in need is rooted in her love for God, and was inspired by her biblical namesake, Ruth.

God's laws allowed the poor or the foreigner to glean (harvest) from the edges of the fields (Leviticus 19:9–10). Ruth (in the Bible) was a foreigner, and was therefore allowed to work in the fields, gathering food for her and her mother-in-law. Gleaning in Boaz's field, a close relative, led to Ruth and Naomi ultimately finding a home and protection. Ruth used her ingenuity and effort in the work of the day—gathering food from the edges of the field—and God blessed her.

The passion of my friend Ruth and the dedication of the biblical Ruth stir me to give thanks to God for how He cares for the poor and downtrodden. They inspire me to seek ways to help others in my community and more broadly as a means of expressing my thanks to our giving God. How might you worship God through extending His mercy to others?

Amy Boucher Pye

God cares for the vulnerable.

The Joy of Fellowship

Read 1 John 1

We proclaim to you what we have seen and heard, so that you also may have fellowship with us. And our fellowship is with the Father and with his Son, Jesus Christ. *1 John 1:3*

In his book *The Roots of Righteousness*, A. W. Tozer wrote, "The fellowship of God is delightful beyond all telling. He communes with His redeemed ones in an easy, uninhibited fellowship that is restful and healing to the soul. He is not sensitive nor selfish nor temperamental. What He is today we shall find Him tomorrow and the next day and the next year.

"He is not hard to please, though He may be hard to satisfy. He expects of us only what He has Himself supplied. He is quick to mark every simple effort to please Him, and just as quick to overlook imperfections when He knows we meant to do His will. He loves us for ourselves and values our love more than galaxies of new created worlds."

Are you longing for that kind of satisfying walk with God? Then follow these simple guidelines found in the first epistle of John. He tells us to walk in light (1:6, 7); never say you are sinless (1:8); keep Christ's commands (2:4); love your brothers (2:10, 11); and love not the world (2:15–17). Use David's prayers, "Search me, God, and know my heart; test me and know my anxious thoughts. See if there is any offensive way in me" (Psalm 139:23–24), and "Create in me a pure heart, O God" (Psalm 51:10). These words can open the door to the joy of fellowship with God and with His Son Jesus Christ.

Dennis DeHaan

The man who walks close to God
will leave no room for the devil to come between.

Our Comforting Advocate

Read John 16:7–14

*I will ask the Father, and he will give you
another advocate to help you.* John 14:16

A missionary to Africa was trying to translate a language, but he couldn't find a tribal word to express the ministry of the Holy Spirit. After three years of searching for just the right phrase, he heard an old chief refer several times to a man as "Nsenga-Mukwashi" during a village court proceeding. When he asked the chieftain what that meant, the elderly leader explained that "Nsenga-Mukwashi" was the title given to the one whose duty it was to stand up for the people of the village if they were in any trouble. On that particular day the "Nsenga-Mukwashi" had eloquently pleaded the cause of a woman who had been unjustly treated. "My people see him as a comforting advocate," said the chief. The missionary recognized that this term could be used to describe the Holy Spirit's work in the life of the believer. It beautifully expressed the idea that God's Spirit is both the Christian's advocate and his comforter.

Think about it. Why are our vague, stammering prayers often answered so specifically? Why is our life richly blessed, even when our faith is weak? Why in sorrow are we able to bear up so well? The answer is in the One who "intercedes for us through wordless groans," who prays for us "in accordance with the will of God" (Romans 8:26, 27).

Yes, our heavenly "Nsenga-Mukwashi" ever stands by to help us in trouble. How blessed is the ministry of that great comforting Advocate!

Henry Bosch

Where the human spirit falls, the Holy Spirit fills.

Marvelous Maker

Read Psalm 104:24–34

How many are your works, LORD! In wisdom you made them all; the earth is full of your creatures. *Psalm 104:24*

As an amateur photographer, I enjoy capturing glimpses of God's creativity with my camera. I see His fingerprints on each delicate flower petal, each vibrant sunrise and sunset, and each cloud-painted and star-speckled sky canvas.

My camera's powerful zoom option allows me to take photos of the Lord's creatures too. I've snapped shots of a chattering squirrel in a cherry blossom tree, a colorful butterfly flitting from bloom to bloom, and sea turtles sunning on a rocky, black beach. Each one-of-a-kind image prompted me to worship my marvelous Maker.

I'm not the first of God's people to praise Him while admiring His unique creations. The writer of Psalm 104 sings of the Lord's many works of art in nature (v. 24). He regards "the sea, vast and spacious, teeming with creatures beyond number" (v. 25) and rejoices in God for providing constant and complete care for His masterpieces (vv. 27–31). Considering the majesty of the God-given life around him, the psalmist bursts with worshipful gratitude: "I will sing to the LORD all my life; I will sing praise to my God as long as I live" (v. 33).

While reflecting on the Lord's magnificent and immense creation, we can look closely at His intentional creativity and attention to detail. And like the psalmist, we can sing to our Creator with thankful praise for how powerful, majestic, and loving He is and always will be. Hallelujah!

Xochitl Dixon

God's works are marvelous, and so is He.

Don't Forget Yourself

Read John 17:1–5

"Father, glorify me in your presence with the glory I
had with you before the world began. *John 17:5*

Some Christians think it's wrong to pray for themselves, but I don't agree. We shouldn't feel guilty about bringing our own needs and concerns to the Lord. A girl listened carefully to her mother's prayers and then said, "Mom, you're always praying for somebody else. You never pray for yourself, but I think you should." This youngster was speaking with a wisdom beyond her years, for we do need to ask the Lord for His guidance, forgiveness, patience, and grace.

It may surprise us to discover that Christ's high-priestly prayer in John 17 began with a petition for himself. But think about it—He was at the most crucial moment of His earthly life; soon He would take up the cross and bear the punishment for the sins of the world. His concern for others was obvious. A few moments after He began to pray, He would specifically mention His disciples, who would be shouldering such heavy responsibility when He was gone. Then He would intercede for His church, which would endure great persecution down through the centuries. But first He prayed for himself.

So, when you spend time in God's presence, tell Him about your hopes, your worries, your desires, and your needs. He'll help you see things more clearly and minister to your aching soul. He'll give you the direction you need. As you go to the Lord in prayer, pray for others, but don't forget yourself.

David Egner

To deny yourself does not mean to neglect yourself.

The Joyous Song of Morning!

Read 2 Corinthians 4:8–18

Weeping may endure for a night,
but joy comes in the morning. *Psalm 30:5 NKJV*

There are many different words in our Bible that are translated by the simple syllable "joy." The one used in Psalm 30:5 (NKJV), however, is seldom used. Freely translated, the Greek word used there means, "loud, joyous singing." Have you ever been so happy that you just could not contain yourself, but felt you must burst into song and shout with delight to express your exuberance? If so, you will understand the meaning of the psalmist.

Charles Spurgeon, while commenting on Psalm 30: 5, writes most comfortingly, "Thy head may be crowned with thorny troubles now, but it shall wear a starry crown before long—thy hand may be filled with cares, but it shall sweep the strings of the harp of heaven soon. How small our troubles and trials will seem when we look back upon them over there! . . . What does it matter though weeping endure for a night, when 'joy comes in the morning.' "

Just as the morning sun in the eastern sky leaps almost instantly above the horizon to shed its bright beams of blessing, so too the sudden coming of Christ will dispel in a moment the long night of earth's darkness and sorrow! Then what singing, what rejoicing, what victory! We can dry our tears and lift our voice in praise. The night is almost gone, and the morning song of joy is about to begin.

Henry Bosch

The best optimism in the world
is bound up with "that blessed hope."

Mighty Waters

Read Revelation 1:9–17

Jesus Christ, who is the faithful witness, the firstborn from the dead, and the ruler of the kings of the earth. Revelation 1:5

While in Brazil, I went to see Iguazu Falls, one of the greatest waterfalls in the world. The massive falls are breathtaking, but what impressed me most at Iguazu was not the sight of the falls or the spray of the water. It was the sound. The sound was beyond deafening—I felt as if I was actually inside the sound itself. It was an overwhelming experience that reminded me how small I am by comparison.

Later, with this scene in mind, I couldn't help but think about John in Revelation 1:15. While on the island of Patmos, he saw a vision of the risen Christ. The apostle described Jesus in the glory of His resurrection, noting both His clothing and His physical qualities. Then John described Christ's voice "as "the sound of rushing waters" (v. 15).

I'm not sure I fully appreciated what that meant until I visited Iguazu and was overwhelmed by the thundering sound of the falls. As those mighty waters reminded me of my own smallness, I better understood why John fell at the feet of Christ as if dead (v. 17).

Perhaps that description will help you grasp the awesomeness of Jesus's presence and prompt you to follow John's example of worshiping the Savior.

Bill Crowder

True worship of Christ changes admiration into adoration.

Unlimited Access

Read Ephesians 2:11–22

Through him we both have access to the Father
by one Spirit. *Ephesians 2:18*

A few years ago, a shocking breach of security occurred when a couple brazenly walked into a White House state dinner—even getting close enough to have their picture taken with the President of the United States. Usually, extensive background checks and careful scrutiny of the guest list screens out the uninvited.

It's a rare day for any of us that our access is not restricted in some way. Signs warn us: Employees Only, Do Not Enter, Authorized Vehicles Only, No Trespassing. None of us want to be told that we are not welcome. But the fact is that there will always be some places from which we will be barred. It makes me grateful that God sets no restriction on who may come to Him.

Believers who approach God encounter no "Keep Out" signs. Through prayer, God the Father allows us immediate and unlimited access to Him because His Son Jesus Christ has opened the way to all who receive Him (Ephesians 2:18). "Come to me, all you who are weary and burdened" (Matthew 11:28). "Whoever comes to me I will never drive away" (John 6:37). "Let anyone who is thirsty come to me and drink" (7:37).

Once you come to Christ for salvation, you can enjoy unrestricted fellowship. The door is always open.

Cindy Hess Kasper

God's throne is always accessible to His children.

In Honor and Memory

Read Revelation 5

In a loud voice they were saying: "Worthy is the Lamb,
who was slain, to receive power and wealth and wisdom and
strength and honor and glory and praise! *Revelation 5:12*

On March 21, 1969, a Marine patrol in Vietnam descended a steep bank to fill their canteens in a stream. As they stooped in two feet of water, the area suddenly exploded with machine-gunfire and grenades. Several men were hit. According to an official report, one soldier, "with complete disregard for his own safety, . . . assisted several Marines. . . . Despite the heavy fire, he made several trips . . . until he himself was wounded and unable to continue."

Twenty-one years later, one of the men who had been pulled out of the water learned that the friend who had rescued him was still alive. He set out to see that he was recognized for his heroism. The Marine eventually found his friend, Jim Lahr, who was now paralyzed from the waist down. With a heart full of appreciation, he saw Jim receive a long-delayed and much-deserved Bronze Star.

I am deeply moved by this Marine's desire to honor the one who saved his life. But that makes me wonder about my lack of emotion for the One who paid a far greater price to save me. No one deserves the honor that Christ does. No one has sacrificed as much. No wonder all heaven will praise Him for ever and ever.

Father, forgive us for not giving your Son the honor He deserves. Fill us with praise.

Mart DeHaan

Man may be worthy of admiration;
only Christ is worthy of adoration.

The Praying Patient

Read John 17:6–19

Holy Father, protect them by the power of your name, the name you gave me, so that they may be one as we are one. John 17:11

The obituary for Alan Nanninga, a man in my city, identified him as "foremost, a dedicated witness for Christ." After a description of his family life and career, the article mentioned nearly a decade of declining health. It concluded by saying, "His hospital stays . . . earned him the honorary title of 'The Praying Patient' " because of his ministry to other patients. Here was a man who, in his times of distress, reached out to pray for and with the people in need around him.

Hours before Judas betrayed Him, Jesus prayed for His disciples. "I will remain in the world no longer, but they are still in the world, and I am coming to you. Holy Father, protect them by the power of your name, the name you gave me, so that they may be one as we are one" (John 17:11). Knowing what was about to happen, Jesus looked beyond himself to focus on His followers and friends.

During our times of illness and distress, we long for and need the prayers of others. How those prayers help and encourage us! But may we also, like our Lord, lift our eyes to pray for those around us who are in great need.

David McCasland

Our troubles can fill our prayers
with love and empathy for others.

Is He Listening?

Read Matthew 26:42; 27:45–46

My God, my God, why have you forsaken me? *Matthew 27:46*

"Sometimes it feels as if God isn't listening to me." Those words, from a woman who tried to stay strong in her walk with God while coping with an alcoholic husband, echo the heart cry of many believers. For eighteen years, she asked God to change her husband. Yet it never happened.

What are we to think when we repeatedly ask God for something good—something that could easily glorify Him—but the answer doesn't come? Is He listening or not?

Let's look at the life of the Savior. In the garden of Gethsemane, He agonized for hours in prayer, pouring out His heart and pleading, "May this cup be taken from me" (Matthew 26:39). But the Father's answer was clearly "No." To provide salvation, God had to send Jesus to die on the cross. Even though Jesus felt as if His Father had forsaken Him, He prayed intensely and passionately because He trusted that God was listening.

When we pray, we may not see how God is working or understand how He will bring good through it all. So we have to trust Him. We relinquish our rights and let God do what is best. We must leave the unknowable to the all-knowing One. He is listening and working things out His way.

Dave Branon

When we bend our knees to pray, God bends His ear to listen.

God-Forsaken

Read Mark 15:16–37

At three in the afternoon Jesus cried out in a loud voice, "Eloi, Eloi, lema sabachthani? (which means "My God, my God, why have you forsaken me?"). *Mark 15:34*

An English doctor conducted an experiment to study the effects of isolation on people. He built a soundproof room 9' x 9' in size and suspended it by nylon rope. The participants wore padded fur gloves and heavy woolen socks to eliminate the sensations of touch. Special translucent goggles limited their vision. After just one hour of isolation, some people found it impossible to concentrate. This was followed by feelings of anxiety and panic. Many could not stay in the room more than five hours.

This reminds me of a much more terrible isolation—the aloneness experienced by the Lord Jesus as He hung on the cross. In the awfulness of those hours, Jesus endured a suffering worse than even the agonizing physical pain of crucifixion: He was forsaken by the Father. When Christ took our sins upon himself to pay the death penalty for us, God turned away from His beloved Son. This isolation from the Father caused Jesus to cry out, "My God, my God, why have you forsaken me?" (Mark 15:34).

Whenever we think of Calvary, we should remember the great sacrifice Jesus made there. Let's praise Him for what He endured. His great love made it possible for us to be restored to God.

Richard DeHaan

Christ became a curse for us to remove the curse from us.

A Day of Rest

Read Exodus 23:10–13

Six days do your work, but on the seventh day
do not work. *Exodus 23:12*

One Sunday, I stood by the gurgling stream that wends its way through our North London community, delighting in the beauty it brings to our otherwise built-up area. I felt myself relax as I watched the cascading water and listened to the birds chirping. I paused to give the Lord thanks for how He helps us to find rest for our souls.

The Lord instituted a time of Sabbath—a time for rest and renewal—for His people in the ancient Near East because He wanted them to thrive. As we see in the book of Exodus, He tells them to sow their fields for six years and rest on the seventh. So too with working six days and resting on the seventh. His way of life set apart the Israelites from other nations, for not only they but also the foreigners and slaves in their households were allowed to follow this pattern.

We can approach our day of rest with expectancy and creativity, welcoming the chance to worship and do something that feeds our souls, which will vary according to our preferences. Some will like to play games; some to garden; some to share a meal with friends and family; some to take an afternoon nap.

How can we rediscover the beauty and richness of setting apart a day to rest, if that's missing from our lives?

Amy Boucher Pye

In our faith and service, rest is as important as work.

Watch and Pray

Read Mark 14:32–42

Watch and pray so that you will not fall into temptation. *Mark 14:38*

From my window I can see a 1,700-meter hill called the Cerro del Borrego or "Hill of the Sheep." In 1862, the French army invaded Mexico. While the enemy camped in the central park of the city of Orizaba, the Mexican army established its position at the top of the hill. However, the Mexican general neglected to guard access to the top. While the Mexican troops were sleeping, the French attacked and killed 2,000 of them.

This reminds me of another hill, the Mount of Olives, and the garden at its foot where a group of disciples fell asleep. Jesus rebuked them, saying, "Watch and pray so that you will not fall into temptation. The spirit is willing, but the flesh is weak" (Mark 14:38).

How easy it is to sleep or become careless in our Christian walk. Temptation strikes when we are most vulnerable. When we neglect certain areas of our spiritual lives—such as prayer and Bible study—we become drowsy and let our guard down, making us easy targets for our enemy, Satan, to strike (1 Peter 5:8).

We need to be alert to the possibilities of an attack and pray to maintain vigilance. If we remain watchful and pray—for ourselves and for others—the Spirit will enable us to resist temptation.

Keila Ochoa

Satan is powerless against the power of Christ.

Obedience in Worship

Read 1 Samuel 15:13–23

To obey is better than sacrifice,
and to heed is better than the fat of rams. *1 Samuel 15:22*

While I was traveling with a chorale from a Christian high school, it was great to see the students praise God as they led in worship in the churches we visited. What happened away from church was even better to see. One day the group discovered that a woman had no money for gas—and they spontaneously felt led by God to take up a collection. They were able to give her enough money for several tankfuls of gas.

It's one thing to worship and praise God at church; it's quite another to move out into the real world and worship Him through daily obedience.

The students' example causes us to think about our own lives. Do we confine our worship to church? Or do we continue to worship Him by obeying Him in our daily life, looking for opportunities to serve?

In 1 Samuel 15 we see that Saul was asked by the Lord to do a task; but when we review what he did (vv. 20–21), we discover that he used worship (sacrifice) as an excuse for his failure to obey God. God's response was, "To obey is better than sacrifice" (v. 22).

It's good to be involved in worship at church. But let's also ask God to show us ways to continue to give Him the praise He deserves through our obedience.

Dave Branon

Our worship should not be confined to times and places;
it should be the spirit of our lives.

Productive Praying

Read James 5:13–18

Therefore confess your sins to each other and pray for
each other so that you may be healed. The prayer
of a righteous person is powerful and effective. *James 5:16*

I can well remember the boyish enthusiasm I had as a youngster when I'd ask my father for something I really wanted. Sometimes, in an effort to escape my unending pleas, he would finally say, "That's enough, son; I'll take care of everything." Do we have that youthful fervency when we bring our needs to our heavenly Father?

Puritan preacher Thomas Brooks (1608–1680) described what often happens with prayer: "Cold prayers are as arrows without heads, as swords without edges, as birds without wings; they pierce not, they cut not, they fly not up to heaven. Cold prayers always freeze before they reach heaven." To become more effective in our praying, we should heed these words of Bishop Hall: "It is not the rhetoric of our prayers, how eloquent they be; nor the geometry of our prayers, how long they be; nor the music of our prayers, how sweet our voice may be; nor the method of our prayers, how orderly they may be; nor even the theology of our prayers, how good the doctrine may be—which God cares for. Fervency of spirit is that which availeth much."

James reminds us that Elijah "prayed earnestly." And what answers he received—the very forces of nature were changed! Fervent prayer, if it be for God's glory and presented in the name of His Son, will accomplish great things for time and eternity.

Paul Van Gorder

Productive prayer requires earnestness, not eloquence.

Five-Minute Rule

Read Psalm 102:1–17

He will respond to the prayer of the destitute;
he will not despise their plea. *Psalm 102:17*

I read about a five-minute rule that a mother had for her children. They had to be ready for school and gather together five minutes before it was time to leave each day.

They would gather around Mom, and she would pray for each one by name, asking for the Lord's blessing on their day. Then she'd give them a kiss and off they'd run. Even neighborhood kids would be included in the prayer circle if they happened to stop by. One of the children said many years later that she learned from this experience how crucial prayer is to her day.

The writer of Psalm 102 knew the importance of prayer. This psalm is labeled, "A prayer of an afflicted person who has grown weak and pours out a lament before the Lord." He cried out, "Hear my prayer, Lord . . . ; when I call, answer me quickly" (vv. 1–2). God looks down "from his sanctuary on high, from heaven [He views] the earth" (v. 19).

God cares for you and wants to hear from you. Whether you follow the five-minute rule asking for blessings on the day, or need to spend more time crying out to Him in deep distress, talk to the Lord each day. Your example may have a big impact on your family or someone close to you.

Anne Cetas

Prayer is an acknowledgment of our need for God.

Great Is Our Lord

Read Psalm 147:1–5

Great is our LORD and mighty in power;
his understanding has no limit. *Psalm 147:5*

Nearly 200 years before Christ, the astronomer Hipparchus catalogued about 850 stars—the total number, he thought. Some 300 years later his figures were still considered accurate. But with the invention of the telescope by Galileo, millions of new heavenly bodies could be viewed, and the world soon learned that the earlier count was incomplete. No one today can tell us exactly how many there are, but astronomers estimate that an average of 100 billion stars are found in a single galaxy, and that 10 billion galaxies are within range of the largest telescopes. The numbers are almost inconceivable!

The magnitude and complexity of nature fill us with awe. Even with the vast resources of science and increasing computer technology, we have only scratched the surface of exploring God's creation. Certainly the psalmist expressed our deepest feelings when he said, "Great is the LORD and most worthy of praise; his greatness no one can fathom" (Psalm 145:3).

Linked with our amazement at the marvels of the universe is the equal wonder that God cares for us! The same Almighty One who placed the multiplied billions of stars in space now stands ready to heal the brokenhearted and bring peace to weary souls. He was so concerned for us that He sent His only Son to pay the ransom for sin and secure our eternal redemption. In adoration we exclaim, "Great is our Lord!"

Paul Van Gorder

The same God whose orderly creation reveals His greatness
provides a salvation which reveals His grace.

Thanks for Unanswered Prayer

Read Psalm 28

Praise be to the LORD,
for he has heard my cry for mercy. *Psalm 28:6*

When the Lord Jesus was here on earth, He prayed and expressed His thanks for a number of things: food (John 6:11), the simplicity of the gospel (Matthew 11:25), and even for His own death (Matthew 26:26–27). He also gave thanks for answered prayer (John 11:41). He set an example for us. Like our Lord, we should express our sincere gratitude to God when our requests are granted.

In a seacoast town where ships often departed stood a small church. At the end of each year, the pastor printed a statistical report for his congregation. One year the parishioners noted an unusual entry. Among the records was this notation: "Missing at sea: nine." The members of the congregation didn't know of any of their number who had been lost at sea, so someone asked the pastor what he meant. "Well," he replied, "during the year, eleven of you asked me to pray for family members or friends who were going out to sea. Because I heard only two of you ever publicly thank the Lord for the safe return of your loved ones, I assumed the remaining nine were still missing. So, I included them in the report!"

This faithful pastor was teaching his people a lesson we all need to learn. When God answers our prayers, we should be quick to show our appreciation to Him—even as the Savior did. Our heavenly Father is pleased when we thank Him for answered prayer.

David Egner

The fragrance of thankful praise
should rise from the blossom of answered prayer.

The Only King

Read Matthew 2:1–12

[The Magi] opened their treasures and presented [Jesus] with gifts of gold, frankincense and myrrh. *Matthew 2:11*

As five-year-old Eldon listened to the pastor talk about Jesus leaving heaven and coming to earth, he gasped when the pastor thanked Him in prayer for dying for our sins. "Oh, no! He died?" the boy said in surprise.

From the start of Christ's life on earth, there were people who wanted Him dead. Wise men came to Jerusalem during the reign of King Herod inquiring, "Where is the one who has been born king of the Jews? We saw his star when it rose and have come to worship him" (Matthew 2:2). When the king heard this, he became fearful of one day losing his position to Jesus. So he sent soldiers to kill all the boys two years old and younger around Bethlehem. But God protected His Son and sent an angel to warn His parents to leave the area. They fled, and He was saved (vv. 13–18).

When Jesus completed His ministry, He was crucified for the sins of the world. The sign placed above His cross, though meant in mockery, read, "THIS IS JESUS, THE KING OF THE JEWS" (27:37). Yet three days later He rose in victory from the grave. After ascending to heaven, He sat down on the throne as King of kings and Lord of lords (Philippians 2:8–11).

The King died for our sins—yours, mine, and Eldon's. Let's allow Him to rule in our hearts.

Anne Cetas

To have an upright life, lean on Jesus.

When People Pray

Read Acts 4:13–31

After they prayed, the place where they were meeting was shaken. Acts 4:31

Peter and John were in danger. The religious leaders in Jerusalem opposing the gospel had warned them to cease their missionary efforts (Acts 4:18). When the apostles reported this to the other believers, they immediately held a prayer meeting.

What happened next is thrilling. The believers first praised God. Then they asked for boldness that they might continue the work. The results were dramatic. The house shook, and the believers were filled with the Holy Spirit. They boldly witnessed, enjoyed spiritual unity, and gave unselfishly to those in need (vv. 31–37).

I've never felt a building shake at a prayer meeting, but I have seen God's power at work. When I've tried to help repair a broken marriage or a divided church, I've asked those involved to pray. Sometimes they refused. Other times, though, they mumbled carefully worded prayers. Those meetings failed.

But occasionally someone would pray in earnest. Almost immediately the atmosphere would change. Confession and forgiveness soon replaced charges and countercharges.

When we pray sincerely, praising God and seeking His glory, great things happen. Prayer must always come from the heart.

Herb Vander Lugt

Sincere intercession is the key to God's intervention.

The Olive Press

Read Mark 14:32–39

They went to a place called Gethsemane. *Mark 14:32*

If you visit the village of Capernaum beside the Sea of Galilee, you will find an exhibit of ancient olive presses. Formed from basalt rock, the olive press consists of two parts: a base and a grinding wheel. The base is large, round, and has a trough carved out of it. The olives were placed in this trough, and then the wheel, also made from heavy stone, was rolled over the olives to extract the oil.

On the night before His death, Jesus went to the Mount of Olives overlooking the city of Jerusalem. There, in the garden called Gethsemane, He prayed to the Father, knowing what lay ahead of Him.

The word Gethsemane means "place of the olive press"—and that perfectly describes those first crushing hours of Christ's suffering on our behalf. There, "in anguish, he prayed . . . and his sweat was like drops of blood falling to the ground" (Luke 22:44).

Jesus the Son suffered and died to take away "the sin of the world" (John 1:29) and restore our broken relationship with God the Father. "Surely he took up our pain and bore our suffering. . . . He was pierced for our transgressions, he was crushed for our iniquities; the punishment that brought us peace was on him, and by his wounds we are healed" (Isaiah 53:4–5).

Our hearts cry out in worship and gratitude.

Bill Crowder

Gone my transgressions, and now I am free—
all because Jesus was wounded for me.

Great Power

Read John 14:8–14

"If you believe, you will receive whatever you ask for in prayer." Matthew 21:22

If the veil of our understanding could be lifted for a brief moment so we could see the hidden workings of God in response to our prayers, we would say with conviction, "Prayer does change things. "

But do we really believe in the power of prayer? Do we actually pray in faith, trusting that God will answer? Too often we seek our own solutions first. Peter Marshall, chaplain of the US Senate in the 1940s, once said, "I am sure that each of you has read this statement many times: 'Prayer Changes Things.' You have seen it painted on posters which adorn the walls of our Sunday school rooms. You have . . . heard it from the pulpit, oh, so many times. But do you believe it? Do you actually, honestly, believe that prayer changes things? Have you ever had prayer change anything for you? Your attitudes, your circumstances, your obstacles, your fears?"

Can we answer Marshall's probing questions with a resounding yes? If so, we know the power of prayer. But if we must honestly say no, then we need to begin obeying the scriptural instructions about prayer.

Each of us must go to the Lord daily with our specific requests. Then we should surrender to His will. We will soon learn from first-hand experience that great power is available through prayer.

David Egner

A life without prayer is a life without power.

The Power of a Song

Read Psalm 98:1–6

*Speaking to one another with psalms, hymns,
and songs from the Spirit. Ephesians 5:19*

When the joy of the Lord is in your heart, it will overflow from your lips in songs. This old story illustrates the point: Willy wasn't well known or very talented. He was only a young newsboy on a city street corner. But something very big and very important had happened to him recently. At Sunday school he had accepted Jesus as his personal Savior. Now he wanted to tell others about Him.

So every evening on the busy corner Willy lifted the tune "Jesus Loves Me," which was his favorite hymn. One stormy night a drunkard staggered out of a tavern and stopped to listen. "What are you whistling, boy?" he asked. "It's a hymn I learned at Sunday school called 'Jesus Loves Me!'" "Well, Jesus certainly doesn't love an old drunkard like me," the man muttered. "O yes, He does, mister!" Willy insisted. "Come with me and I'll prove it to you." He led the man to a nearby mission, where he was given food and a clean bed—all in the name of Jesus. He was deeply touched and gave himself to the Savior—all because little Willy had whistled for the Lord Jesus."

Are you a singing Christian? It's a wonderful way of spreading the blessed news of salvation to needy hearts.

Henry Bosch

The devil views with dread a joyous singing Christian.

The Darkest Day

Read Matthew 26:17–30

The stone the builders rejected has become
the chief cornerstone. *Psalm 118:22*

To celebrate Passover, Jewish worshipers sing Psalms 113–118, a section called the "Egyptian Hallel." The ceremony builds to a crescendo of appreciation for freedom and the beauty of life given by God. It ends with participants singing and praising God both to please Him and to express their own pleasure. One rabbi explains it as experiencing the "emotional joy of freedom."

Near the end of the Passover meal, the second half of these Hallel psalms are sung. According to the gospel of Matthew, Jesus and His disciples sang a hymn and "went out to the Mount of Olives" after celebrating their last Passover together (26:30). They may well have sung this psalm:

The stone the builders rejected;
    has become the chief cornerstone;
the Lord has done this,
    and it is marvelous in our eyes.
The Lord has done it this very day;
    let us rejoice today and be glad. (Psalm 118:22–24)

Regardless of which hymn they sang, the confidence Jesus had in the goodness of His heavenly Father is astounding. He was able to praise His Father even though He knew He was about to experience His darkest day.

Julie Ackerman Link

Praise has the power to lighten our heaviest burden.

Fellowship of Love

Read Philippians 2:1–4

*Not looking to your own interests but each of
you to the interests of the others. Philippians 2:4*

God's children should rally in support of a needy brother or sister
in the Lord.

Some years ago a pastor went to Texas to attend a Christian convention. While he was there, he received word that his wife had
suddenly been stricken with a serious illness. Immediately he hur-
ried to catch the first train home. During the long, sleepless hours
of the night his heart was filled with anxiety. The next morning the
conductor handed him a telegram, saying, "It must be important, for
it was specially relayed to us at the last station."

"I believe it is bad news, perhaps even a death notice," the minister replied as he took the yellow envelope. Then with deep emotion
and trembling hands he slowly opened it. As he read the words,
tears filled his eyes. He was overwhelmed, not with sorrow but with
joy. This was the message: "Convention in session all night. Prayed
for you and your wife. She will get well!" When he arrived home,
he found that she had begun to improve from the hour he left the
meeting. Although the pastor and his loved one were unaware of it
at the time, both of them had been upheld in prayer by Christians
in a fellowship of love.

May we never become so concerned about our "own things" that
we fail to intercede for the enrichment and strengthening of the
entire Body of Christ.

Paul Van Gorder

The "tie that binds" should stretch
to all saints and strengthen under strain!

God's World

Read Psalm 24

The earth is the LORD's, and everything in it. *Psalm 24:1*

I knew my son would enjoy receiving a map of the world for his birthday. After some shopping, I found a colorful chart of the continents, which included illustrations in every region. A birdwing butterfly hovered over Papua, New Guinea. Mountains cascaded through Chile. A diamond adorned South Africa. I was delighted, but I wondered about the label at the bottom of the map: Our World.

In one sense, the earth is our world because we live in it. We're allowed to drink its water, mine its gold, and fish its seas—but only because God has given us the go-ahead (Genesis 1:28–30). Really, it's God's World. "The earth is the LORD's, and everything in it, the world, and all who live in it" (Psalm 24:1). It amazes me that God has entrusted His incredible creation to mere humans. He knew that some of us would mistreat it, deny He made it, and claim it as ours. Still, He allows us to call it home and sustains it through His Son (Colossians 1:16–17).

Today, take a moment to enjoy life in God's world. Savor the taste of some fruit. Eavesdrop on a bird and listen to its song. Revel in a sunset. Let the world you inhabit inspire you to worship the One who owns it.

Jennifer Benson Schuldt

The beauty of creation gives us reasons to sing God's praise.

Work and Pray

Read Matthew 9:35–38

Ask the LORD of the harvest. *Matthew 9:38*
Your labor in the LORD is not in vain. *1 Corinthians 15:58*

The fact that hard work and prayerful dependence on God go hand-in-hand was indelibly impressed upon me by an incident during my boyhood in North Dakota. One spring, area farmers prepared their soil and planted grain as usual.

But the crops grew poorly because of a long dry spell. As the tiny sprouts baked in the hot sun, the farmers became increasingly alarmed. They knew there would be no harvest if it didn't rain soon, so they called for prayer services in nearby churches. A few days later the sky darkened, lightning flashed, and thunder pealed, signaling the answer to the prayers of God's people. As the first drops fell, the farmers rejoiced. The harvest was assured because of hard work—and fervent prayer.

That same combination of hard work and prayer is needed in evangelism. Puritan pastor Richard Baxter, for example, went from house to house in Kidderminster, England, working more than twelve hours a day. But he also had a prayer life that Dwight L. Moody described as "staining his study walls with praying breath." No wonder the vast majority of the people in Kidderminster were converted!

Jesus told His disciples that the "harvest is plentiful" (Matthew 9:37). Then He directed them to pray. And Paul spoke in 1 Corinthians of sowing, watering, and reaping, but he also said, "God has been making it grow" (3:6). Yes, hard work and prayer produce results. They always have, and they always will.

Herb Vander Lugt

Work as if everything depends on you;
pray as if everything depends on God.

What Really Matters

Read Psalm 30

You, LORD, brought me up from the realm of the dead; you
spared me from going down to the pit. Sing the praises of the Lord,
you his faithful people; praise his holy name. *Psalm 30:3–4*

As a deadly tornado ripped through Will County, Illinois, a young father sat cradling his infant child, born just three weeks before. When the fierce, howling winds finally subsided and calm had returned, the man's house was gone—and so was his baby. But according to a news report, the father found his child in a field near his house—alive and well! And so was the rest of his family.

When asked by a reporter if he was angry that he had lost everything he owned, he replied, "No, I just thank God I have my baby and my family. Some people don't have that. Nothing else is important."

Often it takes times of tragedy to remind us what really matters in life. When things are going well, we can easily get preoccupied with what we own. We become tied to so many nonessential, unimportant things. We tend to grow overly concerned about cars, houses, furniture, appliances, clothes, and countless other trappings of modern life. But when life is reduced to the essentials, as it was in the Illinois tornado, we recall again that life itself is enough reason to praise God.

Have you spent time today praising God for life and for the people He has given you to share your life with? That's what really matters.

Dave Branon

Nothing can fill the place in our heart that was intended for God.

Ordinary vs. Extraordinary

Read Romans 8:12–26

The Spirit you received brought about your adoption to sonship. And by him we cry, "*Abba*, Father." *Romans 8:15*

For more than a century, the pinnacle of golf has been to score 59—a score that had been recorded only three times in PGA Tour history before 2010. Then, in 2010, Paul Goydos scored a 59—only to be equaled a month later by Stuart Appleby's 59. Consequently, some sportswriters speculated that the most coveted achievement in golf was now becoming commonplace! It's amazing to see two 59s in the same season, but it would be a mistake to begin to view this as ordinary.

For those who follow Jesus Christ, it is also a mistake to view the remarkable as ordinary. Think about prayer, for instance. At any moment we can talk to the Creator God who spoke the universe into existence! Not only are we welcomed into His presence but we are also invited to enter boldly: "Let us then approach God's throne of grace with confidence, so that we may receive mercy and find grace to help us in our time of need" (Hebrews 4:16).

There is nothing ordinary about access to God—yet sometimes we take this privilege for granted. He is almighty God, but He is also our Father who loves us and allows us to call on Him at any moment of any day. Now that's extraordinary!

Bill Crowder

God is always available to hear the prayers of His children.

Beauty in the Church

Read Exodus 36:1–7

"All who are skilled among you are to come and make
everything the LORD has commanded." *Exodus 35:10*

When my husband, Jay, and I decided to build a new house, we
didn't recruit friends and family who enjoy working with power
tools; instead, we hired a skilled builder to create something both
functional and beautiful.

Beauty in the church building, however, is not always a high
priority. Some associate it with impracticality, so anything ornate
or decorative is considered wasteful. But that wasn't God's attitude
when He established a place of worship for the ancient Israelites. He
didn't recruit just anybody to set up an ordinary tent. He appointed
skilled craftsmen, Bezalel and Oholiab (Exodus 36:1), to decorate
the tabernacle with finely woven tapestries and intricately designed
ornaments (37:17–20).

I think the beauty was important then because it reminded the
people of the worth of God in their worship. During the dry and
dusty days of desert wanderings, they needed a reminder of God's
majesty.

The beauty created by God's people in worship settings today
can serve the same purpose. We offer God our best talents because
He is worthy. Beauty also gives us a glimpse of heaven and whets
our appetites for what God is preparing for our future.

Julie Ackerman Link

Beauty reflects God.

Always Pray and Don't Give Up

Read Luke 18:1–8

Jesus told his disciples a parable to show them that
they should always pray and not give up. *Luke 18:1*

Are you going through one of those times when it seems every attempt to resolve a problem is met with a new difficulty? You thank the Lord at night that it's taken care of but awake to find that something else has gone wrong and the problem remains.

During an experience like that, I was reading the gospel of Luke and was astounded by the opening words of chapter 18: "Then Jesus told his disciples a parable to show them that they should always pray and not give up" (v. 1). I had read the story of the persistent widow many times but never grasped why Jesus told it (v. 2–8). Now I connected those opening words with the story. The lesson to His followers was very clear: "Always pray and never give up."

Prayer is not a means of coercing God to do what we want. It is a process of recognizing His power and plan for our lives. In prayer we yield our lives and circumstances to the Lord and trust Him to act in His time and in His way.

As we rely on God's grace not only for the outcome of our requests but for the process as well, we can keep coming to the Lord in prayer, trusting His wisdom and care for us.

Our Lord's encouragement to us is clear: Always pray and don't give up!

David McCasland

Prayer changes everything.

A Sincere Thank You

Read Psalm 9:1–2

I will give thanks to you, Lord, with all my heart;
I will tell of all your wonderful deeds. *Psalm 9:1*

In preparation for Xavier's first job interview, my husband, Alan, handed our son a pack of thank-you cards for him to send out after he met with prospective employers. He then pretended to be a hiring interviewer, using his decades of experience as a manager to ask Xavier questions. After the role-playing, our son tucked several copies of his resume into a folder. He smiled when Alan reminded him about the cards. "I know," he said. "A sincere thank-you note will set me apart from all the other applicants."

When the manager called to hire Xavier, he expressed gratitude for the first handwritten thank-you card he'd received in years.

Saying thanks makes a lasting impact. The psalmists' heartfelt prayers and grateful worship were preserved in the book of Psalms. Though there are one hundred and fifty psalms, these two verses reflect a message of thankfulness: "I will give thanks to you, Lord, with all my heart; I will tell of all your wonderful deeds. I will be glad and rejoice in you; I will sing the praises of your name, O Most High" (Psalm 9:1–2).

We will never be able to finish expressing our gratitude for all God's wonderful deeds. But we can start with a sincere thank you through our prayers. We can nurture a lifestyle of grateful worship, praising God and acknowledging all He's done and all He promises He'll do.

Xochitl Dixon

Worship begins in a grateful heart.

With All My Art

Read Exodus 35:30–35

[The LORD] has filled him with the Spirit of God . . .
to make artistic designs. *Exodus 35:31–32*

"Why plant flowers? You can't eat them," said my father-in-law after witnessing my spring ritual of filling pots with fragrant and colorful treasures from the garden store. Jay's dad is an engineer—a practical sort of person. He can make anything work, but making it beautiful is not a priority. He values function over form, usefulness over aesthetics.

God created us with different gifts. Engineers who work for the glory of God design machines that make life easier. The Lord also created artists, who make life more pleasant by creating beautiful things for the glory of God and the enjoyment of others.

When we think of art in worship, we usually think of music. But other art forms have long had a role in glorifying God. The calling of Bezalel demonstrates God's regard for fine art (Exodus 35:30–35). God commissioned him to beautify the first official place of worship: the tabernacle. God's purpose for the arts, says Gene Edward Veith, is "to glorify God and to manifest beauty."

When artistic talent is enlivened by the Spirit of God, it becomes an act of worship that then can become a witness to point people to Christ. God has greatly enriched our lives with beauty. And we in turn express our gratitude by displaying His glory in our art.

Julie Ackerman Link

Do all things for the glory of God.

Make a Joyful Noise

Read Psalm 98

Shout for joy to the LORD, all the earth,
burst into jubilant song with music. *Psalm 98:4*

Back when I was searching for a church to attend regularly, a friend invited me to a service at her church. The worship leaders led the congregation in a song I particularly loved. So I sang with gusto, remembering my college choir director's advice to "Project!"

After the song, my friend's husband turned to me and said, "You really sang loud." This remark was not intended as a compliment! After that, I self-consciously monitored my singing, making sure I sang softer than those around me and always wondering if the people around me judged my singing.

But one Sunday, I noticed the singing of a woman in the pew beside me. She seemed to sing with adoration, without a trace of self-consciousness. Her worship reminded me of the enthusiastic, spontaneous worship that David demonstrated in his life. In Psalm 98, in fact, David suggests that "all the earth" should "burst into jubilant song" in worship (v. 4).

Verse one of Psalm 98 tells us why we should worship joyfully, reminding us that "[God] has done marvelous things." Throughout the psalm, David recounts these marvelous things: God's faithfulness and justice to all nations, His mercy, and salvation. Dwelling on who God is and what He's done can fill our hearts with praise.

What "marvelous things" has God done in your life? Recall His wondrous works and give God thanks. Lift your voice and sing!

Linda Washington

We can never praise Jesus too much.

Panic Prayers

Read Psalm 37:1–8

Commit your way to the LORD;
trust in him and he will do this. *Psalm 37:5*

In her book *Beyond Our Selves*, Catherine Marshall wrote about learning to surrender her entire life to God through a "prayer of relinquishment." When she encountered situations she feared, she often panicked and exhibited a demanding spirit in prayer: "God, I must have thus and so." God seemed remote. But when she surrendered the dreaded situation to Him to do with it exactly as He pleased, fear left and peace returned. From that moment on, God began working things out. In Psalm 37, David talked about both commitment and surrender: "Commit your way to the LORD," he said, "trust in him" (v. 5). Committed believers are those who sincerely follow and serve the Lord, and it's appropriate to urge people to have greater commitment. But committing ourselves to God and trusting Him imply surrendering every area of our lives to His wise control, especially when fear and panic overtake us. The promised result of such wholehearted commitment and trust is that God will do what is best for us.

Instead of trying to quell your fears with panic prayers, surrender yourself to God through a prayer of relinquishment, and see what He will do.

Joanie Yoder

Prayer is the bridge between panic and peace.

Giving Thanks Always

Read Ephesians 5:1–20

*Always giving thanks to God the Father for everything,
in the name of our Lord Jesus Christ. Ephesians 5:20*

Two men were passing through a country field when they were charged by an enraged bull. They took off for the nearest fence, but they weren't going to make it. One man said, "Put up a prayer, John. We're in for it!" John answered, "I can't. I never made a public prayer in my life." "But you must! The bull is going to get us." "All right," panted John, "I'll give you a prayer my father used to repeat at supper: 'O Lord, for what we are about to receive, make us truly thankful!'" We may smile at this story, yet it is true that no matter what trials we may face we should give thanks "for everything" (Ephesians 5:20).

While traveling to Cleveland for a speaking engagement, I had a flat tire at seventy miles an hour. As I pulled the car to a stop without losing control, I breathed a prayer of thanks. But I forgot one thing—I didn't praise God for the blowout! I should have been thankful even for that seeming inconvenience.

We can give thanks "in all things" because "we know that in all things God works for the good of those who love him, who have been called according to his purpose" (Romans 8:28).

In a world filled with trials and discouragements, it's a joy to know that things never happen by chance to the true believer. That's why we can give thanks in all things!

Richard DeHaan

If you find yourself wearing a "spirit of heaviness,"
try a "garment of praise"!

Stars & Sand

Read Psalms 147:1–11

He determines the number of the stars
and calls them each by name. *Psalm 147:4*

A team led by an Australian astronomer calculated the number of stars in the known universe to be seventy sextillion—seven followed by twenty-two zeros. That unfathomable number is said to be more than the grains of sand in every beach and every desert on earth. The calculation was the by-product of research on the development of galaxies. One team member said, "Finding the number of stars is not really the research we were doing, but it was a nice result to play around with."

Having an estimate of the number of stars can help us praise God with greater awe and wonder. Psalm 147 says: "How good it is to sing praises to our God, how pleasant and fitting to praise him! . . . He determines the number of the stars and calls them each by name. Great is our Lord and mighty in power; his understanding has no limit" (vv. 1, 4–5).

This psalm not only presents God's majesty but it also affirms His personal concern for each of us. He "heals the brokenhearted" (v. 3), "sustains the humble" (v. 6), and "delights in those who fear him, who put their hope in his unfailing love" (v. 11).

Let's praise the great God of stars and sand, for He knows and cares for each of us.

David McCasland

All creation points to the almighty Creator.

Plenty to Praise

Read Psalm 48

Great is the LORD, and most worthy of praise. *Psalm 48:1*

God—have you ever just sat back and marveled at how grand and glorious He is? Today, let's pause to ponder His majesty and greatness.

To help us do that, here are a few descriptions of God that I found while reading Psalms 1–48.

The Lord is a shield (3:3), my source of safety (4:8), my King (5:2), the Judge (7:8), the Most High (7:17), my refuge (9:9), the helper of the fatherless (10:14), the King forever (10:16), righteous (11:7).

God is my strength, rock, fortress, stronghold (18:1–3; 28:1; 31:4), my deliverer (18:2), my support (18:18), my Redeemer (19:14).

He is my shepherd (23:1), the King of glory (24:7), the LORD Almighty (24:10), the God my Savior (25:5), my light and my salvation (27:1), my strength and shield (28:7).

He is the God of glory (29:3), the living God (42:2), my ever-present help in trouble (46:1), the King over all the earth (47:2).

That should be enough to meditate on for one day. No, that's enough for an eternity!

Let's start today to worship our God in earnest—the One who gives us so many reasons to praise Him.

Dave Branon

You can never praise God too much.

Where Do I Start?

Read Luke 11:1–10

I call on the LORD in my distress, and he answers me. *Psalm 120:1*

Several years ago, I was driving down the freeway when my car died. I pulled over to the side of the road, got out of the car, and opened the hood. As I looked at the engine I thought, *A lot of good this does me. I know nothing about cars. I don't even know where to start!*

That's how we might sometimes feel about prayer: Where do I start? That's what the disciples wanted to know when they asked Jesus, "Teach us to pray" (Luke 11:1). The best place to look for instruction is in the example and teaching of Jesus. Two questions you may have are the following:

Where should we pray? Jesus prayed in the temple, in the wilderness (Luke 4), in quiet places (Matthew 14:22–23), in the garden of Gethsemane (Luke 22), and on the cross (Luke 23:34, 46). He prayed alone and with others. Look at His life, follow His example, and pray wherever you are.

What should we pray? In the Lord's Prayer, Jesus taught us to ask that God's name be honored and that His will be done on earth as it is in heaven. Ask Him for your daily provisions, for forgiveness of sin, and for deliverance from temptation and evil (Luke 11:2–4).

So if you're looking for a good place to start, follow the example of the Lord's Prayer.

Anne Cetas

If Jesus needed to pray, how can we do less?

God: The Father of Rain

Read Psalm 135:1–7

He makes clouds rise from the ends of the earth;
he sends lightning with the rain and brings out
the wind from his storehouses. Psalm 135:7

Scientists tell us that there is as much as thirty-seven million billion gallons of water in the atmosphere at any given time. Our Creator God employs a remarkable process to make that moisture fall as rain. The molecules of water, which are 784 times denser than air, are changed into vapor by the heat of the sun's rays (Psalm 135:7). In this state they are lighter than air and become the invisible "water balloons of the universe," which ascend to form clouds.

Now the question arises, how does the Creator transform this vapor into rain? He uses the lightnings and "any of the dust of the earth" (Proverbs 8:26). As vapor molecules rub together, they set up electrical currents, even though there may be no visible flashes of lightning. These minute drops of moisture are separated into positive- and negative-charged groups. A tiny particle of dust is also required to serve as the nucleus of each raindrop. But where are billions of these microscopic pieces of ash to come from? The answer is found in the estimated 100 tons of dust and sand-size particles that reach our planet every day.

God asked Job, "Does the rain have a father?" (Job 38:28). The patriarch was silent, for this marvelous phenomenon could never spring from human ingenuity. Only the Almighty could devise a way to send continuous life-sustaining showers upon the earth. Truly He who is the Father of the rain is greatly to be praised!

Henry Bosch

The acts of God in nature reveal the attributes of God in heaven.

Out of the Mouths of Babes

Read Matthew 21:14–16

Out of the mouth of babies and infants,
you have established strength because of your foes,
to still the enemy and the avenger. *Psalm 8:2 esv*

After watching ten-year-old Viola using a tree branch as a microphone to mimic a preacher, Michele decided to give Viola the opportunity to "preach" during a village outreach. Viola accepted. Michele, a missionary in South Sudan, wrote, "The crowd was enraptured. . . . A little girl who had been abandoned stood in authority before them as a daughter of the King of kings, powerfully sharing the reality of God's Kingdom. Half the crowd came forward to receive Jesus" (Michele Perry, *Love Has a Face*).

The crowd that day hadn't expected to hear a child preach. This incident brings to mind the phrase "out of the mouths of babes," which comes from Psalm 8. David wrote, "Out of the mouth of babies and infants, you have established strength because of your foes" (v. 2 esv). Jesus later quoted this verse in Matthew 21:16, after the chief priests and scribes criticized the children calling out praise to Jesus in the temple at Jerusalem. The children were a nuisance to these leaders. By quoting this Scripture, Jesus showed that God took seriously the praise of these children. They did what the leaders were unwilling to do: give glory to the longed-for Messiah.

As Viola and the children in the temple showed, God can use even a child to bring Him glory. Out of their willing hearts came a fountain of praise.

Linda Washington

Prayer comes naturally to those who count their blessings.

Sharpen Your Spiritual Tools

Read Mark 1:22–39

Very early in the morning, while it was still dark,
Jesus got up, left the house and went off to a
solitary place, where he prayed. *Mark 1:35*

The Lord Jesus had to keep in touch with the heavenly Father through daily prayer and meditation to carry out His ministry on earth. That should say something to us. The blessings of a holy life are ours if we stay connected to our God. To have power for service, we must get alone daily with Him.

A discerning pastor observed that sometimes our activities, though good, take the place of that all-important relationship. He said, "The demand seems to be for outward activity, not quiet adoration; for banquets, not Bible study; for peppy meetings, not prayerful meditation; for showy works, not sacred worship." He was saying that we sometimes get sidetracked and forget that simply being occupied with Christ and His Word should be our satisfaction. He went on to say, "What would we think of a carpenter who was so busy building that he never stopped to keep his tools in working condition, or a farmer who wouldn't take time to oil his machinery? The child of God who neglects to strengthen his character by prayer, Bible study, and fellowship with Jesus is just as foolish."

Let's not let anything keep us from intimate fellowship with Christ through prayer and meditation on God's Word. The instruments of our spiritual service can become dull very quickly. We need to keep them sharp every day.

Henry Bosch

Religious activity can be the death of genuine spirituality.

One More Miracle

Read Exodus 15:1–21

I will sing to the LORD, for he is highly exalted. *Exodus 15:1*

If you are looking for a praise and worship pattern, look no further than Exodus 15.

There you find the Israelites heaping honor on God. The people were just hours removed from one of the greatest rescues in history. The Lord had protected them from the rampaging Egyptians, and their praises reflected the renewed trust in God that this event brought them.

It's appropriate to pour out our unbridled praise on God when we see Him work in great and miraculous ways. But those aren't the only times He deserves our adoration. Too often we wait for God to perform a big answer to prayer before we feel like singing His praises.

But think about this: God doesn't owe us any miracles. He doesn't need to do anything to prove His greatness. He has already given us an incredible display of His power in His creation. He has made the ultimate sacrifice to purchase our redemption. Through His power, He has conducted the most miraculous transaction known to mankind—He brought us from spiritual death to spiritual life.

Waiting for a miracle? God's done plenty of them already. Recalling what He has done and echoing the praise in Exodus 15, let's give God our unconditional worship.

Dave Branon

Praise flows naturally from a grateful heart.

Calling Myself

Read Psalm 26

Vindicate me, LORD, for I have led a blameless life. *Psalm 26:1*

As I was moving my laptop, cell phone, and assorted books and papers from one room to another, the landline phone rang. I hurriedly set down my stuff and rushed to answer the call before the answering machine kicked in. "Hello," I said. No reply. I said hello again when I heard rustling, but still no response. So I hung up and went back to my stuff on the floor. When I picked up my cell phone, I realized that I had accidentally speed-dialed my home phone number!

I laughed at myself, but then wondered: How often are my prayers more like calling myself than calling on God?

For example, when I am falsely accused, I plead with God for vindication. I want my name cleared and the guilty person held accountable for the harm done to my reputation. But then I get impatient with God and try to vindicate myself. I may as well be praying to myself.

Vindication does not come from self-defensive arguments; it stems from integrity (Psalm 26:1). It requires that I allow God to examine my mind and heart (v. 2) and that I walk in His truth (v. 3). This, of course, requires patient waiting (25:21).

When we call on God, He will help us—but in His perfect time and in His perfect way.

Julie Ackerman Link

The purpose of prayer is not to get what we want,
but to become what God wants.

A Worthy Offering

Read Genesis 4:12–7

If you do well, will you not be accepted? And if you do
not do well, sin lies at the door. *Genesis 4:7 (NKJV)*

I gave my neighbor a Bible. But my neighbor told me she stopped reading it because she couldn't understand why God would be so unfair as to reject Cain's offering. "After all," she said, "as a farmer, he simply brought to God what he had. Did God expect him to buy a different kind of sacrifice?" Sadly, she had missed the point.

It wasn't that God didn't like vegetables. Rather, He knew that Cain's offering was masking an unrighteous attitude. Cain wasn't fully committed to God, as expressed by the fact that he wasn't living according to His ways.

It's easy to worship God on the outside while stubbornly keeping territory from Him on the inside. Jude writes about outwardly religious people who use religious activities to cover the reality of their sinful lives: "Woe to them! For they have gone in the way of Cain" (Jude 11 NKJV). We can faithfully serve God, sing His praises, and give sacrificially to His work. But God doesn't want any of that without our hearts.

Does the Lord take priority over our plans and dreams? Is He worth more than the sin that tempts us? When we express to Him that He is more worthy than anything or anyone else in our lives, it's an offering He won't refuse.

Joe Stowell

What we give our Lord shows how much He is worth to us.

A Most Fitting Response

Read Psalm 40:1–5

He put a new song in my mouth,
a hymn of praise to our God. Many will see
and fear the LORD and put their trust in him. *Psalm 40:3*

Pastor and lecturer Thomas DeWitt Talmage (1832–1902) told the story of an accident that occurred on a ferry on one of the Great Lakes. A little child standing by the rail suddenly lost her balance and fell overboard. "Save my child!" cried the frantic mother. Lying on the deck was a great Newfoundland dog, which plunged into the water at the command of his master. Swimming to the girl, he took hold of her clothing with his teeth and brought her to the side of the boat, where both were lifted to safety. Although still frightened, the little girl threw her arms around that big shaggy dog and kissed him again and again. It seemed a most natural and appropriate thing to do.

Likewise, a response of love and gratitude should flow from every person who has been rescued by the Savior through His self-sacrificing death on the cross. He came from heaven's glory to suffer and die that we might have eternal life. The apostle Paul expressed his gratitude when he wrote, ". . . giving joyful thanks to the Father. . . . For he has rescued us from the dominion of darkness and brought us into the kingdom of the Son he loves" (Colossians 1:12-13).

Is your heart filled with praise and gratitude for all that God has done for you in Christ? It is a most fitting response.

Paul Van Gorder

Praise is the song of a soul set free.

The Leviticus Reminder

Read Leviticus 11:41–45

I am the LORD your God; consecrate yourselves
and be holy, because I am holy. *Leviticus 11:44*

Leviticus may be one of the least-read books in the Bible, and you might be wondering what its purpose really is. Why all those laws and rules about clean and unclean animals? (chapter 11). What message was God giving to the Israelites—and to us?

Bible commentator Gordon Wenham says, "As the laws distinguished clean from unclean animals, so the people were reminded that God had distinguished them from all the other nations on earth to be His own possession. . . . Man's highest duty is to imitate his creator."

Five times in Leviticus God says, "Be holy, because I am holy" (11:44–45; 19:2; 20:7, 26). And forty-five times He says, "I am the LORD" or "I am the LORD your God." One of the most important themes in the book is God's call for His people to be holy. Jesus echoed that theme when He said, "Be perfect, therefore, as your heavenly Father is perfect" (Matthew 5:48).

As you read Leviticus 11, remember that you are special to God and are to "declare the praises of him who called you out of darkness into his wonderful light" (1 Peter 2:9).

We need the Leviticus reminder every day.

Anne Cetas

Study the Bible to be wise; believe it to be safe;
practice it to be holy.

The Power of Private Prayer

Read Matthew 6:1–6

*When you pray, go into your room, close the door
and pray to your Father, who is unseen. Then your Father,
who sees what is done in secret, will reward you.* Matthew 6:6

We all have "private business" with God that can only be transacted in secret. The "pure oxygen" of the inner chamber would revive many Christians who in the smoggy atmosphere of this busy life are about "to faint" (Luke 18:1).

One Saturday night a businessman in Ohio sat down to eat his supper. On the table his wife placed a letter that had just arrived from India. The note revealed that a young girl he was supporting was not only refusing to accept Christ for herself but was also standing in the way of those who wanted to receive Him. Unless there was a change in her attitude, the missionary wrote, they were concerned about her bad influence on the others. The godly man said to his wife, "I must go alone and pray."

He left the table and went into the bedroom. He later learned that while he was interceding on Saturday night, it was Sunday morning in India, and the missionary was teaching the Bible school lesson. God moved that wayward girl to repentance, and she wept, confessed her sins, and received the Lord Jesus. This made such an impact that the other girls one by one followed her example until salvation came to the whole class.

Have you discovered the power of private prayer?

Henry Bosch

One of the blessed and effectual secrets of prayer
is prayer in secret!

Be Glad!

Read Psalm 69:29–36

I will praise God's name in song....
The poor will see and be glad. Psalm 69:30, 32

For several days after my husband and his brother sang a duet in church of "Be Ye Glad," I was unable to get the lyrics by Michael Blanchard out of my mind. But they're good words to get stuck on. They speak clearly about the gladness we encounter because our debts have been paid by God's grace. Five times in one verse, the song says that we should be glad.

Ancient Israel's beloved songwriter and king often wrote about gladness. In three consecutive songs, David spoke of being glad: Psalm 68:3; 69:32; 70:4. His lyrics assure us that it's not the rich or the powerful who have reason to be glad but those who are humble and right with God.

David expanded on this theme in another song: "Blessed is the one whose transgression is forgiven, whose sin is covered. . . . Be glad in the Lord, and rejoice, O righteous; and shout for joy, all you upright in heart!" (32:1, 11 ESV).

If you are feeling poor and powerless today, you can still be glad. You can have something of far more value: a debt-free relationship with God.

When we stop defending our own sinful ways and humbly acknowledge that God's ways are right, true gladness will spring forth in songs of glorious praise.

Julie Ackerman Link

Joy is the result of a right relationship with God.

The Campaign

Read Romans 15:1–7

Let us therefore make every effort to do what leads
to peace and to mutual edification. *Romans 14:19*

Each year young people in our community participate in a "Be Nice" campaign spearheaded by a mental health organization. In one of the events in 2012, 6,000 students spelled out the words BE NICE with their bodies on their schools' sports fields. One principal said, "We want students to come to school and learn without the distraction of fear or sadness or uneasiness around their peers. We are working hard to make sure students are lifting each other up, rather than tearing each other down."

Paul desired that the people in the church at Rome would have an even higher standard of love. Both the strong and weak in the faith were judging and showing contempt for each other (Romans 14:1–12). They despised one another as they argued about what foods were permissible to eat (vv. 2–3) and what holidays they should observe (vv. 5–6). Paul challenged them: "Let us therefore make every effort to do what leads to peace and to mutual edification" (v. 19). He reminded them that their hearts should be concerned with pleasing others, not pleasing themselves. He said, "Even Christ did not please himself" (15:3); He served.

Join the campaign that loves others despite our differences—you'll bring praise to God (v. 7).

Anne Cetas

Kindness is simply love flowing out in little gentlenesses.

No Need Is Too Trivial

Read Isaiah 49:13–18

As a father has compassion on his children, so the LORD
has compassion on those who fear Him. *Psalm 103:13*

Several mothers of small children were sharing encouraging answers to prayer. Yet one woman said she felt selfish about troubling God with her personal needs. "Compared with the huge global needs God faces," she explained, "my circumstances must seem trivial to Him."

Moments later, her little son pinched his fingers in a door and ran screaming to his mother. She didn't say, "How selfish of you to bother me with your throbbing fingers when I'm busy!" She showed him great compassion and tenderness.

As Psalm 103:13 reminds us, this is the response of love, both human and divine. In Isaiah 49, God said that even though a mother may forget to have compassion on her child, the Lord never forgets His children (v. 15). God assured His people, "I have engraved you on the palms of my hands" (v. 16).

Such intimacy with God belongs to those who fear Him and who rely on Him rather than on themselves. As that child with throbbing fingers ran freely to his mother, so may we run to God with our daily problems.

Our compassionate God doesn't neglect others to respond to our concerns. He has limitless time and love for each of His children. No need is too trivial for Him.

Joanie Yoder

God holds His children in the palm of His hand.

Song in Adversity

Read Psalm 20:1–6

Deep calls to deep in the roar of your waterfalls; all your waves and breakers have swept over me. By day the Lord directs his love, at night his song is with me—a prayer to the God of my life. *Psalm 42:7–8*

Lawyer Gong was a prosperous Christian who lived in Fuzhou, China. Each evening his family met for worship, and the sound of their happy singing would drift over to his neighbors—carrying with it a sweet testimony of praise to God. One day his joy was especially deep, for the Lord had blessed him and his wife with their first grandchild.

"No wonder he is so cheerful," said his associates, "God always smiles upon him." Soon, however, trouble struck. The beloved little grandson became ill and died. As Mr. Gong walked in his garden the next morning with a heavy heart, he overheard the man next door say, "Look! In sorrow he is like all the rest of us! Tonight we will hear no glad singing over the garden wall!"

Mr. Gong recognized that he must face this new challenge to his faith like a true believer. He determined not to lose his song of victory. That evening when the family gathered for fellowship, he suggested that they still had much for which they should give thanks. To the astonishment of their unsaved neighbors, they sang their usual hymns of praise. Later one of them was heard to say, "Never until that moment did I understand what being a Christian really meant."

Although the night of trial may settle dark around us, our Lord gives us grace—grace enough to provide us with God-honoring, "midnight melodies"!

Henry Bosch

Sweet are the uses of adversity,
and mellow is the song of the afflicted!

Scriptural Songs

Read Colossians 3:15–17

Let the message of Christ dwell among you richly...
through psalms, hymns, and songs from the Spirit,
singing to God with gratitude in your hearts. Colossians 3:16

The beloved songwriter, John W. Peterson, was a master at using Scripture in his songs. When I was a teenager in the church choir, we performed his cantata *Jesus Is Coming* and sang these words taken from 2 Timothy 3:1–2: "There will be terrible times in the last days. People will be lovers of themselves." Then he wrote of the grim signs that we would recognize in the last days (vv. 2–7). The steady cadence of his music helps me remember that list even today.

While some of us have trouble memorizing verses from God's Word, something in our brain helps us to remember words in songs. If we analyze some of our favorite Christian songs and choruses, we find that they have been derived from Scripture. Thus, we can use the memory boost of music to hide away God-breathed words in our hearts (2 Timothy 3:16). Songs such as "Open the Eyes of My Heart" (Isaiah 6:9–10; Ephesians 1:18) or favorites like "Thy Word Have I Hid in My Heart" (Psalm 119:11, 105) are taken from the Bible. With these words hidden in our memory, a song of praise comes quickly to our lips.

No matter what kind of voice you have, when you sing the words of Scripture back to God, it is sweet music to His ears.

Cindy Hess Kasper

Hymns are the incense of a worshiping soul praising God!

Who Is This?

Read Mark 4:35–41

They were terrified and asked each other, "Who is this?
Even the wind and the waves obey him! Mark 4:41

"Remove everything from your desks, take out a piece of paper and pencil."

When I was a student these dreaded words announced that "test time" had come.

In Mark 4, we read that Jesus's day, which started with teaching by the seaside (v. 1), ended with a time of testing on the sea (v. 35). The boat that had been used as a teaching platform was used to transport Jesus and a handful of His followers to the other side of the sea. During the journey (while an exhausted Jesus slept in the back of the boat), they encountered a swirling storm (v. 37). Drenched disciples woke Jesus with the words, "Teacher, don't you care if we drown?" (v. 38). Then it happened. The One who had exhorted the crowds to "Listen!" earlier in the day (v. 3), uttered a simple, powerful command to the winds of nature—"Quiet! Be still!" (v. 39).

The wind obeyed and the wonder of fear-filled disciples was displayed with the words, "Who is this?" (v. 41). The question was a good one but it would take them a while to honestly and correctly conclude that Jesus was God's Son. Sincere, honest, openhearted questions and experience lead people to the same conclusion today. He is more than a teacher to listen to, He is the God to be worshiped.

Arthur Jackson

"Teacher, I will follow you wherever you go." —Matthew 8:19

Heart of Gratitude

Read Psalm 19:1–6

The heavens declare the glory of God;
the skies proclaim the work of his hands. Psalm 19:1

My boyhood hero was American frontiersman Davy Crockett. In the book *David Crockett: His Life and Adventures,* Davy encounters a beautiful sight that causes him to launch into praise to the Creator. The writer describes it this way: "Just beyond the grove there was another expanse of treeless prairie, so rich, so beautiful, so brilliant with flowers, that even Colonel Crockett, all unaccustomed as he was to the devotional mood, reined in his horse, and gazing entranced upon the landscape, exclaimed, 'O God, what a world of beauty hast Thou made for man! And yet how poorly does he requite Thee for it! He does not even repay Thee with gratitude.'" Crockett recognized that the Creator's handiwork demands a response of thankfulness—a response that is often neglected or ignored.

The psalmist wrote, "The heavens declare the glory of God; the skies proclaim the work of his hands" (Psalm 19:1). God's handiwork is a spectacle that, rightly understood, should not only take our breath away but should also inspire us to worship and praise our God as it did the psalmist.

Davy Crockett was right—encountering the wonders of God's creation should inspire, at the least, a heart of gratitude. Are we grateful?

Bill Crowder

God's glory shines through His creation.

Faster Communication

Read Daniel 9:3–6, 17–23

Before they call I will answer; while they are
still speaking I will hear. *Isaiah 65:24*

I once read a story about the construction of the first telegraph
lines in the Shetland Islands. A passerby watched as the wires were
mounted on the high poles. Someone remarked to him, "What a
wonderful thing this new invention is! When it is finished, we will
be able to send a message 200 miles or more and get an answer
within an hour." The other man seemed unimpressed.

"There's nothing very great about that," he responded. "There isn't?
Can you tell me of anything better or faster?" asked second man.

Thinking of Isaiah 65 the man replied, "Did you ever hear of
getting an answer before the message is sent?"

The man looked dumbfounded, thinking it was just a strange,
meaningless comment. He didn't realize the wisdom of that reply.

In reality, God reads hearts and knows our needs, and often while
we are yet speaking, the desired blessing is already on the way. How
true are the words of the unknown poet, "Before we voice our want,
His power and love can bless; to praying souls He often grants more
than they can express."

In Daniel 9 we find that while the prophet Daniel was still raising his petition, Gabriel began to fly swiftly from God's throne with
the answer from heaven (Daniel 9:20–23). Yes, our prayers ascend
faster than any electronic message and immediately reach God's
ears (Psalm 34:15). With such a swift avenue of communication
open to us, we shouldn't forget to pray!

Henry Bosch

We never get a busy signal on the prayer line to Heaven!

Worship Worthy

Read Psalm 99

Exalt the LORD our God and worship at his footstool;
he is holy. *Psalm 99:5*

As Moses was tending his father-in-law's sheep in the desert, his attention was drawn to a strange sight. A bush burned without being consumed. When Moses turned to look more closely at this phenomenon, God said to him, "Take off your sandals, for the place where you are standing is holy ground" (Exodus 3:5). Joshua had a similar experience when he approached the captain of the host of the Lord. As Joshua drew nearer, he was given this command: "Take off your sandals, for the place where you are standing is holy" (Joshua 5:15).

The experiences of Moses and Joshua vividly teach us that a holy God demands our reverence and respect. True, we are encouraged to "approach God's throne of grace with confidence" (Hebrews 4:16). We can do that because Christ has opened the way for us through His substitutionary death on the cross. But never are we to approach God with disrespect. Our heavenly Father is not "the man upstairs." He is God, the One who is high and lifted up. And because of His majesty and holiness, we are to exalt and worship Him. As the one true God, He is worthy of our adoration. He deserves our highest praise.

Let us therefore enter His presence with reverence.

Let us worship Him with gratitude and exaltation. He is worthy of our heartfelt worship.

Richard DeHaan

True worship acknowledges the true worthship of God.

Let Your Balloon Go!

Read 2 Samuel 22:1–8

Therefore I will praise you, LORD, . . .
I will sing the praises of your name. *2 Samuel 22:50*

The participants at a conference in a church in Nebraska were given helium-filled balloons and told to release them at a point in the worship service when they felt like expressing their joy. All through the service, balloons ascended one by one. But when the meeting was over, one-third of the people had not released their balloons. I wonder if they couldn't think of any reason to praise God.

King David would have let go of his balloon when singing his song of praise recorded in 2 Samuel 22. God had delivered him from all his enemies (v. 1). Earlier, when hiding from King Saul in the rocky desert, David had learned that true security is found only in God (1 Samuel 23:25). David's heart had to "give thanks" and "sing praises," for the Lord had become his rock, fortress, deliverer, stronghold, refuge, and savior (2 Samuel 22:2–3, 50).

What has the Lord been for you throughout your life? Your peace in a chaotic time? Your comforter amid loss? Your forgiver of a sinful choice? Your strength in a difficult task?

Take out a piece of paper and write down your list of thanks. Then take time to praise God for all He is and all He has done.

Let your balloon go!

Anne Cetas

Praise is the overflow of a joyful heart.

Not Worth Mentioning

Read Colossians 3:12–17

Bear with each other and forgive one another
if any of you has a grievance against someone.
Forgive as the Lord forgave you. *Colossians 3:13*

The fellowship between two Christian men was broken. One heard that the other had been talking about him, and he decided to confront him with it. "Will you be kind enough to tell me my faults to my face so I can correct them?" "I certainly will," he replied. They found a place where they could talk. "Before you begin pointing out my failings, will you please kneel with me so we may ask the Lord to show me my weaknesses? You lead in prayer."

When they arose, the man who had criticized said, "After praying over it, my complaints against you look so little they're not worth talking about. The truth is, I wish you'd pray for me and forgive me for the wrong I've done to you."

Quite often this is the case. Many supposed grievances are best forgotten. As we consider the depth of God's forgiveness to us who have wronged Him so shamefully, we should disregard any ill treatment others have directed toward us and willingly clean the slate— forgiving one another as Christ forgave us.

Rather than talking about the faults of our fellow Christians, let's spread their needs before the Lord. We'll discover that divine forgiveness usually brings into focus our own pettiness. Let's allow His boundless, forgiving love to find full expression in our lives.

Paul Van Gorder

He who cannot forgive others breaks the bridge over which he
himself must pass. —Matthew 6:15

Morning, Noon, Night

Read Psalm 55:16–23

Evening, morning and noon I cry out in distress,
and he hears my voice. *Psalm 55:17*

In May 2003, a powerful earthquake struck northern Algeria. TV news images showed distraught people searching the rubble for survivors, while others numbly visited hospitals and morgues to see if their loved ones were alive or dead. Families stood together weeping and crying out for help. Their burden of uncertainty and grief could be seen, heard, and felt.

If you've experienced an intense feeling of loss, you'll appreciate the words of David in Psalm 55, penned during a painful time in his life. Oppressed by the wicked, hated by his enemies, and betrayed by a friend, David spoke of the anxiety and anguish that threatened to crush his spirit: "Fear and trembling have beset me; horror has overwhelmed me" (v. 5).

But instead of caving in to fear, David poured out his heart to God: "As for me, I will call to God, and the LORD saves me. Evening, morning and noon I cry out in distress, and he hears my voice" (vv. 16–17).

Prayer lifts our eyes from personal tragedy to the compassion of God. It enables us to cast our burdens on the Lord instead of breaking under their weight. When our hearts are filled with pain, it's good to call on God in prayer—morning, noon, and night.

David McCasland

In prayer, God hears more than words; He listens to your heart.

Wasted Worship

Read Amos 5:21–27

My sacrifice, O God, is a broken spirit;
a broken and contrite heart. *Psalm 51:17*

If you are able to go to church on Sunday, you probably will. For most Christians, it's almost automatic—and rightly so.

But is it possible that our efforts to go to church for worship might be wasted? Could it all be in vain?

Yes. Before we even enter the church, the worth of our worship can be reduced to nothing because of the way we've lived during the week.

In Amos 5, the Lord had some harsh words for those who attempted to worship Him while bringing with them the guilt of an ungodly lifestyle. His people were constantly angering Him by following false gods (v. 26). When they assembled to worship the Lord through sacrifices and songs, God despised their hypocrisy.

In Isaiah 1, God instructed His people that before they could worship Him, they were to "stop doing wrong. Learn to do right; seek justice" (vv. 16–17).

What a challenge to us! Before we worship God, we are to put things in order by confessing our sins, seeking His forgiveness, and serving Him. Our daily walk with God and our obedience to His commands are the elements that prepare us for church. Anything less will lead to wasted worship.

Dave Branon

Worship that pleases God comes from an obedient heart.

Praiseworthy

Read Revelation 5

I looked and heard the voice of many angels, . . .
They encircled the throne. *Revelation 5:11*

The Grand Rapids Symphony Orchestra and Symphonic Choir were presenting their annual Christmas concert. Near the conclusion, they were joined by the four thousand members of the audience in singing, "Joy to the world, the Lord is come! Let earth receive her King." I got chills when we sang the words, "And heaven and nature sing."

Despite the magnificence of that moment, it was but a faint shadow of the praise that will be raised to the Lamb in heaven. Jesus is worthy of the adoration and praise of all beings: "Worthy is the Lamb, who was slain, to receive power and wealth and wisdom and strength and honor and glory and praise!" (Revelation 5:12).

In Revelation 5, we read John's description of a widening circle of praise to the Lord. It begins with "four living creatures and the twenty-four elders" (v. 8). They are joined by angels numbering "ten thousand times ten thousand" (v. 11).

But that's not all. Every creature in heaven, on earth, and in the sea will one day sing, "To him who sits on the throne and to the Lamb be praise and honor and glory and power, for ever and ever!" (v. 13).

We don't have to wait for that day to sing praise to the Lamb. He is worthy of our praise right now!

David Egner

Praise is the overflow of a joyful heart.

Whatever We Do

Read Proverbs 16:1–9

Kings take pleasure in honest lips; they value the one who speaks what is right. Proverbs 16:13

In *Surprised by Joy*, C. S. Lewis confessed that he came to Christianity at the age of thirty-three, "kicking, struggling, resentful, and darting his eyes in every direction for a chance to escape." Despite Lewis's own personal resistance, his shortcomings, and the obstacles he faced, the Lord transformed him into a courageous and creative defender of the faith. Lewis proclaimed God's truth and love through writing powerful essays and novels that are still being read, studied, and shared more than fifty-five years after his death. His life reflected the belief that a person is never too old to set another goal or dream a new dream.

As we make plans and follow dreams, God can purify our motives and empower us to devote whatever we do to Him (Proverbs 16:1–3). From the most ordinary tasks to the greatest challenges, we can live for the glory of our almighty Maker, who "works out everything to its proper end" (v. 4). Every action, every word, and every thought can become an expression of heartfelt worship, a sacrificial gift to honor our Lord, as He watches over us (v. 7).

God can't be limited by our limitations, our reservations, or our tendencies to settle or dream small. As we choose to live for Him—dedicated to and dependent on Him—He will bring about His plans for us. Whatever we do can be done with Him, for Him, and only because of Him.

Xochitl Dixon

To show His love, Jesus died for us;
to show our love for Jesus, we must live for Him.

Miracle Rain

Read 1 Kings 18:1, 41–45

I am God, and there is no other. *Isaiah 46:9*

Life is hard for the villagers who live on a hilly terrain in the Yunnan Province of China. Their main source of food is corn and rice. But in May 2012 a severe drought hit the region and the crops withered. Everyone was worried, and many superstitious practices were carried out as the people attempted to end the drought. When nothing worked, people started blaming the five Christians in the village for offending the spirits of the ancestors.

These five believers gathered to pray. Before long, the sky darkened and thunder was heard. A heavy downpour started and lasted the whole afternoon and night. The crops were saved! While most of the villagers did not believe God sent the rain, others did and desired to find out more about Him and Jesus.

In 1 Kings 17 and 18 we read of a severe drought in Israel. But in this case, we are told, it was a result of God's judgment on His people (17:1). They had begun to worship Baal, the god of the Canaanites, believing that this deity could send the rain for their crops. Then God, through His prophet Elijah, showed that He is the one true God who determines when rain falls.

Our all-powerful God desires to hear our prayers and answer our pleas. And though we do not always understand His timing or His purposes, God always responds with His best for our lives.

Poh Fang Chia

Through prayer, we draw upon the power of the infinite God.

Seeing Far and Near

Read Psalm 145

The Lord is near to all who call on him. *Psalm 145:18*

Having two healthy eyes is not enough to see clearly. I know this from experience. After a series of eye surgeries for a torn retina, both eyes could see well but they refused to cooperate with each other. One eye saw things far away and the other saw things close up. But instead of working together, they fought for supremacy. Until I could get new prescription glasses three months later, my eyes remained unfocused.

Something similar happens in our view of God. Some people focus better on God when they see Him as "close up"—when they think of Him as intimately present in their daily life. Other Christians see God more clearly as "far away" or far beyond anything we can imagine, ruling the universe in power and majesty.

While people disagree about which view is best, the Bible works like a prescription lens helping us to see that both are correct. King David presents both views in Psalm 145: "The Lord is near to all who call on him" (v. 18) and "Great is the Lord and most worthy of praise; his greatness no one can fathom" (v. 3).

Thankfully, our Father in heaven is near to hear our prayers yet so far above us in power that He can meet every need.

Julie Ackerman Link

God is big enough to care for the smallest needs.

The "Black Dots" of Blessing

Read Psalm 100

*Let the peace of Christ rule in your hearts, since as
members of one body you were called to peace.* Colossians 3:15

An unknown author penned these thought-provoking lines: "We
once saw a man draw some small black ovals on a sheet of paper.
We looked and could make nothing of them. They seemed just an
irregular assemblage of black dots. Then, however, he drew a few
lines, put in a few rests, and a clef sign at the beginning; and we
immediately saw that those black dots were actually musical notes!
On sounding them we were singing, "Praise God from whom all
blessings flow!"

There are many "black spots" in our lives, and we cannot immediately understand why God permitted them to come. However, if
we will wait patiently, the Lord will soon show us through the ad-
ditional lines of His providence and the clef sign of His grace, that
they are actually put there to draw from us the sweet harmonies of
praise that bring honor to His Name.

When we get to heaven and have the perfect perspective of eternity, we will see that the "dark spots" of our earthly life were actually the grace notes of blessing that God placed in our lives to bring
us in harmony with His holy will.

It is said of John Bunyan, who wrote *Pilgrim's Progress*, that he
prayed that the Lord would send him new trials. Then he could
show his love for God by the patient way he endured them.

Are we thankful today—no matter what? Let's allow the peace of
God to rule our hearts.

Henry Bosch

The sure cure for depression is praise!

Things Above

Read Colossians 3:1–13

Set your heart on things above, where Christ is,
seated at the right hand of God. *Colossians 3:1*

Stepping outside and gazing heavenward on a star-studded evening always helps to soothe my soul after a trouble-filled day. When I peer into the night sky, I forget, at least for a moment, the cares of life on earth.

Ancient Israel's prolific songwriter wrote a poem thousands of years ago that still rings true: "When I consider Your heavens, the work of Your fingers, the moon and the stars, which You have ordained, what is man that You are mindful of him, and the son of man that You visit him?" (Psalm 8:3–4 NKJV).

When we try to imagine the immensity of God's heavens, our problems indeed seem trivial. Yet God doesn't think so! With all the galaxies He has to attend to, God is mindful of us. And not only are we on His mind but He also cares for us.

No wonder the apostle Paul advised new believers to set their minds on things above (Colossians 3:2). In doing so, we raise our thoughts above the level of earthly disputes and focus instead on our loving, heavenly Father, who wants us to know Him, to know how to live peacefully with one another, and to know that we can live eternally with Him in a place even more beautiful than the heavens.

"The heavens declare the glory of God" (Psalm 19:1). Let's join creation in praise to Him.

Julie Ackerman Link

Because God gives us everything, we owe Him all our praise.

From Mars?

Read Job 38:4-18

So God created the great creatures of the sea and every
living thing with which the water teems.... Then God said,
"Let us make mankind in our image." *Genesis 1:21, 26*

"Microbes from Mars fell on the very early Earth . . . , and the offspring of those microbes are still here—and they are us." That's how
one astronomer speculated about how life originated on Mars and
then came to Earth.

Some men and women of science are looking to outer space for
the origins of life on earth, not believing the Bible's explanation
that God placed mankind, animals, and plant life on earth through
special creation. But how did that supposed microbial life start on a
hostile planet? The bigger question is this: Why is it so difficult to
accept that the earth, uniquely and singularly fitted for life to exist,
is where God created and placed living creatures?

As humans struggle to accept a miraculous beginning of life from
the breath of God (Genesis 2:7), they choose to trust a miracle of a
far different sort—the miracle of life originating from no first cause
at all. Perhaps they could follow the advice Job received: "Listen to
this, Job; stop and consider God's wonders" (Job 37:14). And maybe
they should try to answer God's question: "Where were you when I
laid the earth's foundations?" (38:4).

Praise God for creating such a wonderful place for us to live! We
stand in awe of His marvelous creation.

Dave Branon

Only God could create the cosmos out of nothing.

The Go-Between

Read Exodus 20:18–26

The people remained at a distance, while Moses approached
the thick darkness where God was. *Exodus 20:21*

Imagine standing at the bottom of a mountain, elbow-to-elbow
with everyone in your community. Thunder and lightning flash;
you hear an earsplitting trumpet blast. Amid flames, God descends
on the mountaintop. The summit is enveloped in smoke; the entire
mountain begins to shake, and so do you (Exodus 19:16–20).

When the Israelites had this terrifying experience near Mount
Sinai, they begged Moses, "Speak to us yourself and we will listen.
But do not have God speak to us or we will die" (20:19). The Israel-
ites were asking Moses to mediate between them and the Almighty.
"The people remained at a distance, while Moses approached the
thick darkness where God was" (v. 21). After meeting with God,
Moses brought God's messages back down the mountain to the
people below.

Today, we worship the same God who displayed His staggering
greatness on Mount Sinai. Because God is perfectly holy and we are
desperately sinful, we cannot relate to Him. Left to ourselves we too
would (and should) shake in terror. But Jesus made it possible for
us to know God when He took our sins on himself, died, and rose
again (1 Corinthians 15:3–4). Even now, Jesus is the go-between
for us to a holy and perfect God (Romans 8:34; 1 Timothy 2:5).

Jennifer Benson Schuldt

Jesus bridges the gap between God and us.

Asking God

Read Psalm 6:4–9

The Lord has heard my cry for mercy;
the Lord accepts my prayer. *Psalm 6:9*

When my husband, Dan, was diagnosed with cancer, I couldn't find the "right" way to ask God to heal him. In my limited view, other people in the world had such serious problems—war, famine, poverty, natural disasters. Then one day, during our morning prayer time, I heard my husband humbly ask, "Dear Lord, please heal my disease."

It was such a simple but heartfelt plea that it reminded me to stop complicating every prayer request, because God perfectly hears our righteous cries for help. As David simply asked, "Turn, Lord, and deliver me; save me because of your unfailing love" (Psalm 6:4).

That's what David declared during a time of spiritual confusion and despair. His exact situation isn't explained in this psalm. His honest pleas, however, show deep desire for godly help and restoration. "I am worn out from my groaning," he wrote (v. 6).

Yet, David didn't let his own limits, including sin, stop him from going to God with his need. Thus, even before God answered, David was able to rejoice, "the Lord has heard my weeping. The Lord has heard my cry for mercy; the Lord accepts my prayer" (vv. 8–9).

Despite our own confusion and uncertainty, God hears and accepts the honest pleas of His children. He's ready to hear us, especially when we need Him most.

Patricia Raybon

Courage to ask is part of God's gift of caring.

Thanks and Selfishness

Read Psalm 92

My eyes have seen the defeat of my adversaries;
my ears have heard the rout of my wicked foes. *Psalm 92:11*

Is it selfish to thank God for special blessings He has bestowed on us or our loved ones? This question was raised in our community several years ago. A powerful tornado had demolished a store building, from which the owner and several people had escaped unhurt. The store owner said he prayed, thanking God for keeping them safe through the ordeal. Someone responded to his statement by saying he thought such a prayer was selfish—especially since others in the area had been killed.

Now, it is possible to pray and give thanks in a selfish spirit. For example, it would have mean and narrow had the businessman said, "Lord, I am thankful that the three people killed in that tornado were members of the Jones family instead of mine." But he didn't pray that way. He simply expressed gratitude to the Lord for what He had done in sparing him and his friends.

Do you possess good health? Thank God for it. Do you live in a comfortable house and have enough to eat? Thank the Lord. The psalmist said, "It is a good thing to give thanks unto the Lord."

But we should not stop there. We should accompany our thanksgiving with intercession for the ill and the needy. Then, we should do what we can to help.

No, it's not selfish to thank the Lord for special favors He has done for us. In fact, it would be selfish if we didn't.

Herb Vander Lugt

A grateful heart is always a prayerful heart.

A "Him" Sing

Read Acts 16:16–26

About midnight Paul and Silas were praying and singing hymns to God, and the other prisoners were listening to them. Acts 16:25

How could Paul and Silas sing in their circumstances? They were in a strange city far away from home. They were risking their lives to proclaim Christ to people who resented them and bitterly opposed their message. Men with selfish motives had spread lies about their work, had convinced the local citizens that they were enemies of the state, and had demanded their arrest. The town officials became extremely angry and ordered that they be beaten and thrown into prison. It was under these conditions that Paul and Silas were singing. But it wasn't the blues their fellow prisoners were hearing; it was praise to the Lord. How can we account for this? The answer is clear. They could sing in the dark because they were being what God intended them to be—His trusting, obedient servants.

The midnight songs of those two men remind me of the nightingale. Observers of this remarkable little bird have often wondered why it continues to sing after sundown. While other birds are quiet, the lilting melodies of this creature can still be heard. The dark does not silence its song. The best explanation is that the nightingale sings at night because that's what it's supposed to do.

The person who walks with the Lord can have a song even in the midst of trouble. He's not discouraged by circumstances. His joy is in being what the Savior wants him to be—one whose greatest delight is to know God and to sing of Him, even in the dark.

Mart DeHaan

There's a song in the night for those who walk in the Light.

Free Prayer

Read Ephesians 6:10–20

Pray in the Spirit on all occasions with all kinds of prayers and requests. With this in mind, be alert and always keep on praying for all the Lord's people. Ephesians 6:18

A pastor was asked to call on a woman in a psychiatric hospital and pray for her. After his visit, he thought how good it would be for somebody to go there regularly and pray for the residents. The "somebody" turned out to be him. On a table in one of the wards, he put up a sign saying "Free Prayer." Later he recalled, "Suddenly I had fifteen people standing in line to get prayed for."

People often ask for our prayers, but do we faithfully pray for them? Many times we see others in great need but find it easier to discuss their plight with friends rather than to intercede for them. But people need and want our prayers.

Paul concluded his call to put on "the full armor of God" (Ephesians 6:13–17) by writing, "Pray in the Spirit on all occasions with all kinds of prayers and requests. With this in mind, be alert and always keep on praying for all the Lord's people" (v. 18).

Oswald Chambers often referred to prayer as "the ministry of the interior" and said, "There is no snare, or any danger of infatuation or pride in intercession; it is a hidden ministry that brings forth fruit whereby the Father is glorified."

Faithful prayer—whether in public or private—is one of the greatest gifts we can give others.

David McCasland

Our intercession may be the key to God's intervention.

True Worship

Read Psalm 96

*"God is spirit, and his worshipers must worship
in the Spirit and in truth." John 4:24*

Occasionally, we catch ourselves simply mouthing words while singing a song in church. Or during the message, we suddenly realize that we are a thousand miles away. Sometimes, we drift away and miss out on genuine worship.

One of the older books in my library includes a story about a man who dreamed that an angel escorted him to church one Sunday. There he saw the instrumentalists playing, but no sound was heard. The congregation began to sing, but he heard no voices. When the minister stood up to pray, his lips moved but he said nothing. The man was amazed as he turned to his guide. "You hear nothing," said the angel, "because there is nothing to hear. These people are not engaged in worship—only in the form of worship. Their hearts are not touched, and this silence is the silence that is yet unbroken by God."

The next time we go to out place of worship, let's go with a sincere desire to enter His presence and honor Him in all we say and do. Let's sing with meaning. Let's pray with sincerity. Let's listen with reverence when God's Word is taught. Only then will we be engaging in true worship. Only then will our praise on earth reach God's throne in heaven.

Richard DeHaan

You can quickly lose interest in worship
if you have nothing invested.

To Whom It Is Due

Read Romans 13:1–10

Give to everyone what you owe them: If you owe taxes,
pay taxes; if revenue, then revenue; if respect, then respect;
if honor, then honor. *Romans 13:7*

My husband and I live in a rural area surrounded by farms where this slogan is popular: "If you ate a meal today, thank a farmer." Farmers definitely deserve our gratitude. They do the hot, hard work of tilling soil, planting seeds, and harvesting the food that keeps us from starving to death.

But every time I thank a farmer, I also try to remember to offer praise to God, for He is the One responsible for producing the food we eat. He gives light, sends rain, and creates the energy within the seed that gives it the strength to push through the soil and produce fruit.

Although the earth and everything in it belong to God (Psalm 24:1), He has chosen humans to be its caretakers. We are responsible to use the earth's resources as He would use them—to do His work in the world (115:16). And just as we are stewards of God's physical creation, we also are stewards of His design for society. We do this by respecting those He has placed in authority, by paying taxes, by giving honor to those who have earned it, and by continuing to pay our debt of love (Romans 13:7–8). But one thing we reserve for God: All praise and glory belong to Him, for He is the One who makes everything possible (Psalm 96:8).

Julie Ackerman Link

God's unsearchable ways deserve our unbounded praise.

Stagecoach Prayer

Read John 15:7–14

*I will do whatever you ask in my name,
so that the Father may be glorified in the Son. John 14:13*

Five-year-old Randy wanted a toy stagecoach for Christmas. While shopping with Mom, he found just the one he wanted. It was about six inches long and had cool wheels and dark brown plastic horses pulling it. "Mommy, I want this one. Pleeeease!" he begged. As young children sometimes do, he threw a tantrum, insisting that he get that stagecoach for Christmas. Mom said, "We'll see," and took him home.

Randy was sure he'd get what he asked for. Christmas morning came, and he opened the package confidently. Sure enough, it was the stagecoach he had begged for. He was so pleased. But then his older brother said, "You really did a dumb thing to insist on getting that coach. Mom bought you a much bigger one, but when you begged for that little one, she exchanged it!" Suddenly the small stagecoach didn't seem so appealing.

Sometimes we're like that with God. We pray about a specific need and tell Him how He ought to answer. We beg and plead—and God may even give us exactly what we ask for. But He may have had something better in mind.

Phillips Brooks once said, "Pray the largest prayers. You cannot think a prayer so large that God, in answering it, will not wish you had made it larger."

Anne Cetas

Large asking results in large receiving.

Try Praising

Read 2 Chronicles 20:17–22

"Give thanks to the LORD,
for his love endures forever." *2 Chronicles 20:21*

When Jehoshaphat, king of Judah, was confronted with a strong enemy, he relied on the Lord for deliverance. In a very strange tactical maneuver, he appointed singers to go before the army and exalt the God of Israel. The Scripture says, "As they began to sing and praise, the LORD set ambushes," (2 Chronicles 20:22) and their enemies were defeated.

In the New Testament we read the thrilling account of Paul and Silas, who were cast into prison at Philippi. Acts 16:25 says that at midnight they "were praying and singing hymns to God." At that point He miraculously brought about their release, and this in turn led to the conversion of the jailer.

I heard of a brave little girl who was taken to the doctor for an operation. Though it was minor, there would be considerable pain and discomfort involved. When everything was ready, the doctor said, "This will hurt, but you may cry as much as you please." The small girl looked up at him and said with a smile, "I'd rather sing." She did, and soon the ordeal was over without a sigh or a tear.

The psalmist admonishes, "Praise the LORD. How good it is to sing praises to our God, how pleasant and fitting to praise him" (Psalm 147:1). When we are experiencing a taunting trial or a dismal discouragement—when our world has come crashing down around us, let's try praising!

Paul Van Gorder

If you find yourself wearing a spirit of heaviness,
replace it with a garment of praise.

Exalt Him

Read Psalm 46

"Be still, and know that I am God; I will be exalted among the nations, I will be exalted in the earth." *Psalm 46:10*

These words from a song sung long ago at the temple in Jerusalem remind us of one of our main tasks—worshiping our awesome God.

One way to do that is to meditate on His many attributes. Exalt God, for He is faithful, eternal, all-knowing, just, unchangeable, gracious, holy, merciful, longsuffering, impartial, and infinite. Our God is perfect.

Exalt God also by realizing that He is all-powerful, almighty, personal, righteous, unsearchable, wise, triune, accessible, self-existent, glorious, and compassionate.

Another way to worship God is to contemplate His names. Exalt God, for He is Creator. He is Love. He is Redeemer. He is Shepherd. He is Savior, Lord, and Father. He is Judge. He is Comforter. He is Teacher. He is I AM. Our God is the Mighty One.

Dwell on His identity. God is our shield. Our stronghold. Our light. Our strength. Our sustainer. Our rescuer. Our fortress.

Meditate on God's attributes. Contemplate His names. Dwell on His identity. Adore Him. Respect Him. Honor Him. Love Him. Exalt Him. Use the rest of your life getting ready to worship our awesome God forever.

Dave Branon

Let everything that has breath praise the Lord. —Psalm 150:6

The Boy Who Couldn't Sleep

Read Daniel 6:4–23

When Daniel learned that the decree had been published,
he went home to his upstairs room where the windows
opened toward Jerusalem. Three times a day he
got down on his knees and prayed. *Daniel 6:10*

It was the 1950s, and a little boy became separated from his mother in New York City. He was picked up by an officer who found him crying. The compassionate policeman took the youngster to the station to await his mother's call, assuring him that if they had not located her by the time he went off duty at 12 o'clock, he would take him home to make sure he was safe. When the youngster stopped crying, he was ushered into the sergeant's office. It was getting late, so they suggested he take a brief nap. The little fellow hesitated, so the sergeant said, "It's all right, go and lie down. We will be taking you home shortly."

The child did as he was told but seemed restless. When the officer asked him, "What's the matter, my boy?" the youngster pleaded, "Would you mind, Sir, if I said my prayers as I do at home?" "Of course not," replied the officer. The boy kneeled down by the couch and, turning his little face heavenward, offered his simple good night petitions. Then, happy and content, he jumped into his "bed away from home" and immediately went to sleep. The officers were strangely silent. Here and there a tear trickled down a cheek.

The child had preached a powerful sermon concerning the influence of a Christian home where prayer was the regular order of the day.

Henry Bosch

A prayerful life is a powerful life!

Our Greatest Ministry

Read Luke 22:31–46

"But I have prayed for you, Simon, that your faith may not fail. And when you have turned back, strengthen your brothers." Luke 22:32

Prayer is the working force of the Christian's life. By word and through example the Lord Jesus taught us that prayer is just as much a ministry as activities like preaching, teaching, witnessing, and doing kind deeds in His name. The Savior did just as much on Peter's behalf by praying for him as He did by exhorting him. We may be assured that we are never useless as long as we can pray.

While very ill, John Knox, the founder of the Presbyterian Church in Scotland, called to his wife and said, "Read me that Scripture where I first cast my anchor." After he listened to the beautiful prayer of Jesus recorded in John 17, he seemed to forget his weakness. He began to pray, interceding earnestly for his fellowmen. He prayed for the ungodly who had thus far rejected the gospel. He pleaded in behalf of people who had been recently converted. And he requested protection for the Lord's servants, many of whom were facing persecution. As Knox was praying, he died. The man of whom Queen Mary had said, "I fear his prayers more than I do the armies of my enemies," ministered through prayer until the moment of his death.

Yes, prayer is our chief duty. If we believe this, we'll spend more time praying. When we are in circumstances that make it impossible for us to do much of anything else, we can still pray. We'll be exercising the greatest of all ministries.

Herb Vander Lugt

God's soldiers fight best on their knees.

The Debt Eraser

Read Psalm 103:1–12

As far as the east is from the west, so far has he
removed our transgressions from us. *Psalm 103:12*

I blinked back tears as I reviewed my medical bill. Considering my husband's severe cut in salary after a lengthy unemployment, even paying half of the balance would require years of small monthly installments. I prayed before calling the doctor's office to explain our situation and request a payment plan.

After leaving me on hold for a short time, the receptionist informed me the doctor had zeroed out our account.

I sobbed a thank you. The generous gift overwhelmed me with gratitude. Hanging up the phone, I praised God. I considered saving the bill, not as a reminder of what I used to owe but as a reminder of what God had done.

My physician's choice to pardon my debt brought to mind God's choice to forgive the insurmountable debt of my sins. Scripture assures us God is "compassionate and gracious" and "abounding in love" (Psalm 103:8). He "does not treat us as our sins deserve" (v. 10). He removes our sins "as far as the east is from the west" (v. 12), when we repent and accept Christ as our Savior. His sacrifice erases the debt we once owed. Completely.

Once forgiven, we aren't defined by or limited by our past debt. In response to the Lord's extravagant gift, we can acknowledge all He's done. Offering our devoted worship and grateful affection, we can live for Him and share Him with others.

Xochitl Dixon

Our greatest debt, caused by sin, is erased by our greater God.

God's Marvelous Creation

Read Psalm 139:13–16

I praise you because I am fearfully and wonderfully made;
your works are wonderful, I know that full well. *Psalm 139:14*

In his book *If I Were an Atheist*, Wilbur Nelson includes a chapter called "If I Were a Medical Doctor." He reasons that medical doctors, of all people, because they are so knowledgeable about the human body with its marvelous functions and complexities, should recognize the Creator who fashioned and made it.

Nelson then gives us a whole series of "Think of's" to ponder. Here are just a few of them: Think of the human body, composed of more than thirty-seven trillion cells. Think of the skin—while water penetrates the skin outwardly, it cannot penetrate it inwardly. Think of the bones—capable of carrying a load thirty times greater than brick will support. Think of the liver—it breaks up old blood cells into bile and neutralizes poisonous substances. Think of the blood—ten or twelve pints of a syrupy substance that distributes oxygen and carries away waste from tissues and organs, and also regulates the body's temperature. Think of the heart—weighing less than a pound, it's a real workhorse. On the average, it pumps 100,000 times every day, circulating 2,000 gallons of blood through 60,000 miles of arteries, capillaries, and veins.

No wonder the psalmist declared to the Lord, "I praise you because I am fearfully and wonderfully made" (Psalm 139:14). We're not here by accident, nor by a process of naturalistic evolution. We are God's marvelous creation!

Richard DeHaan

God's work of creating is done;
our work of praising has just begun.

Faithful Prayer

Read 1 Timothy 2:1–7

[Pray] for kings and all those in authority. *1 Timothy 2:2*

In June 2009, ninety-five-year-old Emma Gray died. For over two decades, she had been the cleaning lady in a big house. Each night as she did her work, she prayed for blessings, wisdom, and safety for the man she worked for.

Although Emma worked in the same place for twenty-four years, the occupants of the residence changed every four years or so. Over the years, Emma offered her nightly prayers for six US Presidents: Dwight Eisenhower, John Kennedy, Lyndon Johnson, Richard Nixon, Gerald Ford, and Jimmy Carter.

Emma had her personal favorites, but she prayed for them all. She followed the instruction we read in 1 Timothy 2 to pray for "all those in authority" (v. 2). The verses go on to speak of how living "peaceful and quiet lives" and being a godly and reverent person "is good, and pleases God our Savior . . . who wants all people to be saved and to come to a knowledge of the truth" (vv. 2–4).

Because God "hears the prayer of the righteous" (Proverbs 15:29), who knows how He used Emma's faithful prayers? In Proverbs 21:1, we read: "In the LORD's hand the king's heart is a stream of water that he channels toward all who please him."

Like Emma, we are to pray for our leaders. Is there someone God is calling you to pray for today?

Cindy Hess Kasper

To influence leaders for God, intercede with God for leaders.

Prayer Circles

Read Luke 18:9–14

All those who exalt themselves will be humbled. Luke 18:14

Around the circle the sixth-grade girls went, taking turns praying for each other in the Bible-study group. "Father in heaven," Anna prayed, "please help Tonya not to be so boy-crazy." Tonya added with a giggle, "And help Anna to stop acting so horrible in school and bothering other kids." Then Talia prayed, "Lord, help Tonya to listen to her mother instead of always talking back."

Although the requests were real, the girls seemed to enjoy teasing their friends by pointing out their flaws in front of the others instead of caring about their need for God's help. Their group leader reminded them about the seriousness of talking to almighty God and the importance of evaluating their own hearts.

If we use prayer to point out the faults of others while ignoring our own, we're like the Pharisee in Jesus's parable. He prayed, "God, I thank you that I am not like other people—robbers, evildoers, adulterers—or even like this tax collector" (Luke 18:11). Instead, we're to be like the man who asked God to be merciful to him, "a sinner" (v. 13).

Let's be careful not to let our prayers become a listing of others' flaws. The kind of prayer God desires flows out of a humble evaluation of our own sinful hearts.

Anne Cetas

The highest form of prayer
comes from the depths of a humble heart.

Keep Praying

Read Luke 11:5–13

Everyone who asks receives; the one who seeks finds; and to the one who knocks, the door will be opened. Luke 11:10

We prayed. Quietly sometimes. Aloud other times. For more than seventeen years we prayed. We prayed for our daughter Melissa's health and direction, for her salvation, and often for her protection. Just as we prayed for our other children, we asked God to have His hand of care on her.

As Melissa rolled into her teenage years, we prayed even more that He would keep her from harm—that He would keep His eyes on her as she and her friends began to drive. We prayed, "God, please protect Melissa."

So what happened? Didn't God understand how much it would hurt so many people to lose such a beautiful young woman with so much potential for service to Him and others? Didn't God see the other car coming on that warm spring night?

We prayed. But Melissa died.

Now what? Do we stop praying? Do we give up on God? Do we try to make it alone?

Absolutely not! Prayer is even more vital to us now. God—our inexplicable sovereign Lord—is still in control. His commands to pray still stand. His desire to hear from us is still alive. Faith is not demanding what we want; it is trusting God's goodness in spite of life's tragedies.

We grieve. We pray. We keep on praying.

Dave Branon

God may deny our request but will never disappoint our trust.

Letters to God

Read Psalm 65:1-8

You who answer prayer, to you all people will come. *Psalm 65:2*

Every year thousands of letters addressed to God find their way to a post office in Jerusalem. One letter, addressed to "God of Israel," requested assistance in getting a job as a bulldozer driver. Another said: "Please help me to be happy, to find a nice job and a good wife—soon." One man asked forgiveness for stealing money from a grocery store when he was a child.

But were those heartfelt requests heard by God? The psalmist said that God is the one who hears prayer (Psalm 65:2). Whether we say our prayers silently, voice them aloud, or write them on paper, they go directly to God. But He does not answer every request as we would wish. Our petitions may be self-serving (James 4:3), or sin may be blocking our fellowship with Him (Psalm 66:18).

More than giving us what we want, the Lord knows our deepest needs, and He wants us to discover the joy of His presence each day. Because of our faith in Christ, praying becomes our means of communion with God, not just a list of things we want from Him.

In His wisdom, God hears all our prayers. In His grace, He offers forgiveness for all our sins. In His love, He gives us eternal and abundant life through His Son.

David McCasland

God hears more than our words—He listens to our heart.

Our Final Tears

Read Revelation 7:9–17

> "For the Lamb at the center of the throne will be their shepherd;
> 'he will lead them to springs of living water.'
> And God will wipe away every tear.'" *Revelation 7:17*

This world has been rightly called "a vale of tears." It seems that everywhere people are wiping their eyes because of some cherished hope crushed to the earth, some loved one snatched from their embrace, or some sin that is bringing sorrow and regret. Thank God, we who are His children can look forward to a better day!

We will arrive on heaven's golden shore, as it were, with tear-stained faces, only to feel the tender hand of God gently clearing our clouded vision with the soothing touch of His eternal comfort. And when that happens, we will have experienced our final tears.

Howard W. Ferrin wrote, "Human hands are poor at removing our tears. If they succeed one time, other tears will come that they cannot wipe away. Only the hand that made the spirit can reach the deep sources of its sorrow or dry up the streams that issue from them. God's handkerchief is embroidered with love and tender sympathy, and it is the pierced hand of Jesus that puts it to the eyes of the weeping ones. He will dry every tear: tears of misfortune and poverty, tears of bereaved affection, tears of doubt and discouragement, tears of pain."

Are you distressed today? Your deep heartache may seem endless, but it will not last forever. "Weeping may stay for the night, but rejoicing comes in the morning" (Psalm 30:5). In heaven, all tears are wiped away. Praise God!

Henry Bosch

The God who washed away our sins
will also wipe away our tears!

Prayer Malfunction

Read 1 John 3:21–24

*This is his command: to believe in the name of his Son,
Jesus Christ, and to love one another.* *1 John 3:23*

In a box of my father's old tools I found a hand drill that was at least sixty years old. I could barely get the wheel to turn. The gears were clogged with dirt, and the pieces that hold the drill bit in place were missing. But I wanted to see if I could get it to work.

I began by wiping the accumulated dirt and sawdust off the gears. Then I oiled them. At first they turned hard and slow, but I kept working them. Soon the gears were turning smoothly. Then I saw a cap at the top of the handle. Unscrewing it, I discovered the missing parts that would hold the bit in place. I placed them in the drill, inserted a bit, and easily bored a neat hole in a piece of wood.

Working with that old drill taught me something about prayer. Jesus said we will receive from God what we ask of Him (Matthew 7:7–8). But there are conditions. For example, John said we must obey God and do what pleases Him (1 John 3:22). This includes believing in His Son and loving one another (v. 23). If we don't meet God's conditions, our prayers will be ineffective—just like that old drill.

If your prayer-life is malfunctioning, make sure you're meeting the conditions. When you do, you can be confident that your prayers will be effective.

David Egner

Faith and love are vital to effective prayer.

Quiet Awe

Read Psalm 104:10–24

> How many are your works, Lord! In wisdom you made
> them all; the earth is full of your creatures. *Psalm 104:24*

My life often feels frenzied and hectic. I hurry from one appointment to the next, returning phone calls and checking items off my seemingly infinite to-do list while on my way. Out of sheer exhaustion one Sunday, I collapsed into the hammock in our backyard. My phone was inside, as were my children and husband. At first I planned to sit for just a moment or two, but in the undistracted stillness, I began to notice things that invited me to linger longer. I could hear the creak of the hammock swinging gently, the buzz of a bee in the nearby lavender, and the flap of a bird's wings overhead. The sky was a brilliant blue, and the clouds moved on the wind.

I found myself moved to tears in response to all God had made. When I slowed long enough to take in the many wonderful things within my eyesight and earshot, I was stirred to worship in gratitude for God's creative power. The writer of Psalm 104 was equally humbled by the work of God's hands, noting "you fill the earth with the fruit of your labor" (v. 13 NLT).

In the midst of a harried life, a quiet moment can remind us of God's creative might! He surrounds us with evidence of His power and tenderness; He made both the high mountains and branches for birds. "In wisdom [God] made them all" (v. 24).

Kirsten Holmberg

We are surrounded by God's creative power.

Waiting for an Answer

Read Psalm 9:1–10

Those who know your name trust in you, for you, LORD,
have never forsaken those who seek you. *Psalm 9:10*

When our daughter was fifteen, she ran away. She was gone more than three weeks. Those were the longest three weeks of our lives. We looked everywhere for her and sought help from law enforcement and friends. During those desperate days, my wife and I learned the importance of waiting on God in prayer. We had come to the end of our strength and resources. We had to rely on God.

It was on a Father's Day that we found her. We were in a restaurant parking lot, on our way to dinner, when the phone rang. A waitress at another restaurant had spotted her. Our daughter was only three blocks away. We soon had her home, safe and sound.

We have to wait on God when we pray. We may not know how or when He will answer, but we can put our hearts constantly before Him in prayer. Sometimes the answers to our prayers don't come when we would hope. Things may even go from bad to worse. But we have to persevere, keep believing, and keep asking.

Waiting is never easy, but the end result, whatever it is, will be worth it. David put it this way: "Those who know your name trust in you, for you, LORD, have never forsaken those who seek you" (Psalm 9:10).

Keep seeking. Keep trusting. Keep asking. Keep praying.

James Banks

Time spent in prayer is always time well spent.

Stray Hearts

Read Exodus 32:21–35

So Moses went back to the LORD and said,
"Oh, what a great sin these people have committed!
They have made themselves gods of gold." *Exodus 32:31*

One day an expressway in my city was shut down for several hours because a cattle truck had overturned. The cattle had escaped and were roaming across the highway. Seeing this news story about stray cattle made me think of something I had recently studied in Exodus 32 about the people of God who strayed from Him.

In the divided kingdom of ancient Israel, King Jeroboam erected two golden calves for the people to worship (1 Kings 12:25–32). But the idea of worshiping hunks of gold had not originated with him. Even after escaping brutal slavery and having seen the Lord's power and glory mightily displayed, the Israelites had quickly allowed their hearts to stray from Him (Exodus 32). While Moses was on Mount Sinai receiving the law from the Lord, his brother Aaron helped God's people stray by constructing an idol in the shape of a golden calf. The writer of Hebrews reminds us of God's anger over this idolatry and those whose hearts "are always going astray" (Hebrews 3:10).

God knows that our hearts have a tendency to stray. His Word makes it clear that He is the Lord and that we are to worship "no other gods" (Exodus 20:2–6).

"The Lord is the great God, the great King above all gods" (Psalm 95:3). He is the one true God!

Cindy Hess Kasper

As long as you want anything very much,
especially more than you want God, it is an idol. —A. B. Simpson

Dancing Before the Lord

Read Mark 14:1–9

*Some of those present were saying indignantly to one
another, "Why this waste of perfume?"* Mark 14:4

A number of years ago, Carolyn and I visited a small church where
during the worship service a woman began to dance in the aisle. She
was soon joined by others. Carolyn and I looked at each other and
an unspoken agreement passed between us: "Not me!" We come
from church traditions that favor a serious liturgy, and this other
form of worship was well beyond our comfort zone.

But if Mark's story of Mary's "waste" means anything at all, it
suggests that our love for Jesus may express itself in ways that others
find uncomfortable (Mark 14:1–9). A year's wages were involved
in Mary's anointing. It was an "unwise" act that invited the disciples' scorn. The word Mark uses to describe their reaction means "to
snort" and suggests disdain and mockery. Mary may have cringed,
fearing Jesus's response. But He commended her for her act of devotion and defended her against His own disciples, for Jesus saw the
love that prompted her action despite what some would consider
the impractical nature of it. He said, "Why are you bothering her?
She has done a beautiful thing to me" (v. 6).

Different forms of worship—informal, formal, quiet, exuber-
ant—represent a sincere outpouring of love for Jesus. He's worthy of
all worship that comes from a heart of love.

David Roper

To worship is to open your heart to the love of God.

A Unique Choir

Read Romans 15:5–13

*That with one mind and one voice you may glorify the God
and Father of our Lord Jesus Christ. Romans 15:6*

When Mitch Miller died several years ago, people remembered
him as the man who invited everyone to sing along. On his popular
1960s TV program *Sing Along with Mitch*, an all-male chorus sang
well-loved songs while the words appeared on the screen so viewers
could join in. A *Los Angeles Times* obituary cited Miller's belief that
one reason for the program's success was the appeal of his chorus:
"I always made a point of hiring singers who were tall, short, bald,
round, fat, whatever—everyday-looking guys." From that unified
diversity came beautiful music in which everyone was invited to
participate.

In Romans 15, Paul called for unity among the followers of
Christ—"that with one mind and one voice you may glorify the
God and Father of our Lord Jesus Christ" (v. 6). From several Old
Testament passages, he spoke of Gentiles and Jews together singing
praise to God (vv. 9–12). A unity that had been considered impossible became reality as people who had been deeply divided began
thanking God together for His mercy shown in Christ. Like them,
we are filled with joy, peace, and hope "by the power of the Holy
Spirit" (v. 13).

What a unique "choir" we belong to, and what a privilege it is to
sing along!

David McCasland

Unity among believers comes from our union with Christ.

Looking Upward

Read Psalm 121

Those who look to him are radiant;
their faces are never covered with shame. *Psalm 34:5*

Sam Haley, a well-known mission worker of the late nineteenth and early twentieth century in New York City, once said, "The night I was converted I went out and looked up at the stars, and thanked God for their beauty. I had not seen them for ten years. As a drunkard, I never looked up." He had come to Christ after more than twenty years of struggling with alcoholism.

Those who never lift their eyes to scan the sky miss a great deal, but a far more tragic fact is that many never look up in faith to God. In these days of worldwide tension and confusion, the only hopeful look is upward. Gazing upon the "things of earth" will only confuse and dishearten us. We are surrounded by unrest, lawlessness, violence, and suffering. Man's wisdom is not sufficient to solve these vexing problems.

David wrote Psalm 34 as an expression of joyous praise because he had sought the Lord, and God had graciously come to his aid. He calls on others to join him in worship. In verse 5 he says that those who seek the Lord are bright with joy and have not been put to shame. Those who take the upward look of faith find peace of soul in believing. Faith enables them to see things from the viewpoint of eternity.

If you are experiencing deep trials or disappointments, take the heavenward look. God is still on the throne, and your eternal welfare is secure.

Herb Vander Lugt

Even as flowers thrive when they bend to the light, so an inner radiance illumines those who constantly turn to the Lord!

Pray First

Read 1 Samuel 23:1–5

[David] inquired of the LORD. *1 Samuel 23:2*

When my husband and I supervise our son's piano practice sessions, we begin by asking God to help us. We pray first because neither my husband nor I know how to play the instrument. Together, all three of us are coming to understand musical mysteries such as the meaning of "staccato" and "legato" and when to use the piano's black keys.

Prayer becomes a priority when we realize that we need God's help. David needed God's assistance in a dangerous situation as he considered fighting the Philistines in the city of Keilah. Before engaging in battle, "[David] inquired of the LORD, saying, 'Shall I go and attack these Philistines?'" (1 Samuel 23:2). God gave His approval. However, David's men admitted that the enemy forces intimidated them. Before a single sword was lifted against the Philistines, David prayed again. God promised him the victory he later claimed (v. 4).

Does prayer guide our lives, or is it our last resort when trouble strikes? We sometimes fall into the habit of making plans and then asking God to bless them, or praying only in moments of desperation. God does want us to turn to Him in moments of need. But He also wants us to remember that we need Him all the time (Proverbs 3:5–6).

Jennifer Benson Schuldt

God wants us to pray before we do anything at all.
—Oswald Chambers

Reasons to Praise

Read Job 38:1–18

"Where were you when I laid the earth's foundation?" *Job 38:4*

How could we forget? How could we be so much like Job? How could we fail to be awestruck by God's majesty?

Yet sometimes we do forget. And like Job, we need to hear anew the details of the wonders of God's creative power.

Job's suffering led him to doubt God, so our heavenly Father reminded him, and us, of His unfathomable ways:

- He laid the earth's foundations (Job 38:4).
- He set the boundaries of the oceans (v. 8).
- He sends the morning sun (v. 12).
- He controls life and death (v. 17).
- He sends the snow, rain, and hail (vv. 22, 26, 30).
- He imprints knowledge on the heart (v. 36).
- He sets the time for the birth of animals (39:1–3).
- He gives creatures like the ostrich their unusual ways of life (vv. 13–18).
- He instills the horse with great power (vv. 19–25).
- He directs the hawk and the eagle (vv. 26–30).

Each day, this earth shouts aloud a song of recognition of its Creator. Let's take some time today to echo that tune and pour out our praise to our mighty Creator-God.

May we never forget God's awesome majesty!

Dave Branon

God's work of creating is done;
our work of praising has just begun.

Misplaced Love

Read Psalm 115

But their idols are silver and gold,
made by human hands. *Psalm 115:4*

Martin Lindstrom, an author and speaker, thinks that cellphones have become akin to a best friend for many owners. Lindstrom's experiment using an MRI helped him discover why. When the subjects saw or heard their phone ringing, their brains fired off neurons in the area associated with feelings of love and compassion. Lindstrom said, "It was as if they were in the presence of a girlfriend, boyfriend, or family member."

Many things vie for our affection and time and attention, and it seems we're always needing to evaluate where we're focusing our lives. Joshua told the people of Israel that they were to give their affection and worship to God alone (Joshua 24:14). This was significant in contrast to the idols worshiped by the nations around them. These idols were made of metal and were only the work of men's hands (Psalm 115:4). They were totally powerless compared to the Lord. Therefore, God's people were exhorted to find their security in Him and not in other gods (Judges 10:13–16). Jesus reiterated this in His discussion of the commandments: "Love the Lord your God with all your heart and with all your soul and with all your mind" (Matthew 22:37).

The Lord alone is our help and shield (Psalm115:9). May we reserve our worship for Him.

Marvin Williams

God is most worthy of our affections.

Too Busy to Pray?

Read Luke 5:12–26

But Jesus often withdrew to lonely places and prayed. *Luke 5:16*

The busier we are, the more we should pray. Scottish pastor James I. Stalker (1848–1927) said as much in a quote in the book *Anthology of Jesus*. Stalker said.

> "Jesus appears to have devoted Himself especially to prayer at times when His life was unusually full of work and excitement. His was a very busy life. . . . Many in our day know what this congestion of occupation is: they are swept off their feet with their engagements and can scarcely find time to eat. We make this a reason for not praying; Jesus made it a reason for praying. Is there any doubt which is the better course? Many of the wisest have in this respect done as Jesus did. When Luther had an especially busy and exciting day, he allowed himself a longer time than usual for prayer beforehand. A wise man once said that he was too busy to be in a hurry; he meant that if he allowed himself to become hurried he could not do all that he had to do. There is nothing like prayer for producing this calm self-possession."

How vital are the importance and privilege of talking to the Lord in prayer! Regardless of the active schedules we maintain, the daily pressures we face, and the various demands placed upon us, we need to take time for regular communion with our heavenly Father.

If we're too busy to pray, we're just too busy!

Richard DeHaan

A prayerless Christian is a powerless Christian.

Sacred Gathering

Read Leviticus 23:33–36, 39–44

On the first day you are to take branches from luxuriant trees—
from palms, willows and other leafy trees—and rejoice
before the LORD your God for seven days. *Leviticus 23:40*

Our group of friends reunited for a long weekend together on the shores of a beautiful lake. The days were spent playing in the water and sharing meals, but it was the evening conversations I treasured the most. As darkness fell, our hearts opened to one another with uncommon depth and vulnerability, sharing the pains of faltering marriages and the aftermath of trauma some of our children were enduring. Without glossing over the brokenness of our realities, we pointed one another to God and His faithfulness throughout such extreme difficulties. Those evenings are among the most sacred in my life.

I imagine those nights are similar to what God intended when He instructed His people to gather each year for the Festival of Tabernacles. This feast, like many others, required the Israelites to travel to Jerusalem. Once they arrived, God instructed His people to gather together in worship and to "do no regular work" for the duration of the feast—about a week! (Leviticus 23:35). The Festival of Tabernacles celebrated God's provision and commemorated their time in the wilderness after leaving Egypt (vv. 42–43).

This gathering cemented the Israelites' sense of identity as God's people and proclaimed His goodness despite their collective and individual hardships. When we gather with those we love to recall God's provision and presence in our lives, we too are strengthened in faith.

Kirsten Holmberg

Worshiping together brings strength and joy.

Benediction Blessing

Read Numbers 6:22–27

The LORD bless you and keep you. *Numbers 6:24*

Our church introduced a new practice for the close of our traditional morning worship service. We turn to one another and sing the familiar Aaronic blessing the Lord gave to Moses to give to Israel: "The LORD bless you and keep you; the LORD make his face shine on you . . ." (Numbers 6:24–26). Our hearts are uplifted as we mutually catch the eye of a fellow believer and extend our blessing to him or her.

One Sunday, I noticed a heartwarming and special exchange that has now become a weekly event. In a pew near the front sat an elderly couple, faithful followers of Jesus Christ and devoted partners for the sixty-two years of their married life. When we began to sing, Oscar reached over and took Marian's hands in his. They sang the opening words of this special blessing to each other before looking to others. Everyone nearby sneaked a peek at the look of love and tenderness on their faces.

A benediction is not simply a ritualistic closing; it's a genuine prayerful wish for God's goodness to follow the other person. In offering it to one another, this couple exemplifies its warmest and deepest meaning. In blessing others, we express gratitude for what God has done for us through Christ's death (Hebrews 13:20–21).

David Egner

God gives blessing to us so we can be a blessing to others.

Fading Flower—Firm Faith

Read Psalm 103:13-18

*The life of mortals is like grass, they flourish like a
flower of the field; the wind blows over it and it is gone,
and its place remembers it no more.* Psalm 103:15–16

Our brief existence on this earth is eloquently expressed by Psalm 103:15–16: Man is like the flower of the field that flourishes and soon is gone. Solomon also describes old age, using imagery that is all too familiar: trembling knees, stooped shoulders, dimming eyes, diminished hearing, and failing mental powers (Ecclesiastes 12:1–7).

This unwelcome decline is experienced even by those of great strength and intellectual stature. Sir Isaac Newton in his latter years, with faculties much impaired, was asked to explain a part of his most important mathematical work. He could only say that at one time he knew the solution and that it was right. An elderly general of great renown, listening to the account of his own campaigns being read to him, had forgotten so much of what he had done that from time to time he asked, "Who commanded those battles?" Yes, we are all "fading flowers"!

Although the sunset years are accompanied by the waning of physical and mental ability, the Christian can rejoice as he reflects on the faithfulness of God. David prayed in his old age, "My mouth is filled with your praise, declaring your splendor all day long" (Psalm 71:8). Looking to the Lord who had preserved him in the past, he was confident that He would continue to sustain him to the end.

No matter where you are in life, take courage and trust in God! With a firm faith in Him, your heart can be filled with praise.

Paul Van Gorder

There is a peculiar beauty about godly old age—the beauty of holiness.

When God Doesn't Hear

Read James 5:13–20

If I had cherished sin in my heart,
the LORD would not have listened. *Psalm 66:18*

Surprising things can happen in a courtroom. A judge might throw out strong evidence against a defendant—even a tape-recorded confession—if the proper rules of jurisprudence were violated in obtaining it. Even if he hears the confession, he disregards it. In a sense, a breach of the rules makes it nonexistent.

A similar thing can happen with prayer. Although God knows our every thought, He may disregard our prayers and petitions if we have allowed sin to destroy our fellowship with Him. The Bible says that God is not obligated to hear us if

- our heart is cherishing some sin (Psalm 66:18)
- we ignore the pleas of the poor (Proverbs 21:13)
- we are living in sinfulness (Isiah 59:1, 2)
- there is discord in the home (1 Peter 3:7)
- we doubt His ability to answer (James 1:6, 7)
- our requests are self-centered (James 4:3)

God wants us to talk to Him, to praise Him, and even to petition Him with our requests. But we cannot assume that He hears us just because we pray. We must first live in a way that honors Him and follows His standards. When we do that, we are assured that He will hear our prayers.

Remember, James said that it's the prayer of the righteous that is effective.

Dave Branon

Prayer must mean something to us if it is to mean anything to God.

Let Loose Your Praise!

Read 2 Samuel 6:12–23

Shout to God with cries of joy.
For the LORD Most High is awesome. *Psalm 47:1–2*

On the left side of the aisle three people sat stiffly in the pew; on the right side sat a man in a wheelchair. When the congregation stood to sing, the man on the right had someone help him stand. The three on the left had their arms folded; the man on the right strained to lift his weak arms toward heaven. As the music swelled to a crescendo, the man on the right closed his eyes and struggled to make his mouth form the words of the familiar song; the three on the left stared straight ahead, their lips sealed.

Obviously, I do not know the hearts of anyone in this story, but when I heard it, I knew I had to examine my own. The story reminded me that I often do more pouting than praising in church. Instead of concentrating on the God I worship, I often criticize the way others are worshiping.

When King David worshiped the Lord exuberantly, his wife called him shameless. He said, "I will become even more undignified than this, and I will be humiliated in my own eyes" (2 Samuel 6:22). He knew that being God-conscious couldn't co-exist with being self-conscious.

Taking worship seriously means taking ourselves less seriously. Worship is not about holding on to our dignity; it's about letting loose our praise.

Julie Ackerman Link

We can never praise God too much!

An Altar of Praise

Read Psalm 34:1–8

Isaac built an altar there and called on the name of the LORD. There
he pitched his tent, and there his servants dug a well. *Genesis 26:25*

In Old Testament times, altars were often erected as memorials of
praise. They hallowed a particular spot where a devout worshiper
had encountered God. That was the type of sacred monument built
by Isaac, as recorded in Genesis 26.

While we no longer follow this practice today, certain places do
hold spiritual significance for us. As we return to them, our hearts
are lifted in praise to the Lord for His goodness.

In the early 1900's a policeman was walking his beat in Chicago
when he observed a man standing before a little mission—acting
rather strange. Thinking the man might be drunk or ill, the policeman approached him. He noticed that his eyes were closed, so he
nudged him and said, "What's the matter, Mac? Sick?" The man
looked up and smiled. "No, sir. My name is Billy Sunday. I was
converted right here in this mission. I never pass this way without
taking the opportunity to stand quietly for a moment and whisper a prayer of thanksgiving." The officer grinned understandingly.
Giving the evangelist's hand a hearty grip, he said warmly, "Put
'er there, Bill! I've heard a lot about you! Keep right on with your
prayer, and I'll see that no one bothers you."

When we think back to the time of our conversion or remember
some other spiritual milestone, we too should lift our souls to God
in humble gratitude. To God's glory, our hearts can be an altar of
praise no matter where we are.

Henry Bosch

God's giving deserves our thanksgiving.

The Power of Prayer

Read 1 Samuel 7:7–14

Do not stop crying out to the LORD our God for us,
that he may rescue us. *1 Samuel 7:8*

One day, when I was deeply concerned about the welfare of someone close to me, I found encouragement in part of the Old Testament story of Samuel, a wise leader of the Israelites. As I read how Samuel interceded for God's people as they faced trouble, I strengthened my resolve to pray for the one I loved.

The Israelites faced the threat of the Philistines, who had previously defeated them when God's people didn't trust in Him (see 1 Samuel 4). After repenting of their sins, they heard that the Philistines were about to attack. This time, however, they asked Samuel to continue praying for them (7:8), and the Lord answered clearly by throwing their enemy into confusion (v. 10). Though the Philistines may have been mightier than the Israelites, the Lord was the strongest of them all.

When we ache over the challenges facing those we love and fear the situation won't change, we may be tempted to believe that the Lord will not act. But we should never underestimate the power of prayer, because our loving God hears our pleas. We don't know how He will move in response to our petitions, but we know that as our Father He longs for us to embrace His love and to trust in His faithfulness.

Are there people in your life who need you to pray for them today? Exercise the power of prayer.

Amy Boucher Pye

God hears us when we pray.

Intercession Is Hard Work

Read 1 Samuel 12:16–25

Therefore confess your sins to each other and pray for each other so that you may be healed. The prayer of a righteous person is powerful and effective. James 5:16

Because prayer is commanded in Scripture, we sometimes think of it as "spiritual work" that must be kept up-to-date. Apparently this was the case with a devout clergyman who lived in the early sixteenth century. He had many parish responsibilities, and he often "got behind" in the number of official prayers he was supposed to say each day. Finally he decided to take time out and "get caught up." For three days he prayed continuously, without food or sleep. At the end of this time he was so mentally exhausted that he lay in bed recuperating for five days. It was weeks before he could even stand the sight of his prayer book.

Genuine prayer is hard work, but it goes deeper than merely keeping current with a spiritual discipline. Intercession for others involves inviting the Holy Spirit to convict us of any wrong attitudes we may have toward the one for whom we are praying. This requires honesty and confession of sin. We must also ask God to fill us with His love and to give us spiritual discernment to see what the person's need really is.

If we are serious about this kind of heart-searching discipline, we will encounter many obstacles. But if we are determined, and are not deterred by these barriers, we'll begin to see others through the eyes of Christ. And that's when we are ready to begin the highly effective work of intercessory prayer.

Dennis DeHaan

Work is life's real recreation; prayer is life's real work.

Big and Little Prayers

Read Matthew 7:7–11

*If you, then, though you are evil, know how to give good
gifts to your children, how much more will your Father
in heaven give good gifts to those who ask him!* Matthew 7:11

One afternoon while driving, my wife heard a radio announcer say, "In the next hour we will be giving away two symphony tickets." "Lord," she prayed, "my husband has been working hard, and he enjoys music. Please let us have those tickets."

Arriving home, she turned on the radio. Within minutes the announcer said, "The second person to call in will win." She called. The next day we enjoyed the world-famous Royal Concertgebouw Orchestra of Amsterdam in Grand Rapids on its US tour.

Several years before, I had pleaded with God for deliverance from the depths of depression. Yet for a long time, the skies remained silent. Relief finally came but left me with many unanswered questions.

What kind of God would instantly answer little prayers yet seem to ignore life-and-death requests? I can only conclude that the answers to our small requests encourage us to trust Him when the big prayers are delayed or not answered as we ask. When the stakes are higher and the spiritual lessons more difficult to learn, divine wisdom sometimes delays the answer or remains silent so that the greatest good can come.

One thing is sure: God delights to give good things, big and small, to all who ask Him.

Dennis DeHaan

God may delay or deny our request,
but He will never disappoint our trust.

Say "Mercy"

Read Philippians 4:1–7

Do not be anxious for anything, but in every situation,
by prayer and petition, with thanksgiving,
present your requests to God. *Philippians 4:6*

You may have played the game when you were a child. You interlace your fingers with someone else's and try to bend the other's hands back until one or the other cries "Mercy!" The winner is the one who gets the other person to surrender.

Sometimes we try to play "Mercy" with God when we pray. We have a request that we desperately want answered in a certain way, so we try to "bend His fingers back" and get Him to give in. When it seems we aren't winning, we try a little harder to convince Him by begging or bargaining. We may even give up grudgingly and say, "Lord, you always win! That's not fair!"

God does want honesty of heart. But occasionally in our honesty a demanding spirit comes out. Deep down we know that prayer is not meant to be a contest with God that we try to win. In our wiser moments, we make our requests known to our Lord, surrender them to Him, rely on His grace, and wait for His answers (Philippians 4:6–7). Author Hannah Whitall Smith said, "Be glad and eager to throw yourself unreservedly into His loving arms, and to hand over the reins of government to Him."

Instead of praying with grudging resignation, "Lord, you always win," surrender to Him. Say "Mercy!"

Anne Cetas

Prayer isn't a time to give orders but to report for duty!

Scripture's Grand Scheme

Read John 5:31–39

And beginning with Moses and all the Prophets,
he explained to them what was said in
all the Scriptures concerning himself. *Luke 24:27*

Henry Ward Beecher, the silver-tongued orator of the nineteenth century, likened Scripture to a Beethoven symphony. From beginning to end, said Beecher, runs the single theme of "man's ruin by sin and his redemption by grace; in a word, Jesus Christ, the Savior."

This redemption was promised in Eden and portrayed in the ceremonies of the Mosaic law. All the key events of the Old Testament paved the way for the coming of Christ. He was the Redeemer looked for by Job. Christ is foretold in the "sublime strains of the lofty Isaiah; in the writings of the tender Jeremiah; in the mysteries of the contemplative Ezekiel; in the visions of the beloved Daniel." With each passing century, the great theme grew clearer and clearer.

Beecher concluded, "Then the full harmony broke out in the [declaration] of the angels, 'Glory to God in the highest. And on earth peace, good will toward men.' And evangelists and apostles taking up the theme, the strain closes in the same key in which it began; the devil, who troubled the first paradise, forever excluded from the second; man restored to the favor of God; and Jesus Christ the keynote of the whole."

Praise God for Scripture's grand theme—Jesus Christ. In Him we have salvation from sin.

Richard DeHaan

Jesus Christ is the recurring theme in the symphony of Scripture.

Nothing's Too Hard for God

Read Genesis 18:1–14

"Is anything too hard for the LORD? I will return to you at the appointed time next year, and Sarah will have a son." *Genesis 18:14*

The Lord is able to meet all our needs, whatever they may be. In Genesis 18:1–14, we see that Sarah needed to learn this truth. God's promise to give Abraham a son named Isaac is recorded in Genesis 17:21. Then, in the next chapter that assurance was repeated to the patriarch as he talked outside his tent with three men sent from God. This time, however, Sarah overheard the conversation. To her, having a child at her advanced age (she was ninety) was an impossibility, so she "laughed to herself" (18:12). It was then that the Lord said to Abraham, "Why did Sarah laugh and say, Will I really have a child, now that I am old? Is anything too hard for the LORD?" (vv. 13–14). The answer to that question, of course, is a definite NO!

As Christians, we can have that same assurance today. Abraham's God is the omnipotent One, the Creator of the universe. Nothing exceeds His power. No problem intimidates Him. No obstacle is too big for Him. Anything—yes, everything is possible with Him. Our heavenly Father is in control of every situation. What comfort we can find in this truth! What confidence it gives us.

The all-knowing, everywhere-present, all-powerful Creator and sovereign God can do anything! That's a great assurance when we present our petitions to our heavenly Father in prayer.

Richard DeHaan

You do not prove the resources of God
until you trust Him for the impossible.

And in Truth

Read Zephaniah 1:1–6; 2:1–3

In his love he will no longer rebuke you,
but will rejoice over you with singing. *Zephaniah 3:17*

Years ago, I attended a wedding where two people from different countries got married. Such a blending of cultures can be beautiful, but this ceremony included Christian traditions mixed with rituals from a faith that worshiped many gods.

Zephaniah the prophet pointedly condemned the mixing of other religions with faith in the one true God (sometimes called syncretism). Judah had become a people who bowed in worship to the true God but who also relied on the god Molek (Zephaniah 1:5). Zephaniah described their adoption of pagan culture (v. 8) and warned that as a result God would drive the people of Judah from their homeland.

Yet God never stopped loving His people. His judgment was to show them their need to turn to Him. So Zephaniah encouraged Judah to "Seek righteousness, seek humility" (2:3). Then the Lord gave them tender words promising future restoration: "At that time I will gather you; at that time I will bring you home" (3:20).

It's easy to condemn examples of obvious syncretism like the wedding I attended. But in reality, all of us easily blend God's truth with the assumptions of our culture. We need the Holy Spirit's guidance to test our beliefs against the truth of God's Word and then to stand for that truth confidently and lovingly. Our Father warmly embraces anyone who worships Him in the Spirit and in truth (see John 4:23–24).

Tim Gustafson

God is always ready to forgive and restore.

Active Worship

Read Psalm 100

Enter his gates with thanksgiving and his courts with
praise; give thanks to him and praise his name. *Psalm 100:4*

In his book *Folk Psalms of Faith*, Pastor Ray Stedman says he wishes
that all churchgoers could stand in the pulpit on a Sunday morning
and watch the faces in the congregation during the sermon.

Although most people seem to give the minister their attention,
many have their minds elsewhere. Stedman writes, "It would be fascinating at the end of a service to know where everybody had been!"

To receive the greatest benefit from a church service, we must
prepare our hearts and become active participants. We must become
wholeheartedly involved in singing the hymns, silently praying as
the pastor leads the congregation in prayer, and worshiping from the
heart as the choir sings.

Finally, we need to discipline ourselves to listen intently with a
receptive heart to the teaching of God's Word. We must develop
a hunger for truth that quiets our spirits, inspires worship, evokes
praise to God, and moves us to serve Him.

It's easy to blame the pastor if we leave the service feeling empty
and discouraged. But he's just one participant; we must do our part.
Those who get the most out of worship are those who put the most
into it.

Richard DeHaan

The heart of worship is worship from the heart.

The Man Who Couldn't Talk

Read Psalm 96

For great is the LORD and most worthy of praise;
he is to be feared above all gods. *Psalm 96:4*

Sitting in his wheelchair at a senior citizens home in Belize, a man joyfully listened as a group of American high school teenagers sang about Jesus. Later, as some of the teens tried to communicate with him, they discovered he couldn't talk. A stroke had robbed him of his ability to speak.

Since they couldn't carry on a conversation with the man, the teens decided to sing to him. As they began to sing, something amazing happened. The man who couldn't talk began to sing. With enthusiasm, he belted out "How Great Thou Art" right along with his new friends.

It was a remarkable moment for everyone. This man's love for God broke through the barriers and poured out in audible worship— heartfelt, joyous worship.

We all have worship barriers from time to time. Maybe it's a relationship conflict or a money problem. Or it could be a heart that's grown a bit cold in its relationship to God.

Our non-talking friend reminds us that the greatness and majesty of our almighty God can overcome any barrier. "O Lord, my God—when I in awesome wonder, consider all the worlds Thy hands have made!"

Struggling in your worship? Reflect on how great our God is by reading a passage such as Psalm 96, and you too may find your obstacles and objections replaced by praise.

Dave Branon

Praise is the song of a soul set free.

More Than Wishing

Read Matthew 6:5–15

Your Father knows what you need before you ask him. *Matthew 6:8*

As a child, C. S. Lewis enjoyed reading the books of E. Nesbit, especially *Five Children and It*. In this book, brothers and sisters on a summer holiday discover an ancient sand fairy who grants them one wish each day. But every wish brings the children more trouble than happiness because they can't foresee the results of getting everything they ask for.

The Bible tells us to make our requests known to God (Philippians 4:6). But prayer is much more than telling God what we want Him to do for us. When Jesus taught His disciples how to pray, He began by reminding them, "Your Father knows what need before you ask him" (Matthew 6:8).

What we call the "Lord's Prayer" is more about living in a growing, trusting relationship with our heavenly Father than about getting what we want from Him. As we grow in faith, our prayers will become less of a wish list and more of an intimate conversation with the Lord.

Toward the end of his life, Lewis wrote, "If God had granted all the silly prayers I've made in my life, where should I be now?"

David McCasland

Our highest privilege is to talk to God;
our highest duty is to listen to Him.

A Pause That Refreshes

Read Job 37:5–15

"Listen to this, Job; stop and consider God's wonders." *Job 37:14*

When was the last time you pondered the greatness of God as revealed in nature? His creation testifies to His grand power, and we can observe His marvelous work. Whether we dwell in a fertile valley or some remote mountain place, in a teeming city or a quiet country town, we can see the evidence of an all-wise, omnipotent God through the wonderful things He has made.

One time I had some speaking engagements in the great Northwest, and I drove through the Cascade Mountains in Washington. What breathtaking grandeur! Even though it was the beginning of summer, the snowplows were busy at Stevens Pass, and the ski slopes were still open. I could see clear streams of water bursting out of rocky crevices high on the mountainside and tumbling down the precipice. Giant trees felled by lightning or broken by avalanches of snow lay silent in the ravines below. Then, as I descended from the mountain pass, a beautiful valley spread before me with its rich orchards. Beyond was a green plateau covered with a new crop of wheat. A swift-flowing river loaded with salmon and trout ran parallel to the highway. As I drove through this beauty, I found myself talking out loud as praise to God leaped from my heart.

We all need to take time for a pause that truly refreshes. As we observe the marvels of creation around us, our soul will be thrilled as we "stop and consider God's wonders."

Paul Van Gorder

It's good to worship God in nature
if it leads us to worship the God of nature!

Battle Praise

Read 2 Chronicles 20:1–22

As they began to sing and praise, the LORD set
ambushes against the men of Ammon and Moab . . .
who were invading Judah. *2 Chronicles 20:22*

Visitors to the Military Museum in Istanbul, Turkey, can hear stirring music that dates back to the early years of the Ottoman Empire. Whenever their troops marched off to war, bands accompanied them.

Centuries earlier, worship singers led the people of Judah into battle, but there was a big difference. Whereas the Ottomans used music to instill self-confidence in their soldiers, the Jews used it to express their confidence in God.

Threatened by huge armies, King Jehoshaphat of Judah knew that his people were powerless to defend themselves. So he cried out to God for help (2 Chronicles 20:12). The Lord's answer came through Jahaziel, who said, "Do not be afraid or discouraged. . . . For the battle is not yours, but God's" (v. 15).

Jehoshaphat responded by worshiping and then by appointing singers to lead the army (vv. 18, 21). As the people sang, "Give thanks to the LORD, for his love endures forever," God confused the invaders and they killed one another (vv. 21–24).

No matter what battles we may face today, the Lord will help us when we cry out to Him. Instead of retreating in fear, we can march ahead with confidence in God's power and sing praise to Him.

Julie Ackerman Link

Praise is the voice of faith.

Praying Like Paul

Read Colossians 1:1–14

*For this reason, since the day we heard about you,
we have not stopped praying for you.* Colossians 1:9

It's dark. It's cold. You've been thrown into prison, and you don't know when you'll get out or when you'll eat your next meal. You bow your head to pray. What will you pray for? Safety? Deliverance? A decent meal?

If you are the apostle Paul, you pray for something far different. You talk to God about a group of people you have never seen.

Colossians 1 gives us a brief record of Paul's prison prayer for the people at the church in Colosse. His words help us see how important intercessory prayer should be—even when we have our own troubles.

In Paul's case, he prayed for what he thought this young church needed. He asked God to give them several things, including spiritual understanding (v. 9), fruitful lives (v. 10), and strength, patience, and joy (v. 11).

Paul gave thanks and prayed for his fellow believers "always" (v. 3). Not just when he felt good. Not just when he was warm and well-fed. Always.

How often is our prayer-life interrupted by circumstances that we turn into excuses? Our friends, our family members—even people we don't know—need our intercession. No matter what our difficulty, let's pray for others.

Dave Branon

The best way to influence people for God
is to intercede with God for people.

God Is Listening

Read Psalm 5

In the morning, Lord, you hear my voice; in the morning
I lay my requests before you and wait expectantly. *Psalm 5:3*

The day before Billy Graham's interview in 1982 on *The Today Show*, his director of public relations, Larry Ross, requested a private room for Graham to pray in before the interview. But when Mr. Graham arrived at the studio, his assistant informed Ross that Mr. Graham didn't need the room. He said, "Mr. Graham started praying when he got up this morning, he prayed while eating breakfast, he prayed on the way over in the car, and he'll probably be praying all the way through the interview." Ross later said, "That was a great lesson for me to learn as a young man."

Prayerfulness is not an event; it is a way of being in relationship with God. This kind of intimate relationship is developed when God's people view prayerfulness as a way of life. The Psalms encourage us to begin each day by lifting our voice to the Lord (Psalm 5:3); to fill our day with conversations with God (55:17); and in the face of accusations and slander, to give ourselves totally to prayer (109:4). We develop prayer as a way of life because we desire to be with God (42:1–4; 84:1–2; 130:5–6).

Prayer is our way of connecting with God in all life's circumstances. God is always listening. We can talk to Him any time throughout the day.

Marvin Williams

In prayer, God hears more than your words—
He listens to your heart.

When Life Seems Unfair

Read Psalm 73

I envied the arrogant when I saw the prosperity
of the wicked. *Psalm 73:3*

Have you ever felt that life is unfair? For those of us who are committed to following the will and ways of Jesus, it's easy to get frustrated when people who don't care about Him seem to do well in life. A businessman cheats yet wins a large contract, and the guy who parties all the time is robust and healthy—while you or your loved ones struggle with finances or medical issues. It makes us feel cheated, like maybe we've been good for nothing.

If you've ever felt that way, you're in good company. The writer of Psalm 73 goes through a whole list of how the wicked prosper, and then he says, "Surely in vain I have kept my heart pure" (v. 13). But the tide of his thoughts turns when he recalls his time in God's presence: "Then I understood their final destiny" (v. 17).

When we spend time with God and see things from His point of view, it changes our perspective completely. We may be jealous of the nonbelievers now, but we won't be at judgment time. As the saying goes, what difference does it make if you win the battle but lose the war?

Like the psalmist, let's praise God for His presence in this life and His promise of the life to come (vv. 25–28). He is all you need, even when life seems unfair.

Joe Stowell

Spending time with God puts everything else in perspective.

In Abundance or Affliction

Read Job 1:13–22

The LORD gave and the LORD has taken away;
may the name of the LORD be praised. *Job 1:21*

Ann Voskamp's book *One Thousand Gifts* encourages readers to search their lives each day for what the Lord has done for them. In it, she daily notes God's abundant generosity to her in gifts both large and small, ranging from the simple beauty of iridescent bubbles in the dish sink to the incomparable salvation of sinners like herself (and the rest of us!). Ann contends that gratitude is the key to seeing God in even the most troubling of life's moments.

Job is famous for a life of such "troubling" moments. Indeed, his losses were deep and many. Just moments after losing all his livestock, he learns of the simultaneous death of all his ten children. Job's profound grief was evidenced in his response: he "tore his robe and shaved his head" (1:20). His words in that painful hour make me think Job knew the practice of gratitude, for he acknowledges that God had given him everything he'd lost (v. 21). How else could he worship in the midst of such incapacitating grief?

The practice of daily gratitude can't erase the magnitude of pain we feel in seasons of loss. Job questioned and grappled through his grief as the rest of the book describes. But recognizing God's goodness to us—in even the smallest of ways—can prepare us to kneel in worship before our all-powerful God in the darkest hours of our earthly lives.

Kirsten Holmberg

We worship a God who is greater
than any of our greatest problems.

Help Needed

Read Hebrews 4:9–16

Let us then approach God's throne of grace with
confidence, so that we may receive mercy and
find grace to help us in our time of need. *Hebrews 4:16*

During World War II, the British Isles represented the last line of resistance against the sweep of Nazi oppression in Europe. Under relentless attack and in danger of collapse, however, Britain lacked the resources to see the conflict through to victory. For that reason, British Prime Minister Winston Churchill went on BBC radio and appealed to the world: "Give us the tools, and we will finish the job." He knew that without help from the outside, they could not endure the assault they were facing.

Life is like that. Often, we are inadequate for the troubles life throws at us, and we need help from outside of ourselves. As members of the body of Christ, that help can come at times from our Christian brothers and sisters (Romans 12:10–13)—and that is a wonderful thing. Ultimately, however, we seek help from our heavenly Father. The good and great news is that our God has invited us to come confidently before Him: "Let us approach God's throne of grace with confidence, so that we may receive mercy and find grace to help us in our time of need" (Hebrews 4:16).

At such times, our greatest resource is prayer—for it brings us into the very presence of God. There we find, in His mercy and grace, the help we need.

Bill Crowder

Don't let prayer be your last recourse in time of need;
make it your first.

When We Praise

Read Acts 16:25–34

At once all the prison doors flew open,
and everyone's chains came loose. *Acts 16:26*

When nine-year-old Willie was abducted from his front yard in 2014, he sang his favorite gospel song "Every Praise" over and over again. During the three-hour ordeal, Willie ignored the kidnapper's repeated orders to keep silent as they drove around. Eventually, the kidnapper let Willie out of the car unharmed. Later, Willie described the encounter, saying that while he felt his fear give way to faith, the abductor seemed agitated by the song.

Willie's response to his dire situation is reminiscent of the experience shared by Paul and Silas. After being flogged and thrown into jail, they reacted by "praying and singing hymns to God, and the other prisoners were listening to them. Suddenly there was such a violent earthquake that the foundations of the prison were shaken. At once all the prison doors flew open, and everyone's chains came loose" (Acts 16:25–26).

Upon witnessing this awesome demonstration of power, the jailer believed in the God of Paul and Silas, and his entire household was baptized along with him (vv. 27–34). Through the avenue of praise, both physical and spiritual chains were broken that night.

We may not always experience a visibly dramatic rescue like Paul and Silas, or like Willie. But we know that God responds to the praises of His people! When He moves, chains fall apart.

Remi Oyedele

"[God], You are holy, enthroned in the praises of Israel."
Psalm 22:3 (nkjv)

Rejoicing in Prayer

Read Psalm 63:1–7

Then Hannah prayed and said,
"My heart rejoices in the LORD." *1 Samuel 2:1*

As we pray, we can sometimes find ourselves being a bit one-sided. Of course, our needs should be presented to God, but we must be careful not to let our expressions be so selfishly motivated that they are nothing but a series of unending "gimme's."

In Psalm 63, the writer spends most of his time praising and blessing God for His goodness, lifting up his hands in holy ardor and fervent zeal (63:3–4). When we turn to Hannah's prayer in 1 Samuel 2, we see that it is also full of exultation and joy. These can be reminders of the balance we need when we pray.

Henry Ward Beecher relates this incident concerning a man named Charles Smith, a farm laborer: "In one corner of his bedroom was a small cot, and as a boy I used to lie there and wonder at the enthusiasm with which he engaged in his devotions. It was a regular thing. First, he would read the New Testament, hardly aware that I was in the room. Then he would alternately pray and sing and laugh. I never saw the Bible enjoyed like that! I thought, 'How that man does enjoy it!' He led me to see that there should be real overflowing gladness and thanksgiving in it all."

As we think about our prayer life, we should ask ourselves: How joyful and full of praise is it?

Henry Bosch

Praise is the fairest blossom of prayer!

A Lifestyle of Praise

Read Psalm 146

I will sing praise to my God as long as I live. *Psalm 146:2*

The mother of American novelist Wallace Stegner (1909–1993) died at the age of fifty. When Wallace was eighty, he finally wrote her a note—"Letter, Much Too Late"—in which he praised the virtues of a woman who grew up, married, and raised two sons in the harshness of the early Western United States. She was the kind of wife and mother who was an encourager, even to those that were less than desirable. Wallace remembered the strength his mother displayed by way of her voice. Stegner wrote: "You never lost an opportunity to sing." As long as she lived, Stegner's mother sang, grateful for blessings large and small.

The psalmist too took opportunities to sing. He sang when the days were good, and when they weren't so good. The songs were not forced or coerced, but a natural response to the "Maker of heaven and earth" (146:6) and how He "gives food to the hungry" (v. 7) and "gives sight to the blind" (v. 8) and "sustains the fatherless and the widow" (v. 9). This is really a lifestyle of singing, one that builds strength over time as daily trust is placed in "the God of Jacob" who "remains faithful forever" (vv. 5–6).

The quality of our voices isn't the point, but our response to God's sustaining goodness—a lifestyle of praise. As the old hymn puts it: "There's within my heart a melody."

John Blase

Maker of heaven and earth, when I pause and reflect, your provision for and protection of me is overwhelming. May my life be a continuous song of praise to you for as long as I live.

Hopeful Praise

Read Psalm 103:1–4

Praise the LORD, my soul, and forget not all his benefits. *Psalm 103:2*

One of my friends was in tears on a beautiful summer day, unable to deal with life's difficulties. Another could not look beyond the life-altering sadnesses of her past. Still another struggled with the closing of the small church he had pastored faithfully. A fourth friend had lost his job at a local ministry.

What can our struggling friends—or any of us—do to find hope? Where do we turn when tomorrow offers no happy promises?

We can praise or "bless" the Lord, as David said in Psalm 103. In the middle of trouble, acknowledging God's role in our lives can redirect our thinking from the hurts of our hearts and force us to dwell instead on the greatness of our God. David knew trouble. He faced the threat of enemies, the consequences of his own sin, and the challenges of sorrow. Yet he also recognized the healing power of praise.

That's why in Psalm 103 he can list reasons to turn our attention to God, who gives us many benefits: He forgives us, heals us, redeems us, crowns us with love and compassion, satisfies our desires, and renews us. David reminds us that God provides justice and righteousness and is gracious and loving.

Take it from David: Praising God's greatness puts hope in our troubled hearts.

Dave Branon

Praise can lighten your heaviest burden.

Thoughtful Praises

Read Psalm 47

God is the King of all the earth;
sing to him a psalm of praise. *Psalm 47:7*

I wonder what God thinks about the way we sing at church. I'm not talking about the quality of our voices, but the honesty of our words. If we're being truthful, the following rewritten hymn titles might more accurately express what's in our hearts as we sing:

"Just As I Am" is "Just As I Pretend To Be."
"O How I Love Jesus" becomes "O How I Like Jesus."
"I Surrender All" is actually "I Surrender Some."
"He's Everything To Me" means "He's Quite A Bit To Me."

Jesus said that we are to worship Him in truth (John 4:24). Singing sincerely and with understanding is a serious challenge (Psalm 47:7).

Let's take up the challenge by seeking God's help to make the original titles of these hymns true for us. In repentance and without pretense, let's turn to Him just as we are. In His forgiving presence, let's declare total love for Jesus by surrendering all to Him. As a result, Jesus truly will become everything to us. Then we will be able to sing honestly about Jesus Christ and our love for Him.

As we make melody in our hearts to the Lord (Ephesians 5:19), let's worship in spirit and in truth.

Joanie Yoder

To sing God's praise, keep your heart in tune with Him.

Worship by Prayer

Read Psalm 66:1–7

Shout for joy to God, all the earth! *Psalm 66:1*

When was the last time you and God met together for a worship service? No praise team. No piano. No order of service. Just you and God and prayer.

Want an example? Listen to the psalmist: "I cried out to [the Lord] with my mouth; his praise was on my tongue. If I had cherished sin in my heart, the Lord would not have listened; but God has surely listened and has heard my prayer. Praise be to God, who has not rejected my prayer, or withheld his love from me!" (Psalm 66:17–20).

Did you notice what was happening in those verses? The psalmist called out to God in praise. He came with a pure heart—cleansed by confession. He was confident that God was listening. God accepted the prayer, and He lavished His love on the person praying. The psalmist's worship included praise, a pure heart, communicating with God—and then God's affirmation and love were poured out. Yes, true worship took place.

What a pattern! Think of the spiritual advantage you gain and the honor God receives when you practice worship by prayer. Anytime, anyplace, you can worship the Lord and He will bless you.

Are you ready to worship?

Dave Branon

God speaks to those who take time to listen,
and He listens to those who take time to pray.

Praise in the Dark

Read Matthew 26:17-30

Through Jesus, therefore, let us continually offer
to God a sacrifice of praise—the fruit of lips
that openly profess his name. *Hebrews 13:15*

Even though my friend Mickey was losing his eyesight, he told me, "I'm going to keep praising God every day, because He's done so much for me."

Jesus gave Mickey, and us, the ultimate reason for such never-ending praise. The twenty-sixth chapter of Matthew tells us about how Jesus shared the Passover meal with His disciples the night before He went to the cross. Verse 30 shows us how they concluded the meal: "When they had sung a hymn, they went out to the Mount of Olives."

It wasn't just any hymn they sang that night—it was a hymn of praise. For millennia, Jews have sung a group of Psalms called "The Hallel" at Passover (*hallel* is the Hebrew word for "praise"). The last of these prayers and songs of praise, found in Psalms 113–118, honors the God who has become our salvation (118:21). It refers to a rejected stone that became a cornerstone (v. 22) and one who comes in the name of the Lord (v. 26). They may very well have sung, "The LORD has done it this very day; let us rejoice today and be glad" (v. 24).

As Jesus sang with His disciples on this Passover night, He was giving us the ultimate reason to lift our eyes above our immediate circumstances. He was leading us in praise of the never-ending love and faithfulness of our God.

James Banks

Praising God helps us recall His goodness that never ends.

Communion on the Moon

Read Psalm 139:1–12

If I go up to the heavens, you are there;
if I make my bed in the depths, you are there. *Psalm 139:8*

Apollo 11 landed on the surface of the moon on Sunday, July 20, 1969. Most of us are familiar with Armstrong's historic statement as he stepped onto the moon's surface: "That's one small step for a man; one giant leap for mankind." But few know about the first meal eaten there.

Buzz Aldrin had taken aboard the spacecraft a tiny communion kit provided by his church. Aldrin sent a radio broadcast to earth asking listeners to contemplate the events of that day and to give thanks.

Then, in radio blackout for privacy, Aldrin poured wine into a silver chalice. He read, "I am the vine; you are the branches. If you remain in me and I in you, you will bear much fruit" (John 15:5). Silently, he gave thanks and partook of the bread and cup.

God is everywhere, and our worship should reflect this reality. In Psalm 139 we are told that wherever we go, God is intimately present with us. Buzz Aldrin celebrated that experience on the surface of the moon. Thousands of miles from earth, he took time to commune with the One who created, redeemed, and fellowshipped with him.

Are you far from home? Do you feel as if you're on a mountaintop or in a dark valley? No matter what your situation, God's fellowship is only a prayer away.

Dennis Fisher

God's presence with us is one of His greatest presents to us.

Let's Celebrate

Read Psalm 150

Praise him with timbrel and dancing,
praise him with the strings and pipe. *Psalm 150:4*

After Ghana's Asamoah Gyan scored a goal against Germany in the 2014 World Cup, he and his teammates did a coordinated dance step. When Germany's Miroslav Klose scored a few minutes later, he did a running front flip. "Soccer celebrations are so appealing because they reveal players' personalities, values, and passions," says Clint Mathis, who scored for the US at the 2002 World Cup.

In Psalm 150, the psalmist invites "everything that has breath" (v. 6) to celebrate and praise the Lord in many different ways. He suggests that we use trumpets and harps, stringed instruments and pipes, cymbals and dancing. He encourages us to creatively and passionately celebrate, honor, and adore the Lord. Because the Lord is great and has performed mighty acts on behalf of His people, He is worthy of all praise. These outward expressions of praise will come from an inner wellspring overflowing with gratitude to God. "Let everything that has breath praise the Lord," the psalmist declares (150:6).

Though we may celebrate the Lord in different ways (I'm not encouraging back flips in our worship services), our praise to God always needs to be expressive and meaningful. When we think about the Lord's character and His mighty acts toward us, we cannot help but celebrate Him through our praise and worship.

Marvin Williams

Praise is the song of a soul set free.

Fearless Giving

Read Malachi 3:8–12

Bring the whole tithe into the storehouse,
that there may be food in my house. *Malachi 3:10*

When my son Xavier was six years old, a friend brought her toddler to visit; and Xavier wanted to give him a few toys. I delighted in our little giver's generosity, until he offered a stuffed animal my husband had searched several stores in different cities to find. Recognizing the high-demand toy, my friend tried to politely decline. Still, Xavier placed his gift into her son's hands and said, "My daddy gives me lots of toys to share."

Though I'd like to say Xavier learned his confident giving from me, I've often withheld my resources from God and others. But when I remember that my heavenly Father gives me everything I have and need, it's easier to share.

In the Old Testament, God commanded the Israelites to trust Him by giving a portion of all He had supplied to the Levite priests, who would in turn help others in need. When the people refused, the prophet Malachi said they were robbing the Lord (Malachi 3:8–9). But if they gave willingly, showing they trusted the Lord's promised provision and protection (vv. 10–11), others would recognize them as God's blessed people (v. 12).

Whether we're managing our finances, our schedules, or the gifts God entrusted to us, giving can be an act of worship. Giving freely and fearlessly can show our confidence in the care of our loving Father—the ultimate generous Giver.

Xochitl Dixon

Fearless giving to God and others
reveals our trust in the Lord's promises and provision.

God is Great; God is Good

Read Nahum 1:1–8

The LORD is slow to anger but great in power. . . .
The LORD is good, a refuge in times of trouble. *Nahum 1:3, 7*

When we were children, my brother and I recited this prayer every night before supper: "God is great, God is good. Let us thank Him for this food." For years I spoke the words of this prayer without stopping to consider what life would be like if it were not true—if God were not both great and good.

Without His greatness maintaining order in the universe, the galaxies would be a junkyard of banged-up stars and planets. And without His goodness saying "enough" to every evil despot, the earth would be a playground ruled by the biggest bully.

That simple childhood prayer celebrates two profound attributes of God: His transcendence and His immanence. *Transcendence* means that His greatness is beyond our comprehension. *Immanence* describes His nearness to us. The greatness of the almighty God sends us to our knees in humility. But the goodness of God lifts us back to our feet in grateful, jubilant praise. The One who is above everything humbled himself and became one of us (Psalm 135:5; Philippians 2:8).

Thank God that He uses His greatness not to destroy us but to save us and that He uses His goodness not as a reason to reject us but as a way to reach us.

Julie Ackerman Link

When you taste God's goodness, His praise will be on your lips.

The Joy of Your Presence

Read Psalm 145:1–18

Great is the LORD and most worthy of praise;
he is to be feared above all gods. *Psalm 96:4*

"Man's chief end is to glorify God and enjoy Him forever," says the Westminster Catechism. Much of Scripture calls for joyful gratitude and adoration of the living God. When we honor God, we celebrate Him as the Source from which all goodness flows.

When we praise God from our heart, we find ourselves in that joyful state for which we were created. Just as a beautiful sunset or a peaceful pastoral scene points to the majesty of the Creator, so worship draws us into a close spiritual union with Him. The psalmist says, "Great is the LORD and most worthy of praise. . . . The LORD is near to all who call on him" (Psalm 145:3, 18).

God does not need our praise, but we need to praise God. By basking in His presence we drink in the joy of His infinite love and rejoice in the One who came to redeem and restore us. "In your presence there is fullness of joy," the psalmist says. "At your right hand are pleasures forevermore" (Psalm 16:11 ESV).

Dennis Fisher

Worship is a heart overflowing with praise to God.

Prayers That Produce

Read James 5:13–18

[God] listens to the godly person who does his will. *John 9:31*

A friend took his young son with him to town one day to run some errands. At lunchtime arrived, they went to a familiar diner. The father sat down on one of the stools at the counter and lifted the boy up to the seat beside him. They ordered lunch, and when the waiter brought the food, the father said, "Son, we'll just have a silent prayer." Dad got through praying first and waited for the boy to finish his prayer, but he just sat with his head bowed for an unusually long time. When he finally looked up, his father asked him, "What in the world were you praying about all that time?" With the innocence and honesty of a child, he replied, "How do I know? It was a silent prayer."

Could our prayers be like that on occasion—not really saying anything to the Lord. Except on those occasions when words truly fail us (Romans 8:26), the Lord needs to hear earnest, heartfelt prayer from us—prompted by the Holy Spirit and offered in the name of the Lord Jesus. The result, according to Paul, is that "the peace of God, which transcends all understanding," will keep our hearts and minds through Christ Jesus (Philippians 4:7).

Let's take prayer seriously! Our requests must be in line with God's Word, and they must come from sincere hearts.

Henry Bosch

True prayer does not require eloquence, but earnestness.

An Old Man's Prayer

Read Daniel 9:3–19

I turned to the Lord God and pleaded with him in prayer. Daniel 9:3

Have you heard the story about the eighty-five-year-old man who was arrested for praying?

You probably have. That's the story of Daniel, an elderly Jewish resident in Babylon sentenced to death for faithfully talking to God (Daniel 6).

Although the prayer that sent Daniel to the lions' den is his most famous talk with God (6:11), it wasn't the only time we see him in prayer.

In Daniel 9, we read another example of how he prayed. Daniel had been reading in his scroll of Jeremiah that the captivity of his people would last seventy years, and the people were at that point sixty-seven years into the exile (Jeremiah 25:8–11). He was eager for it to end.

God had called His people to live righteously, but they weren't doing that. Daniel decided to live righteously despite their lack of faith. He began to pray that God would not delay the end of the captivity.

As he prayed, Daniel focused on worship and confession. His pattern of prayer gives us an important insight into talking to God. We are to recognize that God is "great and awesome" (v. 4) and that "we have sinned" (v. 15). In prayer, we praise and confess.

Let's follow Daniel's lead. To him, prayer was as vital as life itself.

Dave Branon

No one stands as tall as a Christian on his knees.

The Power of God's Music

Read Colossians 3:12–17

Let the message of Christ dwell among you richly . . .
with all wisdom through psalms, hymns,
and songs from the Spirit. *Colossians 3:16*

The Sound of Music, one of the most successful musical films ever produced, was released as a motion picture in 1965. It won many accolades, including five Academy Awards, as it captured the hearts and voices of people around the world. More than a half a century later, people still attend special showings of the film where viewers come dressed as their favorite character and sing along during the performance.

Music is deeply rooted in our souls. And for followers of Jesus, it is a powerful means of encouraging each other along the journey of faith. Paul urged the believers in Colossae, "Let the message of Christ dwell among you richly as you teach and admonish one another with all wisdom through psalms, hymns, and songs from the Spirit, singing to God with gratitude in your hearts." (Colossian 3:16).

Singing together to the Lord embeds the message of His love in our minds and souls. It is a powerful ministry of teaching and encouragement that we share together. Whether our hearts cry out, "Create in me a pure heart, O God" (Psalm 51:10), or joyfully shout, "And he will reign for ever and ever" (Revelation 11:15), the power of music that exalts God lifts our spirits and grants us peace.

Let us sing to the Lord today.

David McCasland

Music washes from the soul the dust of everyday life.

God Hears Your Cry

Read Psalm 34:1-18

The righteous cry out, and the LORD hears them;
he delivers them from all their troubles. *Psalm 34:17*

The psalmist David found that in his hour of trouble he could call upon the Lord and be confident of receiving His help. This was a great comfort to him. In Psalm 34 he told of his trials and praised God for His loving care and deliverance. Still today, Christians can expect the heavenly Father to hear their plea and graciously come to their rescue.

Someone once asked a lifeguard this question: "How can you tell when anyone is in need of help if hundreds of bathers on the beach or in the water are all combining their voices in a veritable hubbub of noise?" He replied, "No matter how great the sounds of confusion may be, there has never been a time when I couldn't distinguish a cry of distress above them all. I could always tell when there was an actual emergency."

Isn't that like our heavenly father? In all of the confusion of life, he always hears the person who is crying out for help in life's storms. He sees us as if there were no other child of His in the whole world. Bending His loving ear to hear our faintest call for help, He hastens to our aid. "The righteous cry out, and the LORD hears them" (Psalm 34:17).

Rejoicing in the way God has come to our deliverance, we exclaim in gratitude with the psalmist, "I will extol the LORD at all times; his praise will always be on my lips" (v. 1).

Henry Bosch

We need not fear the perils around us
as long as the eye of the Lord is upon us.

First Response

Read James 5:13-16

Do not be anxious about anything, but . . . present your requests to God. And the peace of God . . . will guard your hearts and your minds in Christ Jesus. Philippians 4:6–7

When my husband, Tom, was rushed to the hospital for emergency surgery, I began to call family members. My sister and her husband came right away to be with me, and we prayed as we waited. Tom's sister listened to my anxious voice on the phone and immediately said, "Cindy, can I pray with you?" When my pastor and his wife arrived, he too prayed for us (James 5:13–16).

Oswald Chambers wrote: "We tend to use prayer as a last resort, but God wants it to be our first line of defense. We pray when there's nothing else we can do, but God wants us to pray before we do anything at all."

At its root, prayer is simply a conversation with God, spoken in the expectation that God hears and answers. Prayer should not be a last resort. In His Word, God encourages us to engage Him in prayer (Philippians 4:6). We also have His promise that when "two or three gather" together in His name, He will be "there in the midst of them" (Matthew 18:20).

For those who have experienced the power of the Almighty, our first inclination often will be to cry out to Him. Nineteenth-century pastor Andrew Murray said: "Prayer opens the way for God himself to do His work in us and through us."

Cindy Hess Kasper

Pray first!

Abby's Prayer

Read Ephesians 6:16–20

*I urge . . . that petitions, prayers, intercession
and thanksgiving be made for all people.* 1 Timothy 2:1

When Abby was a sophomore in high school, she and her mom heard a news story about a young man who'd been critically injured in a plane accident—an accident that took the lives of his father and stepmother. Although they didn't know this person, Abby's mom said, "We just need to pray for him and his family." And they did.

Fast forward a few years, and one day Abby walked into a class at her university. A student offered her the seat next to him. That student was Austin Hatch, the plane crash victim Abby had prayed for. Soon they were dating, and in 2018 they were married.

"It's crazy to think that I was praying for my future husband," Abby said in an interview shortly before they were married. It can be easy to limit our prayers to our own personal needs and for those closest to us, without taking the time to pray for others. However, Paul, writing to the Christians at Ephesus, told them to "pray in the Spirit on all occasions with all kinds of prayers and requests. With this in mind, be alert and always keep on praying for all the Lord's people" (Ephesians 6:18). And 1 Timothy 2:1 tells us to pray "for all people," including those in authority.

Let's pray for others—even people we don't know. It's one of the ways we can "carry each other's burdens" (Galatians 6:2).

Dave Branon

God's answers to our prayers may exceed our expectations.

In Brief

Read Psalm 117

Great is his love toward us. *Psalm 117:2*

I counted once and discovered that Abraham Lincoln's Gettysburg Address contains fewer than 300 words. This means, among other things, that words don't have to be many to be memorable.

That's one reason I like Psalm 117. Brevity is its hallmark. The psalmist said all he had to say in twenty-nine words (actually just seventeen words in the Hebrew text).

Praise the Lord, all you nations; extol him, all you peoples. For great is his love toward us, and the faithfulness of the Lord endures forever. Praise the Lord!

Ah, that's the good news! Contained in this hallelujah psalm is a message to all nations of the world that God's covenant love is "great . . . toward us" (v. 2).

Think about what God's love means. God loved us before we were born; He will love us after we die. Not one thing can separate us from the love of God that is in Jesus our Lord (Romans 8:39). His heart is an inexhaustible and irrepressible fountain of love!

As I read this brief psalm of praise to God, I can think of no greater encouragement for our journey than its reminder of God's merciful kindness. Praise the Lord!

David Roper

What we know about God
should lead us to give joyful praise to Him.

What's in Your Mouth?

Read Psalm 126

It was said among the nations,
"The LORD has done great things for them." *Psalm 126:2*

Communications experts tell us that the average person speaks enough to fill twenty single-spaced, typewritten pages every day. This means our mouths crank out enough words to fill two books of 300 pages each month, twenty-four books each year, and 1,200 books in fifty years of speaking. Thanks to phones, voicemail, texts, and face-to-face conversations, words comprise a large part of our lives. Therefore, the kinds of words we use are important.

The psalmist's mouth was filled with praise when he wrote Psalm 126. The Lord had done great things for him and his people. Even the nations around them noticed. Remembering God's blessings, he said, "Our mouths were filled with laughter, and our tongue with songs of joy" (v. 2).

What words would you have used in verse 3 had you been writing this psalm? So often, our attitude may seem to be: "The Lord has done great things for us, and I—

. . . can't recall any of them right now."

. . . am wondering what He'll do for me next."

. . . need much more."

Or can you finish it by saying, "And I am praising and thanking Him for His goodness"? As you recall God's blessings today, express your words of praise to Him.

Anne Cetas

Let no thought linger in your mind
that you would be ashamed to let out of your mouth.

Thankfulness Transforms

Read Psalm 107:1-8

Give thanks to the LORD, for he is good;
his love endures forever. *Psalm 107:1*

In the early days of the settlement of the western part of the United States, travelers encountered considerable difficulty. One party of pioneers on the Oregon Trail had suffered greatly from a scarcity of water for themselves and grass for their horses. Some of the wagons had broken down, causing delays in the stifling heat. Optimism and cheer were gone.

One night a meeting was called for the purpose of airing their complaints. When the pioneers had gathered around the campfire, one of them arose and said, "Before we do anything else, I think we should first thank God that we have come this far with no loss of life and that we have enough strength left to finish our journey." After the prayer, there was silence. No one had any grievances that they felt were important enough to voice. Thankfulness often transforms a grumbling spirit into one of contentment, enabling us to see the many mercies of God that we ordinarily would overlook. A grateful heart finds God-given blessing in every hour of distress.

Are you experiencing frustrations and difficulties? As the burdens rest heavily upon you and the temptation to murmur increases, take time to thank God for His enduring mercies. In counting your blessings you will find that thankfulness will change pessimism to praise.

Paul Van Gorder

The sure cure for depression is praise.

Night

Read Psalm 42

> By day the LORD directs his love,
> at night his song is with me. *Psalm 42:8*

In his riveting and unsettling book *Night*, Elie Wiesel describes his boyhood experiences as one of the countless victims of the Holocaust. Ripped from his home and separated from everyone in his family except his father (who would die in the death camps), Wiesel suffered a dark night of the soul such as few will experience. It challenged his views and beliefs about God. His innocence and faith became sacrifices on the altar of man's evil and sin's darkness.

David experienced his own dark night of the soul, which many scholars believe motivated his writing of Psalm 42. Harried and hounded, probably as he was pursued by his rebellious son Absalom (2 Samuel 16–18), David echoed the pain and fear that can be felt in the isolation of night. It's the place where darkness grips us and forces us to consider the anguish of our heart and ask hard questions of God. The psalmist lamented God's seeming absence, yet in it all he found a night song (v. 8) that gave him peace and confidence for the difficulties ahead.

When we struggle in the night, we can be confident that God is at work in the darkness. We can say with the psalmist, "Put your hope in God, for I will yet praise him, my Savior and my God" (Psalm 43:11).

Bill Crowder

When it is dark enough, men see the stars. —Emerson

Time Together

Read Psalm 147:1–11

The LORD delights in those who fear him,
who put their hope in his unfailing love. *Psalm 147:11*

On the two-hour drive home from a family member's wedding, my mom asked me for the third time what was new in my job. I once again repeated some of the details as if telling her for the first time, while wondering what might possibly make my words more memorable. My mom has Alzheimer's, a disease that progressively destroys the memory, can adversely affect behavior, and eventually leads to the loss of speech—and more.

I grieve because of my mom's disease, but I am thankful she is still here and we can spend time together—and even converse. It thrills me that whenever I go to see her she lights up with joy and exclaims, "Alyson, what a pleasant surprise!" We enjoy each other's company; and even in the silences when words escape her, we commune together.

This perhaps is a small picture of our relationship with God. Scripture tells us, "The Lord delights in those who fear him, who put their hope in his unfailing love" (Psalm 147:11). God calls those who believe in Jesus as their Savior His children (John 1:12). And although we may make the same requests over and over again or lack for words, He is patient with us because He has a loving relationship with us. He is happy when we converse with Him in prayer—even when the words escape us.

Alyson Kieda

God delights to hear from us!

Worship and Obey

Read Psalm 95

Come, let us sing for joy to the LORD. . . .
Do not harden your hearts as you did at Meribah. *Psalm 95:1, 8*

Millions of Christians gather every Sunday to worship God as their Creator and Redeemer. Whether formal and liturgical or free and spontaneous, church services are occasions to declare God's worthiness and to give Him praise. But centuries of church history reveal how quickly worship can degenerate into empty ritualism. This occurs whenever God's people harden their hearts and fail to obey His Word.

The psalmist knew this to be true from Israel's experience. Under the leadership of Moses, they had been miraculously delivered from slavery in Egypt and had fervently praised the Lord (Exodus 12–15). But almost immediately they began to doubt God's goodness and trustworthiness. They complained bitterly and found fault with the Lord and His servant Moses. They ignored His instructions, and their worship became hollow. This angered God and resulted in their wandering for forty years in a desert they could have crossed in a short time. And few among them were allowed to enter the Promised Land!

Lord, fill us with wonder and gratitude for your marvelous salvation. Help us to give you the praise you deserve, and enable us to be faithful in our love and obedience to you.

Herb Vander Lugt

Our worship is right only when we are right with God.

He Knows My Name

Read John 10:1–4

The sheep listen to his voice. He calls his own sheep by name and leads them out. John 10:3

When we attended a large church, we learned new things, joined a great small group, and enjoyed the worshipful music. But I didn't realize for a long time that I missed something—the pastor had no idea who I was. Because of the thousands in attendance, I understood that it would be impossible for him to know each person by name.

Then, when we began attending a much smaller church, I received a handwritten welcome note from the pastor. After a few more weeks, Pastor Josh was calling me by name and chatting with me about my recent surgery. It felt good to be personally acknowledged.

All of us have a desire to be known—especially by God. A song by Tommy Walker, "He Knows My Name," reminds us that God knows our every thought, sees each tear that falls, and hears us when we call. We read in the gospel of John, "The sheep listen to his voice. He calls his own sheep by name. . . . I am the good shepherd; I know my sheep" (John 10:3, 14).

For the One who made heaven and earth, knowing a few billion people is not a problem. God loves you immensely (John 3:16), He thinks about you all the time (Psalm 139:17–18), and He knows your name (John 10:3).

Cindy Hess Kasper

No Christian is anonymous to God.

Wonderfully Made

Read Psalm 139:12–18

*I praise you because I am fearfully
and wonderfully made. Psalm 139:14*

While getting an eye exam recently, my doctor hauled out a piece of equipment that I hadn't seen before. I asked him what the device was, and he responded, "I'm using it to take a picture of the inside of the back of your eye."

I was impressed that someone had invented a camera that could do that. But I was even more impressed by what my doctor could learn from that picture. He said, "We can gather a lot of details about your current general health simply by looking at the back of your eye."

My doctor's comment amazed me. It is remarkable that a person's overall health can be measured by the health of the eye. What care the Lord has taken to place these details in the bodies He has created! It immediately brings to my mind the words of David, the psalmist, who reveled in God's creativity: "I praise you because I am fearfully and wonderfully made; your works are wonderful, I know that full well" (Psalm 139:14).

The enormous complexities of our bodies reflect the genius and wisdom of our great Creator. The wonder of His design is more than breathtaking—it gives us countless reasons to worship Him!

Bill Crowder

All life is created by God and bears His autograph.

Everyone Sings!

Read Revelation 5:8–14

"To him who sits on the throne and to the Lamb be praise and honor and glory and power, for ever and ever!" Revelation 5:13

Each summer I enjoy attending many of the free outdoor concerts presented in our city. During one performance by a brass band, several of the members briefly introduced themselves and told how much they enjoyed practicing and playing together.

The pleasure of sharing music in community has drawn people together for centuries. As followers of Christ, whether we are in small groups, choirs, or congregations, bringing praise to God is one of the key elements in our own expression of faith. And one day, we'll be singing in a concert that defies imagination.

In a sweeping vision of the tumultuous events at the end of time, John records a chorus of praise that begins with a few and swells to a company beyond number. In honor of the Lamb of God, who with His blood has redeemed people from every tribe and nation (Revelation 5:9), the song begins at the throne of God, is joined by multiplied thousands of angels, and finally includes every creature in heaven, earth, and sea. Together we will sing, "To him who sits on the throne and to the Lamb be praise and honor and glory and power, for ever and ever!" (v. 13).

What a choir! What a concert! What a privilege to start rehearsing today!

David McCasland

Those who know Christ now will sing His praise forever.

Praise for Pure Hearts

Read Psalm 51:7–17

A broken and contrite heart you, God,
will not despise. *Psalm 51:17*

During my friend Myrna's travels to another country, she visited a church for worship. She noticed that as people entered the sanctuary they immediately knelt and prayed, facing away from the front of the church. My friend learned that people in that church confessed their sin to God before they began the worship service.

This act of humility is a picture to me of what David said in Psalm 51: "My sacrifice, O God, is a broken spirit; a broken and contrite heart you, God, will not despise" (v. 17). David was describing his own remorse and repentance for his sin of adultery with Bathsheba. Real sorrow for sin involves adopting God's view of what we've done—seeing it as clearly wrong, disliking it, and not wanting it to continue.

When we are truly broken over our sin, God lovingly puts us back together. "If we confess our sins, he is faithful and just and will forgive us our sins and purify us from all unrighteousness" (1 John 1:9). This forgiveness produces a fresh sense of openness with Him and is the ideal starting point for praise. After David repented, confessed, and was forgiven by God, he responded by saying, "Open my lips, Lord, and my mouth will declare your praise" (Psalm 51:15).

Humility is the right response to God's holiness. And praise is our heart's response to His forgiveness.

Jennifer Benson Schuldt

Praise is the song of a soul set free.

The Prayerful Attitude

Read 1 Thessalonians 5:5–18

Pray continually. *1 Thessalonians 5:17*

Once in an assembly of ministers, the question was raised as to how one could comply with the command to "pray without ceasing" (1 Thessalonians 5:17 NKJV). A variety of answers was offered, and at length someone was appointed to write an essay on the subject, to be read at the next meeting. A custodian who overheard that asked, "What? A whole month to explore the meaning of that text? I believe it is one of the easiest and best in the Bible!"

"Well," said an old minister, "what can you tell us about it? Can you truly pray all the time even when you have so many things to do?"

"Why, sir, the more I have to do, the more I pray. When I awake in the morning, I ask the Lord to open the eyes of my understanding. Then while I am dressing, I pray that I may be clothed with the robe of His righteousness; and when I wash I ask for the cleansing of the Holy Spirit as I go about my tasks. As I begin to work, I pray that I may have strength equal to my day! As I sweep I beseech Him that my heart may be cleansed from all its impurities. And so all day long everything I do furnishes me with a thought for prayer!"

"Praise the Lord," said the preacher, "I think, brethren, we can dispense with next month's essay!"

Henry Bosch

To "pray without ceasing" one must
constantly keep his "lines" up to heaven—
seeking "moment by moment" instruction and guidance!

Five-Finger Prayers

Read James 5:13–18

Pray for each other. *James 5:16*

Prayer is a conversation with God, not a formula. Yet sometimes we might need to use a "method" to freshen up our prayer time. We can pray the Psalms or other Scriptures (such as the Lord's Prayer), or use the ACTS method (Adoration, Confession, Thanksgiving, and Supplication). I recently came across this "Five-Finger Prayer" to use as a guide when praying for others:

- When you fold your hands, the thumb is nearest you. So begin by praying for those closest to you—your loved ones (Philippians 1:3–5).
- The index finger is the pointer. Pray for those who teach— Bible teachers and preachers, and those who teach children (1 Thessalonians 5:25).
- The next finger is the tallest. It reminds you to pray for those in authority over you—national and local leaders, and your supervisor at work (1 Timothy 2:1–2).
- The fourth finger is usually the weakest. Pray for those who are in trouble or who are suffering (James 5:13–16).
- Then comes your little finger. It reminds you of your smallness in relation to God's greatness. Ask Him to supply your needs (Philippians 4:6, 19).

Whatever method you use, just talk with your Father. He wants to hear what's on your heart.

Anne Cetas

It's not the words we pray that matter;
it's the condition of our heart.

Don't Forget to Hoe

Read Matthew 9:35–38

Ask the LORD of the harvest, therefore, to send out workers
into his harvest field. *Matthew 9:38*

Driving through a small village in Pennsylvania, we saw these
words on a church bulletin board: "Pray for a good harvest, but
keep on hoeing." An excellent bit of advice, indeed! How foolish
it would be for a farmer to ask the Lord for a good crop but fail to
plant the seed!

Yet how often we fail to apply this principle in other areas of
life. We bend our knees in earnest petition for one who is needy,
and then we promptly refuse to give of our own abundance to help
provide the necessary relief. We pray that the Lord will "send forth
workers into his harvest," but we are not willing to be one of the
workers ourselves. We ask in faith that a brother who has been
alienated might be brought back into fellowship, yet we never go
out of our way to say a kind word, or outwardly manifest any love
toward him.

Jesus said: "Ask the Lord of the harvest, therefore, to send out
workers into his harvest field." (Matthew 9:38). Yes, it is necessary
to "pray for a good harvest" but note, the petition is for workers! We
have to "keep on hoeing!"

Richard DeHaan

That which is prefaced by prayer should be punctuated by practice!

The Universe Is God's

Read Psalm 104:31–35

[The Lord] touches the mountains, and they smoke. *Psalm 104:32*

Rising more than six miles from its base on the ocean floor and stretching seventy-five miles across, Hawaii's Mauna Loa is the largest volcano on Earth. But on the surface of the planet Mars stands Olympus Mons, the largest volcano yet discovered in our solar system. The altitude of Olympus Mons is three times higher than Mount Everest and 100 times more massive than Mauna Loa. It's large enough to contain the entire chain of the Hawaiian Islands!

Long ago, David looked up at the night skies and stood in awe at the wonder of his Creator's universe. He wrote, "The heavens declare the glory of God; the skies proclaim the work of his hands" (Psalm 19:1).

But the stars and the sky were not all that stirred the wonder of ancient writers. Earthquakes and volcanoes also inspired awe for the Creator. Psalm 104 says, "[God] looks at the earth, and it trembles, who touches the mountains, and they smoke" (v. 32).

As space probes explore more of our solar system, they will continue to discover unknown wonders. But whatever they find is the work of the same Creator (Genesis 1:1).

The wonders of the universe should move us to praise God, just as they moved a shepherd boy long ago as he gazed up at the heavens (Psalm 8:3–5).

Dennis Fisher

All of creation bears God's autograph.

Praise the Lord

Read Psalm 112

Praise the LORD. I will extol the LORD with all my heart in
the council of the upright and in the assembly. *Psalm 111:1*

I had a friend who answered his phone by saying, "Praise the Lord!"
instead of "Hello."

Of course, it's easy to say, "Praise the Lord" when things are running smoothly and you're in good health, have a nice job, and enjoy
a lovely family. But how about it when you are suffering pain?

Well, my friend had to have serious surgery, and I am told that
the last thing he said as the anesthesiologist placed the mask over his
face was, "Praise the Lord!" When he came to, his mumbling words
were also, "Praise the Lord." Clearly, he had a wonderful habit!

David says in Psalm 147: "How good it is to sing praises to our
God!" (v. 1). We should feel perfectly at home and at ease in praising
God.

A nineteenth-century British preacher named Billy Bray was redeemed out of a terrible life of drunkenness and sin. After his conversion he experienced much trouble, but he never stopped praising
the Lord. At one time, he came to the place where all he had to
eat was a mess of small potatoes that a friend had given him. Bray
had bowed his head to offer thanks when he felt that the devil was
saying to him, "How can you thank God for such small potatoes?"
Billy replied, "Go away, Devil—when I was serving you, I didn't
even have small potatoes. I had no potatoes at all!" Yes, praise the
Lord even for small potatoes!

M. R. DeHaan

The praise life is so important because it wears out the self life!

Postures of the Heart

Read 2 Chronicles 6:7–9, 12–15

[Solomon] knelt down before the whole assembly of Israel and spread out his hands toward heaven. *2 Chronicles 6:13*

When my husband plays the harmonica for our church praise team, I have noticed that he sometimes closes his eyes when he plays a song. He says this helps him focus and block out distractions so he can play his best—just his harmonica, the music, and him—all praising God.

Some people wonder if our eyes must be closed when we pray. Since we can pray at any time in any place, however, it might prove difficult to always close our eyes—especially if we are taking a walk, pulling weeds, or driving a vehicle!

There are also no rules on what position our body must be in when we talk to God. When King Solomon prayed to dedicate the temple he had built, he knelt down and "spread out his hands toward heaven" (2 Chronicles 6:13–14). Kneeling (Ephesians 3:14), standing (Luke 18:10–13), and even lying face down (Matthew 26:39) are all mentioned in the Bible as positions for prayer.

Whether we kneel or stand before God, whether we lift our hands heavenward or close our eyes so we can better focus on God—it is not the posture of our body but of our heart that is important. Everything we do "flows from [our heart]" (Proverbs 4:23). When we pray, may our hearts always be bowed in adoration, gratitude, and humility to our loving God, for we know that His eyes are "open and [His] ears attentive to the prayers" of His people (2 Chronicles 6:40).

Cindy Hess Kasper

The highest form of prayer
comes from the depths of a humble heart.

Celebration of Praise

Read Exodus 15:1–18

Who among the gods is like you, LORD? *Exodus 15:11*

You've probably never been to a worship service quite like the one the Israelites held after they reached the safe side of the Red Sea.

The people had just seen God save them from certain, watery death. They had come within an eyelash of being pushed into the sea by the charging forces of Pharaoh's army. Relentlessly, the charioted soldiers had chased them down (Exodus 14:5–9). In panic, the children of Israel had cried out for help (v. 10).

The Lord parted the sea, allowing the people to cross (vv. 16, 21–22). But when the Egyptians rode onto the seabed, God caused the waters to cascade down on them (v. 28).

That's when the celebration began! Joyously, the people praised God for His strength and salvation (Exodus 15:2), His power (v. 6), His greatness (v. 7), His holiness (v. 11), His love, redemption, and guidance (v. 13), and His eternal reign over them (v. 18). They poured out their hearts in worship to the God of their salvation.

Look over the attributes for which the Israelites praised God. Review how His character has touched your life. Find ways to honor Him in worship. The God who parted the sea is the God who makes a way for you. Give Him your celebration of praise!

Dave Branon

God's great power deserves our grateful praise.

Effective Prayer

Read Matthew 7:7–11

Everyone who asks receives; the one who seeks finds. *Matthew 7:8*

A twelve-year-old Cambodian boy named Lem Cheong began to question his family's religious beliefs. He had been taught that a person seeking guidance should go to a temple and shake a container of numbered bamboo slivers until one fell out. The priest then interpreted the meaning of the number. But this practice didn't satisfy Cheong's longing for clear answers, nor did it fill the void in his heart that only God could fill.

According to Harold Sala in his book *Touching God*, Cheong asked his uncle, a priest, if he had ever had a prayer answered. The man was shocked by the brashness of his nephew's question, but he admitted that he couldn't remember a single time one of his prayers had been answered.

Later Cheong asked a Christian if God had ever answered his prayers. The man recounted several instances. Cheong was so impressed that he accepted Jesus as his Savior that day. Since then, prayer has become a vital part of his life.

Jesus said, "Ask and it will be given to you; seek and you will find; knock and the door will be opened to you" (Matthew 7:7). Christian prayer is effective because God is the living and true God who hears and answers according to His will. And His will is always good.

Vernon Grounds

Through prayer, finite man draws upon
the power of the infinite God.

The Unfinished Work of Christ

Read Hebrews 7:11–28

He is able to save completely those who come to God through him,
because he always lives to intercede for them. *Hebrews 7:25*

Even as Jesus prayed for Peter in a time when he was experiencing severe temptation (Luke 22:32), so our Lord now constantly intercedes on our behalf. This work of the Savior will never be completed as long as we need help, comfort, and blessing. Scottish minister Robert M'Cheyne (1813–1843) remarked, "If I could hear Christ praying for me in the next room, I would not fear a million enemies. Yet the distance makes no difference; He is praying for me!"

When facing a personal crisis, I realized the truth of these words in Hebrews 7 in a wonderful new way. I asked the Lord to pray and intercede in my behalf, for Satan seemed to be seeking to "sift" me in his sieve (Luke 22:31). I recognized the impotence of my own weak prayers and the need of special grace. The next day a problem of several months was solved by the Lord's intervention. Never before had I so fully appreciated the high-priestly work of our risen Savior.

If there is a great problem in your life and your prayers seem of no avail, tell Jesus about it and ask Him to pray for you! He will take your request and present it to the Father—perfumed with the everlasting incense of His own merits. Because of His wonderful intercessory work on your behalf, you too may experience the remarkable results that only His all-powerful prayers can obtain.

Henry Bosch

It is the power of Christ's prayer that defeats Satan!

The Way to Praise Him

Read Luke 19:28–38

Blessed is the king who comes in the name of the LORD! *Luke 19:38*

The triumphal entry of Jesus into Jerusalem a few days before His death focused attention on Christ as Lord. When Jesus sent His disciples to get the colt He was to ride, He instructed them to tell its owners, "The Lord needs it" (Luke 19:31). And when the crowds shouted their praise, they quoted Psalm 118:26, saying, "Blessed is the king who comes in the name of the Lord!" (Luke 19:38).

Jesus is Lord. His is "the name that is above every name" (Philippians 2:9). The word *Lord* refers to His sovereignty. He is the King, and every believer in Him is a member of His kingdom.

We make Jesus the Lord of our lives by bowing to His authority as King. This means we live in obedience to Him. We shouldn't be like the man who claimed to be a Christian but who chose to live in sin. When his minister confronted him, he glibly replied, "Don't worry, pastor. It's okay. I'm just a bad Christian."

It's not okay. Not at all! Not for a member of Christ's kingdom (Luke 6:43–49).

Let's make sure we are honoring Jesus with our deeds as well as with our words. Then we can join with others in proclaiming, "Jesus is Lord!"

David Egner

To follow Christ is to take Him as our Savior and our Lord.

The Power of Praise

Read Isaiah 61:1–3

The LORD has anointed me . . . to bestow . . .
a garment of praise instead of a spirit of despair. *Isaiah 61:1, 3*

Praise is powerful! No matter what difficulties we face, singing praises to our God can dispel our despondency and bring us encouragement. That's why all Christians should have a song of praise in their hearts.

Troubled at times with a coldness of heart toward the things of the Lord, Scottish pastor Robert M'Cheyne would sing the praises of God until he felt revived in his spirit. One day, while he was trying to prepare his heart for preaching, he wrote in his journal: "Is it the desire of my heart to be made altogether holy? . . . Lord, You know all things . . . Felt much deadness and much grief that I cannot grieve for this deadness. Toward evening revived. Got a calm spirit through psalmody [singing psalms] and prayer." M'Cheyne had been uplifted by praising God. Those in his household were often able to tell what hour he awoke because he began the day with a psalm of praise.

Perhaps you feel as if you are mired in despair. Lift a song of praise to the Lord! The psalmist said, "I will sing of the LORD's great love forever" (89:1). When we do that, the praise will flow not only from our lips but also from the heart. The Lord delights to give "the oil of joy instead of mourning, and a garment of praise instead of a spirit of despair" (Isaiah 61:3).

Yes, "how good it is to sing praises to our God"—at all times (Psalm 147:1).

Paul Van Gorder

If you find yourself wearing a spirit of heaviness,
put on a garment of praise.

Thank God for Music

Read 2 Chronicles 5:7–14

The trumpeters and musicians joined in unison, . . . to give
praise and thanks to the LORD. . . . The glory of the LORD
filled the temple of God. *2 Chronicles 5:13–14*

Music plays a big part in the Bible. From Genesis to Revelation,
God enlists musicians to work on His behalf. He uses music to call
people to worship and to send them to war, to soothe ragged emotions and to ignite spiritual passion, to celebrate victories and to
mourn losses. Music is an all-occasion, all-inclusive art form. There
are followers and leaders, simple songs and complex songs, easy instruments and difficult instruments, melodies and harmonies, fast
rhythms and slow rhythms, high notes and low notes.

Music is a wonderful metaphor for the church, because everyone
participates by doing what he or she does best. We all sing or play
different notes at different times, but we all perform the same song.
The better we know our parts, and the better we follow the conductor, the more beautiful the music.

One of the best uses for music is praise. When Solomon's temple
was completed, the musicians praised and thanked God. As they
did, "the glory of the LORD filled the temple of God" (2 Chronicles
5:14).

We thank God for beautiful music, for it's like a preview of
heaven, where the glory of God will dwell forever and where praise
for Him will never cease.

Julie Ackerman Link

Those who praise God on earth will feel at home in heaven.

Breathtaking Glory

Read 1 Chronicles 29:10–13

Yours, LORD, is the greatness and the power and the glory
and the majesty and the splendor. *1 Chronicles 29:11*

One of the pleasures of a trip to Europe is visiting the grand cathedrals that dot the landscape. They are breathtakingly beautiful as they soar toward the heavens. The architecture, art, and symbolism found in these amazing buildings present a spellbinding experience of wonder and magnificence.

As I thought about the fact that these structures were built to reflect God's magnificence and His all-surpassing splendor, I wondered how we could possibly recapture in our hearts and minds a similar feeling of God's grandeur and be reminded again of His greatness.

One way we can do that is to look beyond man's grand, regal structures and contemplate the greatness of what God himself has created. Take one look at a starry night sky and think of God's power as He spoke the universe into existence. Hold a newborn baby in your arms and thank God for the miracle of life itself. Look at the snow-covered mountains of Alaska or the majestic Atlantic Ocean teeming with millions of God-designed creatures and imagine the power that makes that ecosystem work.

Mankind is not wrong to reach for the sky with structures that are intended to point us to God. But our truest admiration should be reserved for God himself as we say to Him, "Yours, Lord, is the greatness and the power and the glory and the majesty and the splendor" (1 Chronicles 29:11).

Dave Branon

God alone is worthy of our worship.

A Pattern for Prayer

Read Daniel 2:1–18

Daniel returned to his house and explained the matter to his friends. . . . He urged them to plead for mercy from God. *Daniel 2:17–18*

Daniel had many wonderful traits. Evidently, he was handsome, intelligent, and possessed outstanding abilities. Furthermore, he had deep convictions and great courage, and dared to stand for the right—even though it would bring disfavor from the king.

One of his finest characteristics was that he was a man of prayer! In Daniel 2, we find him calling his friends to pray in time of an extreme emergency. In chapter 6 we see him kneeling three times a day according to his custom, and in chapter 9 we hear him utter one of the most outstanding petitions of confession in the entire Word of God.

Note three facts concerning Daniel's prayerlife from chapter 2. In verse 16 he is found doing everything possible to answer his own requests! Aware of the crisis he and his friends are facing, he goes without delay to the king himself, asking for more time. In verses 17 and 18, he tells his companions, Shadrach, Meshach, and Abednego, to begin praying with him that the God of heaven would reveal the king's dream. Then in verse 19, after Daniel's request has been granted, he gives thanks and praise to the Lord for His gracious answers! We can pray like Daniel: First, we do all we can to answer our own petitions. Next, we call for the prayers of others. Finally, we give thanks. Always.

Be a modern-day Daniel: a praying, working, thanking Christian!

Richard DeHaan

Prayer with obedience is power;
prayer without obedience is presumption!

Our Prayers, God's Timing

Read Luke 1:5–17

Now to him who is able to do immeasurably
more than all we ask or imagine, according to his power
that is at work within us.... *Ephesians 3:20*

Sometimes God takes His time in answering our prayers, and that isn't always easy for us to understand.

That was the situation for Zechariah, a priest whom the angel Gabriel appeared to one day near an altar in the temple in Jerusalem. Gabriel told him, "Do not be afraid, Zechariah; your prayer has been heard. Your wife Elizabeth will bear you a son, and you are to call him John" (Luke 1:13).

Zechariah had probably asked God for a child *years* before. Elizabeth was now well beyond childbearing age. And *now* God was going to answer this prayer?

God's memory is perfect. He is able to remember our prayers not only for years but also for generations beyond our lifetime. He never forgets them and may move in response long after we first brought our requests to Him. Sometimes His answer is "no," other times it is "wait"—but His response is always measured with love. God's ways are beyond us, but we can trust that they are good.

Zechariah learned this. He asked for a son, but God gave him even more. His son John would grow up to be the very prophet who would announce the arrival of the Messiah.

Zechariah's experience demonstrates a vital truth that should also encourage us as we pray: God's timing is rarely our own, but it is always worth waiting for.

James Banks

When we cannot see God's hand at work,
we can still trust His heart.

A Dangerous Challenge

Read 2 Chronicles 20:1, 15–22

The battle is not yours, but God's. *2 Chronicles 20:15*

While millions watched on television, Nik Wallenda walked across Niagara Falls on a 1,800-foot wire that was only two inches in diameter. He took all the precautions he could. But adding to the drama and danger of both the height and the rushing water below, a thick mist obscured Nik's sight, wind threatened his balance, and spray from the falls challenged his footing. Amid—and perhaps because of—these perils, he said that he "prayed a lot" and praised God.

The Israelites also praised God in the middle of a dangerous challenge. Theirs involved a large group of warriors who had gathered to fight them (2 Chronicles 20:2). After humbly asking God for help, King Jehoshaphat appointed a choir to march out into battle in front of the Israelite army. The worshipers sang: "Give thanks to the Lord, for his love endures forever" (v. 21). When they began to sing, the Lord caused the enemy forces to attack and destroy each other.

Praising God in the midst of a challenge may mean overriding our natural instincts. We tend toward self-protection, strategizing, and worry. However, worshiping can guard our hearts against troubling thoughts and self-reliance. It reminds us of the lesson the Israelites learned: "The battle is not [ours], but God's" (v. 15).

Jennifer Benson Schuldt

No matter what is in front of us, God is always behind us.

Alone with God

Read Mark 1:32–39

Very early in the morning, while it was still dark,
Jesus got up, left the house and went off
to a solitary place, where he prayed. Mark 1:35

The gospel of Mark portrays the Lord Jesus as Christ the Servant. The inspired record is filled with the mighty deeds and activities of the One who said, "For even the Son of Man did not come to be served, but to serve" (Mark 10:45). Yet amid the intense activity of His daily service, Jesus set aside times for quietness and prayer—like the occasion mentioned in Mark 1:35. What an example this is to us, His followers!

William Wilberforce, Christian statesman of Great Britain in the late eighteenth and early nineteenth centuries, once said, "I must secure more time for private devotions. I have been living far too public for me. The shortening of private devotions starves the soul. It grows lean and faint." Following a failure in Parliament, he remarked that his problems may have been due to the fact that he spent less and less time in his private devotions in which he could earnestly seek the will of God. He concluded, "God allowed me to stumble."

If the Lord Jesus took time from His crowded days and busy nights to be alone with the Father in prayer, how much greater is our need!

Getting alone with God is the best way to prepare for the day ahead.

Paul Van Gorder

To walk with God, we must make it a practice to talk with God.

Prelude to Praise

Read Psalm 150

I will ever sing in praise of your name
and fulfill my vows day after day. *Psalm 61:8*

We enter a concert hall, find our seats, and listen with anticipation as the members of the orchestra tune their instruments. The sound is discordant, not melodic. But the tuning is simply a prelude to the symphony.

C. S. Lewis suggested that's how it is with our devotional practices and even our worship services. Sometimes they sound discordant, but God hears our prayers and praises with fatherly delight. We are really preparing for participation in the glorious symphony of heaven. Now we are making a minuscule contribution to the harmonies of angelic and redeemed hosts. But our adoration, though feeble, pleases the heart of the Divine Listener more than the finest rendition of earth's greatest orchestra.

Are we eagerly awaiting our participation in heaven's symphony of praise? Are we joyfully participating in the adoration that delights the heart of God? Or do we regard devotion as more of a discipline than a delight?

Our attitudes will be transformed when we realize that praise delights God's heart. Praise helps us to tune our lives to heavenly harmonies.

Praise is an indispensable preparation for the worship that will be our eternal joy. "Let everything that has breath praise the LORD" (Psalm 150:6).

Vernon Grounds

The heart filled with praise brings pleasure to God.

Keep On
Read Psalm 66:1–10

All the earth bows down to you; they sing praise to you. *Psalm 66:4*

"Keep on travelin'. Keep on . . ." sang the teenagers from an American high school while visiting a country church in Jamaica. They sang the first five words of their Sunday evening concert when everything went dark. All power was gone.

Well, not all power. Not true power.

The students kept singing. Flashlights were found to shine on the chorale as they sang their entire repertoire without accompaniment.

Midway through the concert, the director, my daughter Lisa, asked the congregation to sing along. It was goosebump time as God's name was lifted high in that darkened church. "Hallelujah" never seemed so heavenly.

Before the concert, everyone had worked hard to make sure all the electrical equipment was working. But the best thing that happened was for that power to go out. As a result, God's power was highlighted. God's light, not electric light, shone through. Jesus was praised.

Sometimes our plans break down and our efforts fall short. When things happen that we can't control, we must "keep on travelin'" and remember where the real power for godly living and true praise comes from. When our efforts falter, we need to keep praising and lifting up Jesus. It's all about Him anyway.

Dave Branon

God's great power deserves our grateful praise

Only By Prayer

Read Mark 9:14–29

Everything is possible for one who believes. Mark 9:23

My friend called me late one night during her cancer treatment. Grieved by her uncontrollable sobs, I soon added my own tears and a silent prayer. *What am I supposed to do, Lord?*

Her wails squeezed my heart. I couldn't stop her pain, fix her situation, or find one intelligible word of encouragement. But I knew who could help. As I wept with my friend, stumbling through a prayer, I whispered repeatedly, "Jesus. Jesus. Jesus."

Her cries quieted to sniffs and whimpers, until her breathing slowed. Her husband's voice startled me. "She's asleep," he said. "We'll call tomorrow."

I hung up, weeping prayers into my pillow.

The gospel of Mark shares a story of another person who wanted to help his loved one. A desperate father brought his suffering son to Jesus (Mark 9:17). Doubt clung to his plea, as he reiterated the impossibility of their circumstances (vv. 20–22) and acknowledged his need for Jesus to empower his belief (v. 24). The father and son experienced freedom, hope, and peace when Jesus stepped in and took control (vv. 25–27).

When loved ones are hurting, it's natural to want to do the right things and say the perfect words. But Christ is the only One who can truly help us. When we call on the name of Jesus, He can enable us to believe and rely on the power of His presence.

Xochitl Dixon

The name of Jesus is the powerful prayer
that leads us into His mighty presence.

Of Birds and Stars

Read Job 12:1–9

"Ask the animals, and they will teach you." *Job 12:7*

Nature teaches us much about God.

For one thing, it shows His kindness in providing animals and birds with inborn impulses and patterns that aid them greatly in adjusting to what is often a hostile environment.

For instance, some birds would perish if they had to stay all year in areas that have huge temperature changes. Therefore, the Lord has graciously given them migrating instincts. It's been discovered that the small indigo bunting (a member of the finch family) steers his way 2,000 miles south every year just by looking at the northern sky! This night-flying bird does not seem to rely on any one star or constellation, says zoology expert Stephen T. Emlen. Rather, the bird recognizes the whole geometrical pattern of the stars within thirty-five degrees of the North Star. It can be confused only when that part of the sky is entirely blocked off by clouds. The bunting then wisely discontinues his flight until it can once again get a clear view. The prophet Jeremiah says the Lord gave these "ordinances of . . . the stars for a light by night" (Jeremiah 31:35 NKJV). Apparently, they not only aid man in navigation but also assist our feathered friends.

As we observe nature, so crammed with beauty, wonder, and design, we should be taught by the beasts and the "fowls of the air" (Job 12:7 KJV) that there is a gracious heavenly Father who provides for His creatures in wisdom. This in turn should call forth our adoration and praise!

Henry Bosch

God's signature of wisdom and power
is clearly impressed on the world of nature!

Gracias!

Read 1 Chronicles 16:7–10, 23–36

Give praise to the LORD. *1 Chronicles 16:8*

When I visited Mexico, I wished I knew how to speak Spanish. I could say "gracias" (thank you), "muy bien" (very good), and "hola" (hello). But that was about it. I grew tired of just saying "gracias" to everyone who talked with me or did something for me.

But we should never grow tired of giving words of thanks to God. David knew the importance of saying thanks. After he became king over Israel and had a tent constructed to house the ark of the covenant (where God's presence dwelt), he appointed some of the Levites "to extol, thank, and praise the LORD" (1 Chronicles 16:4). Many people remained there to offer sacrifices and give thanks to God daily (vv. 37–38).

David also committed to Asaph and his associates a song of thanks (1 Chronicles 16:8–36). His psalm gave thanks for what the Lord had done: "His deeds among the peoples" (v. 8 NKJV), "His wonderful acts" (v. 9), "the wonders he has done, his miracles and the judgments he pronounced" (v. 12), and His "salvation" (v. 35 NKJV). David's song also gave praise for who the Lord was: good, loving, and holy (vv. 34–35).

Like David, we should never grow tired of saying "gracias" to God for who He is and for all He's done for us. Take time today to offer your sacrifice of praise to Him.

Anne Cetas

The heart filled with praise brings pleasure to God.

Not Shut Out

Read 1 Thessalonians 5:12–28

Brothers and sisters, pray for us. *1 Thessalonians 5:25*

One of the greatest ministries a Christian can have is that of praying for the needs of others. That's why a person who is forced to rest after an accident or illness never needs to feel useless or uninvolved in the Lord's work. A unique opportunity of Christian service becomes open to him or her—to uphold family, friends, church, pastor, and missionaries in prayer.

In his book *Keep on Keeping On*, Harold L. Fickett Jr. told about his call on a woman who had suffered a severe heart attack. Confined to her home, she was very discouraged. She complained to Pastor Fickett about her uselessness. Oh, how she wanted to do some meaningful work for the Lord! Fickett told her kindly that in her new situation she could minister with power. "You have time on your hands," he said. "You have no place to go. You can use your time in praying for God's servants all over the world. Begin by remembering me as your pastor before the throne of God, and then pray for all of the Christian workers you know." The woman followed her pastor's advice, and she found joy and a new sense of purpose in life.

Prayer for others, especially God's servants, is a much-needed ministry, and it's something every Christian can do. There's no reason any believer has to feel shut out from the Lord's work.

Richard DeHaan

The best way to influence people for God
is to intercede with God for people.

Pray about It

Read Luke 18:1–8

In return for my friendship they accuse me,
but I am a man of prayer. *Psalm 109:4*

In a bygone era, a newsboy was complaining of his discouragements and problems, and an older Christian friend was trying to tell him how to take them to Jesus. The little fellow couldn't easily comprehend the mystery of prayer.

Finally, putting his finger on the boy's forehead, the gentleman said, "What do you do in there?" "I think," said the little fellow. "Well now," said the other, "God can look down and see your thoughts. Suppose, therefore, that you just think a little prayer every time you are in difficulty; God will look down and read it, and it will become a telegram to heaven."

The next time the gentleman met his young friend, the boy looked bright and happy. He explained, "It's all right since I began sending those sky telegrams. Jesus answers my prayers and is blessing me so much. I am now selling twice as many newspapers as I used to."

Nothing is too small to bring to our blessed Lord and King. We may tell Him everything—pray about it! Are you alone and need a friend? God can send you just the right one; pray about it! Are your difficulties severe? Are you full of doubt and fear? Trust Him here and now, and pray about it! With thanksgiving make your request. Whatever concerns you, pray about it.

Henry Bosch

The best therapy for despair is prayer.

"I Will Praise the Lord"

Read Psalm 146

I will praise the LORD all my life; I will sing praise
to my God as long as I live. *Psalm 146:2*

Missionary Allen Gardiner experienced many physical difficulties throughout his service to the Savior. Despite his troubles, he said, "While God gives me strength, failure will not daunt me." In 1851, at age fifty-seven, he died of disease and starvation while serving on Picton Island at the southern tip of South America. When his body was found, his diary lay nearby. It bore the record of hunger, thirst, wounds, and loneliness. The last entry in his little book showed the struggle of his shaking hand as he tried to write legibly. It read, "I am overwhelmed with a sense of the goodness of God." Think of that! No word of complaint, no whining, no grumbling at the circumstances—just praise for God's goodness.

The seventeenth-century Scottish theologian Samuel Rutherford wrote, "Some of the people of God slander God's grace in their souls, as some wretches used to do, who complain and murmur for want. 'I have nothing,' say they, 'all is gone, the ground yields but weeds'; when their fat harvest and their money makes them liars . . . I advise you to speak good of Christ for His beauty and sweetness, and speak good of Him for His grace."

If we were to add up the blessings God has sent and the benefits of His presence with us, the assets would overwhelm us. No matter what our circumstances, we could say with the psalmist, "I will praise the Lord."

Paul Van Gorder

If you can think of nothing for which to give thanks,
think of what God has given you in Christ.

Behind the Scenes

Read Daniel 10:1–14

Your words were heard, and I have come
in response to them. *Daniel 10:12*

My daughter sent a text message to a friend in hopes of having a question answered quickly. Her phone indicated that the recipient had read the message, so she waited anxiously for a reply. Mere moments passed, yet she grew frustrated, groaning her annoyance at the delay. Irritation eroded into worry; she wondered whether the lack of response meant there was a problem between them. Eventually a reply came, and my daughter was relieved to see their relationship was fine. Her friend had simply been sorting out the details needed to answer the question.

The Old Testament prophet Daniel also anxiously awaited a reply. After receiving a frightening vision of great war, Daniel fasted and sought God through humble prayer (10:3, 12). For three weeks, he received no reply (vv. 2, 13). Finally, an angel arrived and assured Daniel his prayers had been heard "since the first day" (v. 12). In the meantime, the angel had been battling on behalf of those prayers. Though Daniel didn't know it at first, God was at work during each of the twenty-one days that elapsed between his first prayer and the angel's coming.

Our confidence that God hears our prayers (Psalm 40:1) can cause us to become anxious when His reply doesn't come when we want it to. We are prone to wonder whether He cares. Yet Daniel's experience reminds us that God is at work on behalf of those He loves even when it isn't obvious to us.

Kirsten Holmberg

God is always at work on behalf of His people.

The Right Way to Pray

Read Matthew 6:5–15

*When you pray, go into your room, close the door
and pray to your Father, who is unseen.* Matthew 6:6

I admire people who record prayer requests in journals tattered from daily handling, those who keep track of every prayer and praise and then faithfully update their lists. I'm inspired by those who gather with others to pray and whose kneeling wears out the carpet at their bedsides. For years, I tried to copy their styles, to emulate a perfect prayer life, and to imitate the eloquence of the so-much-more-articulate-than-me folks. As I longed to learn the right way to pray, I strived to unravel what I thought was a mystery.

Eventually, I learned that our Lord simply desires prayer that begins and ends with humility (Matthew 6:5). He invites us into an intimate exchange through which He promises to listen (v. 6). He never requires fancy or memorized words or phrases (v. 7). He assures us that prayer is a gift, an opportunity to honor His majesty (vv. 9–10), to display our confidence in His provision (v. 11), and to affirm our security in His forgiveness and guidance (vv. 12–13).

God assures us that He hears and cares about every single spoken and unspoken prayer, as well as the prayers that slip down our cheeks as silent tears. As we place our trust in God and His perfect love for us, we can be sure praying with a humble heart that's surrendered to and dependent on Him is always the right way to pray.

Xochitl Dixon

Calling on Jesus as our loving Savior and Lord
is the right way to pray.

The Life of Praise

Read Revelation 19:1–7

Sing joyfully to the LORD, you righteous. *Psalm 33:1*

From the book of Revelation we learn that heaven is a place characterized by praise. We read of people around the throne of God falling down before it and joyously bursting into song. The grand climax, however, is described in Revelation 19, where, in glad anticipation of the reign of Jesus Christ as King of Kings, the cry is raised, "Salvation and glory and power belong to our God; . . . For our Lord God Almighty reigns" (vv. 1, 6).

Yes, heaven will be filled with praise. God, however, doesn't want us to wait until we get there to render our worship and adoration. He wants our devotion now. With the psalmist we should say every morning, "My tongue will proclaim your righteousness, your praises all day long" (Psalm 35:28).

The words praise and praises can be found more than 350 times in the Bible. In the Psalms alone the expression is used on 182 occasions. One example is Psalm 107 where we read, "Let them give thanks to the Lord for his unfailing love and his wonderful deeds for mankind" (v. 31).

In the light of who God is and what He does, our lives should be filled with joyous adoration—both now and forever! Has His praise been on your lips today?

Richard DeHaan

Hem your blessings with praise lest they unravel!

Our Prayer; God's Will

Read 2 Corinthians 12:7–10

Three times I pleaded with the LORD
to take it away from me. *2 Corinthians 12:8*

The handwritten prayer request was heartbreaking in its seeming impossibility: "Please pray—I have multiple sclerosis, weak muscles, trouble swallowing, increased pain, diminishing sight." The woman's body was breaking down, and I could sense despair in her plea for intercession.

But then came the hope—the strength that trumps the physical damage and degradation: "I know our blessed Savior is in full control. His will is of utmost importance to me."

This person may have needed my prayers, but I needed something she had: unabated confidence in God. She seemed to present a perfect portrait of the truth God taught Paul when he asked for relief from his difficulty—what he called his "thorn in my flesh" (2 Corinthians 12:7). His quest for relief turned out to be not just a seeming impossibility; his request was turned down flat by his heavenly Father. Paul's continual struggle, which was clearly God's will, was a valuable lesson: Through his weakness, God's grace could be displayed and God's strength was "made perfect" (v. 9).

As we pour out our hearts to God, let's be even more concerned with seeking His will than we are with receiving the answer we want. That's where the grace and the strength come from.

Dave Branon

We pray not to obtain our will in heaven,
but to effect God's will on earth.

In God's House

Read Psalm 84

My soul yearns, even faints, for the courts of the LORD; my heart and my flesh cry out for the living God. *Psalm 84:2*

Tobias, who recently turned three, loves to go to church. He cries when he isn't able to attend. Each week when he arrives for the children's program of Bible stories, games, singing, and dinner, he runs into the building and enthusiastically announces to the leaders and other children: "Let's get this party started!" The Lord must smile at this child's excitement about being in what he thinks is God's house.

The author of Psalm 84, one of the sons of Korah, also had a love for God's house. Some commentators have speculated that for a time he, a temple singer, was unable to go to the temple—either because of sickness or circumstances. So as he wrote this psalm, his soul was especially longing and crying out to be in "the courts of the Lord" (v.2). He believed that one day of worship in God's house gave more satisfaction than a thousand days spent anywhere else (v. 10).

There's something special about praising God together with His people, and we should take every opportunity we can to do so. But if we can't, like the psalmist, we can still express our love for the living God and our longing to know Him (v. 2). The Lord is pleased and we'll be blessed when our heart's desire is to be with Him and His people.

Anne Cetas

A good indicator of our spiritual temperature
is our eagerness to worship God.

Praying about Little Things

Read Luke 11:5-10

Hear my cry, O God; listen to my prayer. *Psalm 61:1*

Charles H. Spurgeon once remarked, "I remember hearing it said of a godly man: 'Mr. So-and-So is very strange. The other day he prayed about a key he had lost.' The person who told me this was astonished at bothering God about something so trivial. . . . 'What! Bother the Lord about a lost key?' 'That's right,' I replied. 'Tell me, how big must a care be before you talk to Him about it? If a certain size is required, we should be told in the Bible so that we may learn the mathematics of prayer. Small matters often cause us great concern and sometimes are harder to deal with than bigger things. If we couldn't voice them to God, it would bring great loss of comfort to us all.'"

Small requests sometimes receive dramatic answers. In an earlier era, a preacher prayed for $10 to buy a license for his car. He had to speak at a penitentiary and needed transportation. So he told the Lord that if He wanted him to preach there, He would have to supply the money. As he got up from his knees, his wife came into the room with an envelope in her hand. "Someone just shoved this through the letter slot," she said. In it was $10.

The Lord knows our needs, and He bends His loving ear to every request that's in keeping with His will. He answers prayer—even for the little things!

Henry Bosch

Anything that's big enough to worry about
is big enough to pray about.

That's the Spirit

Read Psalm 148

Whatever you do, work at it with all your heart, as working
for the Lord, not for human masters. *Colossians 3:23*

For more than three decades in the mid to late 1900s, Bob Ufer was
the enthusiastic radio voice of University of Michigan football. Until
shortly before he died in 1981, he delighted listeners with his emotional play-by-play coverage of the Wolverines. Anyone who heard
him knew at once whose side he was on. His audience would often
hear him exclaim something like this: "History will record that on
a bee—yoo—tiful overcast Saturday afternoon here in little Ann
Arbor town more than 100,000 fans came out to see MEESH—
EE—GUN battle Ohio State!" The loyal following Bob Ufer built
up through the years indicates how appealing a person can be if he
gives himself wholeheartedly to a cause he loves.

His fervor reminds us how natural it is to respond with intensity
to something close to our hearts. That's especially true in our relationship to God. The Scriptures give many examples of men who
served the Lord with great enthusiasm. To celebrate the return of
the ark of the covenant, David went shouting and jumping through
the streets of Jerusalem. Centuries later, Jesus burned with godly
zeal as He chased the money-changers from the temple. And when
the early church needed dependable workers, men like Stephen
came to the fore because they were full of the Spirit.

Do people quickly recognize by our enthusiasm that we love and
serve God and are filled with His Spirit? Do our lives give evidence
of wholehearted praise?

Mart DeHaan

Nothing great was ever achieved without enthusiasm. —Emerson

Persevering Prayer

Read Genesis 32:24–29

Then the man said, "Let me go, for it is daybreak." But Jacob replied, "I will not let you go unless you bless me." *Genesis 32:26*

One day George Mullen began praying for five of his friends. After many months, one of them came to the Lord. Ten years later, two others were converted. It took twenty-five years before the fourth man was saved. Mullen persevered in prayer until his death for the fifth friend, and throughout those fifty-two years he never gave up hoping that he would accept Christ! His faith was rewarded, for soon after Mullen's funeral the last one was saved.

In Genesis 32, we read that the angel of the Lord wrestled with Jacob. Two important lessons about persevering prayer can be learned from this experience. First, the patriarch was alone when God appeared to him. Likewise, our most effective intercession is usually made in a quiet place where we are undistracted by the world. Second, although Jacob recognized his own weakness, he continued to cling to God, for he had a compelling desire to receive a blessing. The Lord rewarded his night long quest and blessed him. So too, when we come to the end of our own resources and rely entirely on God, we begin to experience power with God and with men.

We too must remain steadfast as we offer our petitions to the Lord (see Colossians 4:2).

Keep praying. God honors persevering prayer!

Henry Bosch

Delay is not denial—PRAY ON!

The Warbler's Witness

Read Romans 1:18–25

Many, LORD my God, are the wonders you have done. *Psalm 40:5*

A tiny bird, the lesser whitethroat warbler, summers in Germany and winters in Africa. As the days grow short, the adult birds head south, leaving their little ones behind. Several weeks later, the young fly across thousands of miles of unfamiliar land and sea to join their parents. How do they find a place totally unknown to them? Experiments have shown that they have an instinctive knowledge of longitude, latitude, and an ability to tell direction by the stars. God has given them a calendar, a clock, and all the navigational data they need to fly those thousands of uncharted miles to their parents' side.

The evolutionist says that our amazing and complex world developed by chance. But is this easier to accept than to believe that God created this amazing warbler, and thousands of other such creatures? To me, ascribing this to chance is absurd.

God's wisdom is plainly observable in the works of His creation. His handiwork in nature speaks so strongly for His existence and power that Paul used it as an argument to establish man's guilt and condemnation. Paul wrote that man is without excuse if he does not respond in faith to the God who made it all (Romans 1:20).

Our Creator-God deserves our recognition and our praise!

David Egner

He is spiritually deaf who cannot hear the voice of God in nature.

Being Real with God

Read 1 Peter 5:6–10

Cast all your anxiety on him because he cares for you. *1 Peter 5:7*

I bow my head, close my eyes, lace my fingers together and begin to pray. "Dear Lord, I'm coming to you today as your child. I recognize your power and goodness. . . ."

Suddenly, my eyes snap open. I remember that my son hasn't finished his history project, which is due the next day. I recall that he has an after-school basketball game, and I imagine him awake until midnight finishing his schoolwork. This leads me to worry that his fatigue will put him at risk for the flu!

C. S. Lewis wrote about distractions during prayer in his book *The Screwtape Letters.* He noted that when our minds wander, we tend to use willpower to steer ourselves back to our original prayer. Lewis concluded, though, that it was better to accept "the distraction as [our] present problem and [lay] that before [God] and make it the main theme of [our] prayers."

A persistent worry or even a sinful thought that disrupts a prayer may become the centerpiece of our discussion with God. God wants us to be real as we talk with Him and open up about our deepest concerns, fears, and struggles. He is not surprised by anything we mention. His interest in us is like the attention we would receive from a close friend. That's why we're encouraged to give all of our worries and cares to God—because He cares for us (1 Peter 5:7).

Jennifer Benson Schuldt

Distractions don't have to derail our prayers.

The Prayers of a Little Girl

Read Matthew 5:43–48

"I tell you, love your enemies
and pray for those who persecute you." *Matthew 5:44*

In *Christianity Today*, psychiatrist Robert Cole told an amazing story of a girl who had learned to pray for those who were hostile to her. Cole was in New Orleans in 1960 when a federal judge ruled that the city schools must be integrated. A six-year-old girl, Ruby Bridges, was the only black child to attend the William T. Franz School. Every day for weeks as she entered and left the building, a mob would be standing outside to scream at her and threaten her. They shook their fists, shouted obscenities, and threatened to kill her. One day her teacher saw her lips moving as she walked through the crowd, flanked by burly federal marshals. When the teacher told Cole about it, he asked Ruby if she was talking to the people. "I wasn't talking to them," she replied. "I was just saying a prayer for them." Cole asked her, "Why do you do that?" "Because they need praying for," came her reply.

Cole later said that if he had been in that situation he would have found it difficult to pray for those people. And I must admit I would too. But this little first-grader gave us a stirring example of the fact that it is possible to pray for our enemies. Like Ruby Bridges, we can learn to pray for those who persecute us.

David Egner

Nothing makes us love our enemies so much as praying for them.

Reasons for Praise

Read Psalm 92:1–5; 100

Praise the LORD. Give thanks to the LORD,
for he is good; his love endures forever. *Psalm 106:1*

Years ago a believer with a spirit of gratitude regularly attended the services of a rescue mission in Chicago. One day he had a bandage on his thumb and explained that he had smashed it with a hammer. Then he added, "But praise the Lord! I have my thumb yet!" On another occasion he purchased a steak with his meager earnings and was on his way home with it when a shoelace became untied. As he laid the package on the sidewalk to tie his shoe, a large dog grabbed the choice meat and made off with it. Later, as this humble believer recounted his exasperating experience, he said with characteristic cheerfulness, "Praise the Lord. I still have my appetite left!" He always found reasons to be grateful.

People who themselves have never discovered the inner joy he possessed may find it hard to believe these accounts; nevertheless, they are true. No matter how skeptical they may be, however, all Christians must agree that the inspired writer of Psalm 92 was right when he declared, "It is good to praise LORD" (v. 1). An unsaved person does not understand God and is often unaware of reasons for thanksgiving. But the devout believer, assured of His goodness, rejoices in the knowledge that righteousness will triumph and that those who love the Lord will be vindicated.

Let's look for reasons to say with the psalmist, "Give thanks to the LORD, for he is good; his love endures forever" (106:1).

Herb Vander Lugt

Hem your blessings with praise lest they unravel.

When Yes Means No

Read Romans 8:22–28

I call on the LORD in my distress, and he answers me. *Psalm 120:1*

I thanked God for the privilege of serving as my mom's live-in care-giver during her battle against leukemia. When medicines began to hurt more than help, she decided to stop treatment. "I don't want to suffer anymore," she said. "I want to enjoy my last days with family. God knows I'm ready to go home."

I pleaded with our loving heavenly Father—the Great Physician—confident He could work miracles. But to say yes to my mom's prayers, He would have to say no to mine. Sobbing, I surrendered, "Your will be done, Lord."

Soon after, Jesus welcomed my mama into a pain-free eternity.

In this fallen world, we'll experience suffering until Jesus returns (Romans 8:22–25). Our sinful nature, limited vision, and fear of pain can distort our ability to pray. Thankfully, "the Spirit intercedes for God's people in accordance with the will of God" (v. 27). He reminds us that in all things God works for the good of those who love Him (v. 28), even when His yes to someone else means a heartbreaking no for us.

When we accept our small part in His greater purpose, we can echo my mom's watchword: "God is good, and that's all there is to it. Whatever He decides, I'm at peace." With confidence in the Lord's goodness, we can trust Him to answer every prayer according to His will and for His glory.

Xochitl Dixon

God's answers are wiser than our prayers.

Why Worship?

Read Psalm 27

Wait for the LORD; be strong and take heart
and wait for the LORD. *Psalm 27:14*

Why bother going to church? Some would tell us that it's better to sleep late on Sunday, eat a leisurely breakfast, and lounge around talking with the family. And then maybe have lunch with friends or enjoy a picnic and games with the children. "Make it a day that's different and even restful," some would say, "but don't waste time by going to church on Sunday!"

Worship? Who needs worship anyway? We all do! We need worship because we are unique creatures made in the image of God. We are made for God, so we can't fulfill our purpose unless we develop a right relationship with Him. And worship helps us to do that when we focus on the Lord.

As we join with other worshipers in church, our hearts are lifted out of this temporal world into God's eternal world. According to William Temple, in worship the conscience is quickened by the holiness of God, the mind is fed by the truth of God, the imagination is purged by the beauty of God, the heart is opened to the love of God, and the will is devoted to the purpose of God. And thus we are helped onward in our goal of becoming more like God.

Let's decide now that on Sunday we will be in church with a heart prepared to worship.

Vernon Grounds

What you worship determines what you become.

Your Heart

Read Nehemiah 1

I sat down and wept. For some days I mourned and fasted
. . . before the God of heaven. Nehemiah 1:4

I loved Malcom's prayer at church the other day. Only seven years old, he stood in front of 100 other kids and prayed: "Jesus, thank you that some of us get to play football and go to church, and for safety on the ride here, and for forgiveness of our sins, and for eternal life. We love you, Jesus. Please don't ever forget how much we love you!"

It brought tears to my eyes as he expressed his heart to God. As adults, we may tend to try to polish our prayers a little, thinking that it will sound better to God's ears or to those around us who might hear us. But I think God must delight in hearing just what's on His child's heart.

Nehemiah's heart was filled with concern for the welfare of Jerusalem, his homeland, when he heard that the people were in great distress and that the wall around the city was broken down (Nehemiah 1:3). Wanting to do something, he talked to God about it. He praised God for who He is (v. 5), requested forgiveness for sin (v. 6), reminded Him of His promise (v. 9), and asked for mercy from the king (v. 11). God watched over Nehemiah and His people through the whole rebuilding process.

What is on your mind? Thanks or burdens? Whatever it is, your loving God wants to hear your heart.

Anne Cetas

The highest form of prayer
comes from the depths of a humble heart.

Praying on Target

Read Matthew 14:22-33

*When he saw the wind, he was afraid and,
beginning to sink, cried out, "Lord, save me!"* Matthew 14:30

These three little words spoken by Peter make up one of the shortest prayers recorded in the Bible. The apostle's desperate plea points out a vital aspect of effective communication with God—praying on target. Many of our requests are not answered because we speak in broad generalities. We pile up words and phrases that sound good but have little focus or direction.

George Sweeting, president of Moody Bible Institute, illustrated what it means to pray specifically. In an article entitled, "Harnessing Your Prayer Power," he told of a missionary who was evacuated by a freighter from a South Pacific island during World War II. The vessel had to zigzag through hostile waters to avoid detection by submarines. One day a periscope appeared above the surface of the ocean. "That's when I learned to pray specifically," said the missionary. "While the enemy was looking us over (probably trying to decide whether or not to sink us), we cried, 'Lord, stop his motors! Jam his torpedo tubes! Break his rudder!' "

Most of our heaven-directed words do not arise out of life-and-death situations. Yet we should always make our requests as clear and sharp as if they did. "Lord, control my tongue," for example, is more pointed than "Help me to be a better Christian." The more specific our request, the more definite His response.

I wonder, do we deprive ourselves of God's power because we fail to pray on target?

Dennis DeHaan

In praying, if we aim at nothing, we're bound to hit it.

The Conquering Power of Praise

Read 2 Chronicles 20:14–25

As they began to sing and praise, the LORD set ambushes against the men of Ammon and Moab and Mount Seir who were invading Judah, and they were defeated. *2 Chronicles 20:22*

Through a remarkable incident in the history of the Jewish nation—a story told in 2 Chronicles 20—God gives us a wonderful prescription for victory in the midst of life's adversities.

A great host of enemy warriors had assembled to attack the kingdom of Judah. Fearful and not knowing what to do, King Jehoshaphat prayed to the Lord for help. A startling answer to his plea came from a Levite by the name of Jahaziel. Empowered by the Holy Spirit, he declared that despite the overwhelming superiority of the enemy, God would save His people in an unusual way. They were to sing praises to the Lord and not give in to worry. The next day, instead of ordering his sharpshooters to advance against the foe, Jehoshaphat appointed a choir to go before the army! As they began "to sing and praise," (2 Chronicles 20:22) Judah gained a great victory. The people didn't lift a finger, yet through divine intervention the enemy was conquered. Judah carried away a great spoil of precious jewels.

If we face an insurmountable obstacle, we turn the matter over to the Lord and praise Him for what He is going to do. In this way, we are letting Him work out the problem, and He will never disappoint.

As we give thanks in everything and let a song well up in our heart, victory is assured. That's the conquering of power of praise!

Henry Bosch

To triumph over trial, stop sighing and start singing!

The Prayer and the Chainsaw

Read Nehemiah 1

Lord, let your ear be attentive to the prayer
of this your servant. *Nehemiah 1:11*

I respect my Aunt Gladys's intrepid spirit, even if that very spirit concerns me sometimes. The source of my concern came in the form of news she shared in an email: "I cut down a walnut tree yesterday."

You must understand that my chainsaw-wielding aunt is seventy-six years old! The tree had grown up behind her garage. When the roots threatened to burst through the concrete, she knew it had to go. But she did tell us, "I always pray before I tackle a job like that."

While serving as butler to the king of Persia during the time of Israel's exile, Nehemiah heard news concerning the people who had returned to Jerusalem. Some work needed to be done. "The wall of Jerusalem is broken down, and its gates have been burned with fire" (Nehemiah 1:3). The broken walls left them vulnerable to attack by enemies. Nehemiah had compassion for his people and wanted to get involved. But prayer came first, especially since a new king had written a letter to stop the building efforts in Jerusalem (see Ezra 4). Nehemiah prayed for his people (Nehemiah 1:5–10), and then he asked God for help before requesting permission from the king to leave (v. 11).

Is prayer your response? It's always the best way to face any task or trial in life.

Linda Washington

Make prayer a first priority, instead of a last resort.

Parents Who Pray

Read Matthew 19:13–15

People brought little children to Jesus for him to place
his hands on them and pray for them. *Matthew 19:13*

A young mother sent these lines to a magazine: "I wish I could wrap my children in bubble wrap to protect them from the big, bad world outside."

Author Stormie Omartian understands how that mother feels. In her book *The Power of a Praying Parent*, she writes, "One day I cried out to God, saying, 'Lord, this is too much for me. I can't keep a 24-hours-a-day, moment-by-moment watch on my son. How can I ever have peace?' "

God responded by leading Stormie and her husband to become praying parents. They began to intercede for their son daily, mentioning the details of his life in prayer.

The desire to wrap our children in bubble wrap to protect them is rooted in fear, a common tendency, especially among mothers. Wrapping them in prayer, as Jesus did (Matthew 19:13–15), is a powerful alternative. He cares more about our children than we do, so we can release them into His hands by praying for them. He doesn't promise us that nothing bad will happen to them. But as we pray, He will give us the peace we long for (Philippians 4:6–7).

This challenge is for all parents—even those whose children have grown up: Don't ever stop wrapping your children in prayer!

Joanie Yoder

Every child needs a praying parent.

Julie's Prayer

Read John 14:12–14

*I will do whatever you ask in my name,
so that the Father may be glorified in the Son. John 14:13*

In 2008, a Christian film crew traveled to China on a special assignment—to retrace the life of missionary Eric Liddell, the 1924 Olympic gold medalist whose story was told in the movie *Chariots of Fire*. The crew took with them Eric's three daughters, Patricia, Heather, and Maureen—allowing them to revisit some of the places where the two older sisters had lived in China. Also along on the trip was their elderly Aunt Louise.

On one occasion, after the entourage had arrived in Beijing, they had to walk quite a distance with their luggage. As they did, Aunt Louise grew short of breath. Julie Richardson, a video crew member, sat down beside her, put her hand on her knee, and prayed simply, "Dear Jesus, help Aunt Louise to breathe." Immediately, she began to catch her breath.

Later, Heather retold the story and shared that Julie's prayer had rekindled her faith. Julie's simple act of faith reminded Heather of the continual connection we have with Jesus—a reality she had set aside in her life.

Sometimes we need reminders that God is near. When trials come and God seems far away, remember Julie's prayer and the truth that we are just one prayer from connecting with the God of the universe (John 14:13).

Dave Branon

God delights in the earnest prayers of His people.

He's Waiting

Read Psalm 34:1–15

I sought the LORD, and he answered me;
he delivered me from all my fears. *Psalm 34:4*

Jane Welsh, secretary to Scottish essayist Thomas Carlyle (1795–1881), married him and devoted her life to him and his work. He loved her deeply but was so busy with his writing and speaking that he often neglected her. Some time into their marriage, she became ill and suddenly died.

In a book by John Ortberg, I read that after the funeral Thomas went alone to Jane's room and looked at her diary. He found these words that she had written about him: "Yesterday he spent an hour with me and it was like heaven. I love him so." On another day, she wrote, "I have listened all day to hear his steps in the hall, but now it is late. I guess he will not come today." He wept brokenly, realizing his neglect of her and her desire just to talk with him.

As I read that, I couldn't help but think, God loves me dearly and waits for me to fellowship with Him. How many days do I forget Him?

The Lord welcomes our worship, our prayer, our praise. He has told us in His Word to pray all the time (1 Thessalonians 5:17). As He did with the church in Laodicea in Revelation 3, Christ knocks on the door of our heart and patiently waits (v. 20). He listens attentively for our call, our cry, our prayer. How often does He wait in vain?

David Egner

Talk with God—He longs to hear from you.

Where Did I Come From?

Read Acts 17:22–31

*From one man [God] made all the nations,
that they should inhabit the whole earth. Acts 17:26*

My seven-year-old African American friend Tobias asked me a thought-provoking question the other day: "Since Adam and Eve were white, where did black people come from?" When I told him we don't know what "color" they were and asked him why he thought they were white, he said that's what he always saw in Bible-story books at church and in the library. My heart sank. I wondered if that might make him think he was inferior or possibly not even created by the Lord.

All people have their roots in the Creator God, and therefore all are equal. That's what the apostle Paul told the Athenians: "From one man [God] made all the nations, that they should inhabit the whole earth" (Acts 17:26). We are all "from one blood" (Acts 17:26 NKJV). Bible scholar Darrell Bock, in his commentary on the book of Acts, says, "This affirmation would be hard for the Athenians, who prided themselves in being a superior people, calling others barbarians." However, because we all descended from our first parents, Adam and Eve, no race nor ethnicity is superior or inferior to another.

We stand in awe of our Creator, who made us and gives to all "life and breath and everything else" (v. 25). Equal in God's sight, we together praise and honor Him.

Anne Cetas

God loves each of us as if there were only one of us.

Praying and Doing

Read Exodus 14:1–16

Then the LORD said to Moses, "Why are you crying out to me? Tell the Israelites to move on." *Exodus 14:15*

Bible scholar Adam Clarke was a very slow and deliberate worker. He therefore disciplined himself to rise early every morning and get started on his work. A young preacher who admired Dr. Clarke and wanted to follow his example asked him how he could get up early so consistently. "Do you pray about it?" the man asked. "No," Clarke responded, "I just do it."

Sometimes God wants us to take action rather than pray. Today's Scripture gives us an example. Pharaoh had pursued the Israelites and seemed to have them trapped. The people cried out to God. Moses encouraged them by assuring them that the Lord would destroy the enemy. It was then that God told Moses to move ahead. The time had come to act.

Dwight L. Moody once met for prayer with a group of individuals who were very wealthy. They had gathered to ask the Lord to provide the funds to pay off the debt on their church building. "Men," Moody said, "I don't think, if I were you, that I'd trouble the Lord with that matter." Of course, Moody believed in praying for such needs. But he saw in that group of men the ability to answer their prayers out of their own resources, without feeling a pinch. This too was a time to act.

Yes, sometimes we must stop praying for God's work and start doing His work.

Richard DeHaan

Prayer was never intended as a labor-saving device.

Erev Yom Kippur

Read Matthew 5:21–26

*Leave your gift there in front of the altar. First go and be
reconciled to them; then come and offer your gift. Matthew 5:24*

In Judaism, the holiest day of the year is Yom Kippur, the day of
atonement. On that day, the nation seeks God's forgiveness for sins
both personal and national.

What is interesting, however, is the day before Yom Kippur,
known as Erev Yom Kippur. It represents a person's last opportunity
to seek forgiveness from other people before Yom Kippur begins.
This is important because, in Jewish thought, you must seek forgiveness from other people before you can seek the forgiveness of God.

Today, we are called to do the same. Jesus pointed out that in
order to worship Him with all our heart, we first need to resolve
matters with others. In Matthew 5:23–24, He said, "If you are offering your gift at the altar and there remember that your brother or
sister has something against you, leave your gift there in front of the
altar. First go and be reconciled to them; and then come and offer
your gift."

Even in a matter so basic as our giving, the ability to truly worship God is hindered by the reality of relationships broken by our
wrong actions, attitudes, and words.

So that our worship can be pleasing and acceptable to God, let us
make every effort to be reconciled to one another—today.

Bill Crowder

An offense against your neighbor
is a fence between you and God.

It Pays to Wait

Read Psalm 130

LORD, hear my voice. Let your ears be attentive
to my cry for mercy. *Psalm 130:2*

God listens when His children pray. The apostle Peter told us that "the eyes of the Lord are on the righteous and his ears are attentive to their prayer" (1 Peter 3:12).

A small boy, complaining to his brother, said, "Daddy said he likes it when we ask him for things, but I don't think he meant what he said. I told him a long time ago that I wanted a camera I saw in a store window. But he didn't give it to me. It's no use asking him for anything." Several years passed. Then one morning the father called his son into his study and said, "I suppose you've forgotten all about that camera you wanted." "No, I haven't," replied the boy. "I just figured you didn't want to spend the money on me." The father quickly responded, "No, that wasn't it at all!" Then, handing a camera to him, he said, "Here's the one I wanted you to have. It's a much nicer model than the one you had picked out. And you're old enough now to appreciate and use the one I'm giving you." Although that son had to wait, he received more than he had asked for.

Yes, our heavenly Father not only gives us what is best for us but He also gives it when it's best for us. He knows our needs. He hears our prayers. And the timing of His answers is always right. It pays to wait!

Richard DeHaan

Delay is not denial—pray on!

Don't Forget to Crown Him

Read Romans 14:7–11

"Why do you call me, 'Lord, Lord,'
and do not do what I say?" *Luke 6:46*

Christ wants to be crowned king of our lives. We are to do more than call Him "Lord." We must allow Him to govern all our actions as well.

A heartwarming story in the book *Forward Day by Day* tells about a song that especially delights youngsters. It's called, "Praise Him, All Ye Little Children." Sitting at the piano one day, a father and his young boy were singing that song together. It is one of those gospel hymns that runs on and on with many satisfying but seemingly endless verses. They sang several stanzas: "Praise Him, praise Him, all ye little children; God is love, God is love . . . Love Him, love Him, all ye little children . . . Thank Him, thank Him, all ye little children." And finally, "Serve Him, serve Him, all ye little children." Then the father stopped. The boy looked up in surprise, still expecting more. "Dad, you forgot to crown Him!" he said. And so once again they lifted their voices and sang, "Crown Him, crown Him, all ye little children; God is love, God is love!" Without realizing it, the child had emphasized a great biblical truth. As believers we say we love Christ and may even serve Him, but often we fail to give Him absolute control. Instead, we insist on governing our lives and refuse to yield completely to Him.

Jesus deserves our best, for He has bought us—soul and body. Let's too crown Him Lord of all!

Henry Bosch

If you don't crown Jesus Lord of all,
you really don't crown Him Lord at all.

Praying for Others

Read 2 Corinthians 1:8–11

You help us by your prayers. *2 Corinthians 1:11*

Some Christians feel frustrated because they are not able to serve the Lord as actively as they would like. They may be limited by some physical disease, or perhaps their family or work responsibilities are keeping them from doing more for Christ. They want to help in the Lord's work, but they are restricted.

Any believer, though, can serve the Lord through prayer. Paul spoke about the hardships he suffered in Asia Minor and how the prayers of others helped him. He was under tremendous pressure, but God gave him strength and delivered him. The Christians in Corinth were actively involved in Paul's ministry, for he wrote to them, "You also helping together in prayer for us."

We tend to view prayer as only an indirect involvement in ministry, but it may be the most important thing we can do. God's specially called servants need the faithful prayer support of His people. Whatever their task—pastoring, administering, or teaching—they may be facing tremendous pressure. They may be under attack by the enemy. They may be struggling against physical affliction or making far-reaching decisions Whatever it is, they cannot do it alone. We can be helping them. How? By praying.

Let us never think we can't be active in the Lord's work. We can always help others through prayer.

David Egner

Make sure intercession is part of every prayer session.

Two-Winged Sun

Read Isaiah 38:1–8

[The Lord] says: I have heard your prayer
and seen your tears. *Isaiah 38:5*

For five years, an ancient clay seal remained in a closet in Jerusalem's Institute of Archaeology. After the seal was dug up at the foot of the southern part of Jerusalem's old city wall, initial examination failed to establish the significance of the nearly 3,000-year-old object. But then a researcher carefully scrutinized the letters on the seal, resulting in a major discovery. The inscription, written in ancient Hebrew, reads: "Belonging to Hezekiah [son of] Ahaz king of Judah."

At the center of the seal is a two-winged sun surrounded by two images symbolizing life. The archaeologists who discovered the seal believe that King Hezekiah began using this seal as a symbol of God's protection after the Lord healed him from a life-threatening illness (Isaiah 38:1–8). Hezekiah had been pleading with the Lord to heal him. And God heard his prayer. He also gave Hezekiah a sign that He would indeed do what He had promised, saying, "I will cause the sun's shadow to move ten steps backward" (v. 8 NLT).

The facts related to this archeological artifact give us an encouraging reminder that the people in the Bible were learning, as we are, to call on the Lord who hears us when we cry out to Him for help. And even when His answers are not what we want or expect, we can rest assured that He is compassionate and He is powerful. The One who orders the movement of the sun can certainly move in our hearts.

Poh Fang Chia

Call out to God; He is wanting to hear from you.

A Puzzling Prayer Request

Read Matthew 6:5–15

Lead us not into temptation,
but deliver us from the evil one. Matthew 6:13

It's seems to be a shocking concept that Jesus would pray that God would "lead us not into temptation." It that even possible?

James tells us emphatically, "When tempted, no one should say, 'God is tempting me.' For God cannot be tempted by evil, nor does he tempt anyone" (James 1:13). How shall we resolve this apparent contradiction?

First, Matthew 6 is not suggesting that God deliberately pushes men into impossible situations of peril. The idea of the verse is best expressed, "Let us not be led into temptation or trial." The wilderness of this world through which we as pilgrims are traveling is full of pitfalls and snares. This petition is therefore a natural request for guidance through the maze of temptations that we may not be unduly tested, nor be tried by Satan beyond our capacity to resist the evil that confronts us! While the Lord at times allows us to tread the pathway of trial to strengthen our faith and purify our dross, we may rightly pray that we may not be brought under the "power of temptation" and so lose our spiritual footing.

First Corinthians 10:13 assures us: "No temptation has overtaken you except what is common to mankind. And God is faithful; he will not let you be tempted beyond what you can bear. Bu when you are tempted, he will also provide a way out (1 Corinthians 10:13).

Henry Bosch

Do not keep a longing eye on the temptation
from which you seek deliverance!

Surrounded by Prayer

Read Romans 15:22–33

I urge you, brothers and sisters, . . . to join me in my struggle
by praying to God for me. Romans 15:30

My friend Melissa's nine-year-old daughter Sydnie was in the hospital for chemotherapy and a bone marrow transplant when I had a dream about her. I dreamed she was staying in a central room at the hospital with her parents. Surrounding her room was a block of other rooms where family and friends were staying and continually praying for her during her times of treatment.

In real life, Sydnie wasn't physically surrounded by family and friends in adjacent rooms. But spiritually speaking, she was surrounded by prayer and love.

The apostle Paul seemed to have a desire to be surrounded by prayer. In most of his letters to churches, he requested to be remembered in prayer to the Lord (2 Corinthians 1:11; Ephesians 6:18–20; Colossians 4:2–4; Philemon 1:22). To the believers in Rome, he wrote, "I urge you, brothers and sisters, . . . to join me in my struggle by praying to God for me" (Romans 15:30). He knew that he could not be effective in his service for God without His power.

The Bible tells us that Jesus also prays for us (John 17:20; Hebrews 7:25), as does the Holy Spirit, whose prayers are according to the will of God (Romans 8:27). What a comfort to be surrounded by prayer!

Anne Cetas

Prayer prompted by the Holy Spirit is powerful.

Mountains Can Move

Read Mark 11:20–24

"Have faith in God," Jesus answered. *Mark 11:22*

A familiar slogan about prayer is, "Prayer changes things." But prayer doesn't do this—God does. Some people think that prayer itself is the source of power, so they "try prayer," hoping "it will work" for them. In Mark 11, Jesus disclosed one of the secrets behind all true prayer: "Have faith in God." Not faith in faith, not faith in prayer, but "faith in God" (v. 22).

Jesus told His disciples they could command a mountain to be cast into the sea, and if they believed it would happen, it would. Jesus then gave them His meaning behind that astonishing promise. He said, "Whatever you ask for in prayer, believe that you have received it, and it will be yours" (v. 24). Jesus was speaking about answered prayer. We can ask and receive answers only if our asking is directed to God in faith and according to His will (1 John 5:14).

I've often wished that I could move mountains by faith. Having once lived in Switzerland, I'd like God to move the Alps into my backyard in England. But He has done something much more important: He has removed mountains of worry, fear, and resentment from my heart and cast them into oblivion through my faith in Him. He is still in the mountain-moving business! Have faith in God and pray!

Joanie Yoder

Faith is the key to answered prayer.

Joyfully Worship

Read 2 Chronicles 7:1–11

*They knelt on the pavement with their faces to the ground,
and they worshiped and gave thanks to the LORD.* 2 Chronicles 7:3

It wasn't a normal, run-of-the-mill morning worship service when Solomon dedicated the temple. There was the sacrifice of countless animals (2 Chronicles 5:6). Special music was provided by the Levites on stringed instruments, cymbals, and harps, and by 120 trumpet-playing priests (5:12). There was the thick cloud in which dwelt the glory of the Lord (5:14). There was the dedicatory prayer of Solomon (6:12–42).

The most dramatic event occurred, however, when fire fell from heaven and consumed the offerings (7:1). The people, awed by God's presence, bowed low in worship (7:3). Two weeks later, when Solomon sent them home, they were "joyful and glad in heart for the good things the LORD had done" (7:10).

Although we cannot duplicate the majesty of such a celebration, from it we can learn about the transforming power of worship. And we can be challenged as believers and as churches to seek to worship God more effectively.

As you attend church this week, review the mighty works God has done in your life and in the lives of your fellow worshipers. Bow before the Lord in gratitude for who He is and sing praises to His greatness, power, and glory. In the spirit of the people at the temple, let's joyfully worship the Lord.

Dave Branon

True worship acknowledges the true worth-ship of God.

Mindless Prayer

Read Joshua 1:1–9

*As I was with Moses, so I will be with you;
I will never leave you nor forsake you. Joshua 1:5*

Sometimes I am ashamed of my prayers. Too often I hear myself using familiar phrases that are more like mindless filler than thoughtful, intimate interaction. One phrase that annoys me, and that I think might offend God, is "Lord, be with me." In Scripture, God has already promised not to leave me.

God made this promise to Joshua just before he led the Israelites into the Promised Land (Joshua 1:5). The author of Hebrews later claimed it for all believers: "I will never leave you nor forsake you" (13:5 NKJV). In both cases, the context indicates that God's presence has to do with giving us the power to carry out His will, not our own will, which is generally what I have in mind in my prayers.

Perhaps a better prayer would be something like this: "Lord, thank you for your indwelling Spirit, who is willing and able to direct me in the ways you want me to go. May I not take you where you don't want to go. May I not enlist you to do my will, but humbly submit to doing yours."

When we are doing God's will, He will be with us even without our asking. If we're not doing His will, we need to ask for His forgiveness, change our course, and follow Him.

Julie Ackerman Link

May our prayers not be mindless,
but instead mindful of God's will.

The Ministry of Prayer

Read Romans 12:9–16

Be joyful in hope, patient in affliction,
faithful in prayer. Romans 12:12

English pastor John Henry Jowett (1863–1923) told a story about a young woman named Mary, who worked as a housekeeper for a wealthy family. She had very few opportunities to serve the Lord except to pray for others. Her employer kept her so busy with household duties that she was seldom able to attend church services on Sunday.

While visiting in Mary's home one day, Jowett spoke to her about her busy schedule. "Do you ever feel frustrated because you can do so little for the Lord?" he asked. "Oh, Pastor, I take a newspaper to my bedroom each night," she replied. The minister wondered what that had to do with the question, but before he could inquire she continued, "I always turn to the columns that record births, marriages, and deaths. I pray first that the little babies may be led to the Savior early in life and become a great blessing to others. Then I pray that the brides and grooms may be very happy and may always be true to each other. Finally, I pray for all the bereaved, one by one, that they may turn to the one Source of lasting comfort." Jowett was deeply touched and humbled, for he realized that the church had few who were so unselfish in their praying.

What a challenge Mary leaves us by her example! Can we follow her example of creating our own ministry of prayer?

Henry Bosch

Through prayer you can go on far-reaching errands for God without leaving home.

Singing in the Spirit

Read 2 Chronicles 5:7–14

Be filled with the Spirit, speaking to one another with
psalms, hymns, and songs from the Spirit. *Ephesians 5:18–19*

During the Welsh Revivals of the early twentieth century, Bible
teacher and author G. Campbell Morgan described what he observed. He believed the presence of God's Holy Spirit was moving
on "billowing waves of sacred song." Morgan wrote that he had seen
the unifying influence of music in meetings that encouraged volun-
tary prayers, confession, and spontaneous singing. If someone got
carried away by their feelings and prayed too long, or spoke in a way
that didn't resonate with others, someone would begin to softly sing.
Others would gently join in, the chorus swelling in volume until
drowning out all other sound.

The renewal in song that Morgan describes has its story in the
Scriptures, where music plays a prominent role. Music was used to
celebrate victories (Exodus 15:1–21); in worshipful dedication of the
temple (2 Chronicles 5:12–14); and as a part of military strategy
(20:21–23). At the center of the Bible we find a songbook (Psalms
1–150). And in Paul's New Testament letter to the Ephesians we
read this description of life in the Spirit: "[Speak] to one another
with psalms, hymns, and songs from the Spirit" (Ephesians 5:19).

In conflict, in worship, in all of life, the music of our faith can
help us find one voice. In harmonies old and new we're renewed
again and again, not by might, nor by power, but the Spirit and
songs of our God.

Mart DeHaan

The Spirit has a song for those who listen.

Tell Jesus First

Read Psalm 57

John's disciples came and took his body and buried it.
Then they went and told Jesus. *Matthew 14:12*

When wicked King Herod had John the Baptist beheaded, John's friends "went and told Jesus" (Matthew 14:2). There's no one better to go to than our Savior when we must unburden our hearts.

Biddy Chambers once said of her husband, "Like all teachers of forceful personality, he constantly had people longing to pour out their intimate troubles to him. I remember at the close of one meeting a woman came up to him with the words, 'Oh, Mr. Chambers, I feel I must tell you about myself.' As he led her away to a quiet corner, I resigned myself to a long wait; but he was back again in a few minutes. As we went home, I remarked on the speed with which he managed to free himself, and he replied, 'I just asked her if she had ever told God all about herself. When she said she hadn't, I advised her to go home and pour out before Him as honestly as she could all her troubles, then see if she still needed or wanted to relate them to me.'" Chambers knew the importance of going directly to Jesus when faced with a special need or a trying situation.

Many a burden would be lifted if we would immediately confide in the Lord and prayerfully seek to discover the answer to our problems in His Word. How vital to tell our troubles first to Jesus!

Henry Bosch

When you're sick at heart, talk it over with the Great Physician—
no appointment necessary.

Cornered

Read Luke 6:27–36

Pray for those who mistreat you. *Luke 6:28*

One Sunday morning, Dwight L. Moody entered a house in Chicago to escort some children to Sunday school. During his visit, three men backed him into a corner and threatened him. "Look here," Moody said. "Give a fellow a chance to say his prayers, won't you?" The men actually allowed him to call out to God, and Moody prayed for them so earnestly that they left the room.

Had I been in Moody's situation, I might have called for help or looked for the back door. I'm not sure I would have acted on Jesus's command to His followers: "Pray for those who mistreat you" (Luke 6:28).

Praying for the people who treat us with contempt is one way to "do good to those who hate [us]" (v. 27). Jesus explained that Christians get no credit for swapping acts of kindness with other "nice" people. He said, "Even sinners do that" (v. 33). However, blessing our persecutors (Romans 12:14) sets us apart from them and aligns us with the Most High, because God is kind even to wicked people (Luke 6:35).

Today, if you feel "cornered" by someone, seek safety if the situation calls for it, and follow Jesus's teaching: Pray for that person (Luke 23:34). Prayer is your best defense.

Jennifer Benson Schuldt

Returning good for good is human;
returning good for evil is divine.

"Amen and FM"

Read Luke 11:1–13

Let us then approach God's throne of grace
with confidence, so that we may receive mercy
and find grace to help us in our time of need. Hebrews 4:16

A radio announcer's young son was overheard saying his bedtime prayers. He prayed in a conventional manner until he came to the end, and then he said, 'God bless all the boys and girls everywhere, and be with all the missionaries around the world, in Jesus's name, Amen and FM!'

How thankful we should be that we do not need a radio transmitter or a Wi-Fi connection to communicate with God. Rather, the simplest prayer breathed from the heart of the humblest saint reaches the throne room of almighty God himself. As believers, we have one of the greatest privileges imaginable. We can actually talk to God—sharing with Him our joys and triumphs, as well as our burdens and deepest sorrows. Why is it then that we do not pray more often? Are we too busy?

This brings to mind the example of the prophet Daniel. He had to attend to nearly all of the king's business. He had to pay attention to all his own work, as well as keep an eye on lots of other men; yet he found time to pray—not just now and then, once a day, or when he happened to have a few moments to spare, but "three times a day" (Daniel 6:10).

Have you prayed today? Why not talk to the Lord right now? You have a standing invitation!

Richard DeHaan

Our prayer life is a spiritual barometer;
by it we may know whether it is fair or foul in our hearts.

The Perfect Prayer Partner

Read Romans 8:31–34

[Jesus] is at the right hand of God
and is also interceding for us. *Romans 8:34*

Few sounds are as beautiful as hearing someone who loves you praying for you. When you hear a friend pray for you with compassion and God-given insight, it's a little like heaven touching earth.

How good it is to know that because of God's kindness to us our prayers can also touch heaven. Sometimes when we pray we may struggle with words and feelings of inadequacy, but Jesus taught His followers that we "should always pray and not give up" (Luke 18:1). God's Word shows us that one of the reasons we can do this is that Jesus himself "is at the right hand of God and is also interceding for us" (Romans 8:34).

We never pray alone, because Jesus is praying for us. He hears us as we pray, and He speaks to the Father on our behalf. We don't have to worry about the eloquence of our words, because no one understands us like Jesus. He helps us in every way, presenting our needs before God. He also knows when the answers we ask for would not be good for us, handling every request or concern with perfect wisdom and love.

Jesus is the perfect prayer partner—the friend who intercedes for us with immeasurable kindness. His prayers for us, which are beautiful beyond words, should encourage us to always pray with thankfulness.

James Banks

There's no greater privilege than praying with Jesus.

A Lesson in Praise

Read Psalm 150

Praise the LORD. *Psalm 150:1*

Psalm 150 is not only a beautiful expression of praise but it's also a lesson in praising the Lord. It tells us where to praise, why we're to praise, how we're to praise, and who should offer praise.

Where do we praise? In God's "sanctuary" and "mighty heavens" (v. 1). Wherever we are in the world is a proper place to praise the One who created all things.

Why do we praise? First, because of what God does. He performs "acts of power." Second, because of who God is. The psalmist praised Him for "his surpassing greatness" (v. 2). The all-powerful Creator is the Sustainer of the universe.

How should we praise? Loudly. Softly. Soothingly. Enthusiastically. Rhythmically. Boldly. Unexpectedly. Fearlessly. In other words, we can praise God in many ways and on many occasions (vv. 3–5).

Who should praise? "Everything that has breath" (v. 6). Young and old. Rich and poor. Weak and strong. Every living creature. God's will is for everyone to whom He gave the breath of life to use that breath to acknowledge His power and greatness.

Praise is our enthusiastic expression of gratitude to God for reigning in glory forever.

Julie Ackerman Link

Praise is the overflow of a joyful heart.

Psalms, Incense, Praise

Read Psalm 150

Let everything that has breath praise the LORD. *Psalm 150:6*

The well-known English preacher Charles H. Spurgeon wrote something that would be good to remember at the start of each day: "Let your thoughts be psalms, your prayers incense, and your breath praise." Let's look at each of these phrases.

"Let your thoughts be psalms." The 150 psalms have a variety of themes, including praise, God's character, and expressions of dependence on the Lord. Throughout the day we can turn our thoughts into psalms by meditating on God's holiness, His worthiness of our worship, and how much we need Him.

"Let your prayers be incense." In the tabernacle of the Jews, incense was burned continually to offer a sweet savor to the Lord (Exodus 30:7–8). Our prayers are like incense to God (Psalm 141:2), bringing to His nostrils the pleasing scent of our adoration and need for Him.

"Let your breath be praise." The book of Psalms concludes with the words, "Let everything that has breath praise the LORD. Praise the LORD!" (Psalm 150:6). Talking about God and offering Him words of praise should be as natural to us as breathing.

Keep the Lord in your thoughts, prayers, and speech today.

David Egner

A heart filled with praise brings pleasure to God.

Watch What Happens

Read Colossians 4:2–4, 12–13

Devote yourselves to prayer,
being watchful and thankful. *Colossians 4:2*

When a missionary to Haiti returned to the United States, she reported a wonderful answer to prayer. She explained that while in Haiti she had been faced with the prospect of having cancer. A biopsy was performed and sent away for analysis, but the medical report didn't come back for several weeks. As she waited for word, she could find no peace of mind. She recalled that she had fears of what would happen to her husband and their small children. There seemed to be no relief from her distress. But one evening her anxiety suddenly lifted like a cloud. She had a deep and inexpressible awareness that the Lord would take care of her family and their emotional needs, regardless of the outcome.

As she reflected on this, it occurred to her that it was Wednesday evening—and her church family back home held prayer meetings on that night. And it was the first Wednesday night after friends had been notified of her struggle. She and her husband felt that God had given them an opportunity to sense His answer to the prayers of others on their behalf. The medical report soon came back with the welcome news that there was no cancer.

The emphasis given to prayer in Colossians 4 highlights the kind of support we all should be giving to one another. Let's pray in the Spirit for the needs of others and watch to see what the Lord is going to do.

Mart DeHaan

The best way to influence people for God
is to go to God for people.

The Mercy of a Father's Heart

Read Psalm 103:1–14

As a father has compassion on his children, so the LORD
has compassion on those who fear him. *Psalm 103:13*

Psalm 103 is a hymn of praise that extolls the mercy of God. Plus, it reminds us that the Lord deals with His people as a compassionate father treats his children. It makes me think of David's experience with his son Absalom. This handsome, gifted young man tried to usurp the throne from his father, an effort that drove David out of Jerusalem. He even laid plans to destroy all who were still loyal to the king.

In spite of this treachery, David's deep love for his son was not altered. He told his military leaders, "Be gentle with the young man Absalom for my sake" (2 Samuel 18:5). When news came that this rebellious youth had been killed, his father wept bitterly and uttered one of the most moving laments to be found in all literature. He cried, "'O my son Absalom! My son, my son Absalom! If only I had died instead of you—O Absalom, my son, my son!" (2 Samuel 18:33). Being a parent myself, I know how he must have felt. My heart too would desire mercy for my children no matter what they had done. Such strong family feelings are typical of godly men in every age!

This ought to be an encouragement as we consider our heavenly Father's relationship to us. If we can be filled with deep compassion for our offspring, think of how much more His kindness abounds toward us! Praise God for His loving Father-heart.

Herb Vander Lugt

The mercy of God is infinite love
expressing itself in infinite goodness.

Mayday!

Read Psalm 86:1–13

When I am in distress, I call to you,
because you answer me. *Psalm 86:7*

The international distress signal "Mayday" is always repeated three times in a row—"Mayday-Mayday-Mayday"—so the situation will be clearly understood as a life-threatening emergency. The word was created in 1923 by Frederick Stanley Mockford, a senior radio officer at London's Croydon Airport. That now-closed facility once had many flights to and from Le Bourget Airport in Paris. According to the National Maritime Museum, Mockford coined Mayday from the French word *m'aidez*, which means, "help me."

Throughout King David's life, he faced life-threatening situations for which there seemed to be no way out. Yet, we read in Psalm 86 that during his darkest hours, David's confidence was in the Lord. "Hear my prayer, LORD; listen to my cry for mercy. When I am in distress, I call to you, because you answer me" (vv. 6–7).

David also saw beyond the immediate danger by asking God to lead his steps: "Teach me your way, LORD, that I may rely on your faithfulness; give me an undivided heart, that I may fear your name" (v. 11). When the crisis was past, he wanted to keep walking with God.

The most difficult situations we face can become doorways to a deeper relationship with our Lord. This begins when we call on Him to help us in our trouble and also to lead us each day in His way.

David McCasland

God hears our cries for help and leads us in His way.

Praying Together

Read Ephesians 5:22–33

Each one of you also must love his wife as he loves himself,
and the wife must respect her husband. *Ephesians 5:33*

Louis Evans, former pastor of the Hollywood Presbyterian Church, made an amazing statement. He said that he never knew a couple who went ahead with a divorce after first praying together, on their knees, every day, for a week.

Praying together is both a solvent and a glue. It dissolves resentments and bitterness, and it binds hearts in new and joyous harmony. Swiss psychiatrist Dr. Paul Tournier writes, "It is only when a husband and wife pray together before God that they find the secret of true harmony: that the difference in their temperaments, their ideas, antheir tastes enriches their home instead of endangering it. . . .

"When each of the marriage partners seeks quietly before God to see his own faults, recognizes his sin, and asks the forgiveness of the other, marital problems are no more. . . . They learn to become absolutely honest with each other. . . . This is the price to be paid if partners very different from each other are to combine their gifts instead of setting them against each other."

If praying together can restore a marriage about to break up, think of what it can do to strengthen and enrich a marriage that is lacking in communication and intimacy. It is certainly worth a try.

Dennis DeHaan

Couples who pray together, stay together

Unceasing Prayer

Read 1 Thessalonians 5:12–18

Pray continually. *1 Thessalonians 5:17*

In his book *Keep on Keeping On*, Harold L. Fickett Jr. told about a pastor's wife who had for a long time been perplexed by the command to "pray continually." Spending long sessions on her knees in formal prayer was frustrating to her because she was a busy wife and mother. It just wasn't feasible. Fickett said, "As she thought about this, the answer came to her. She realized, 'I can pray when I am washing the dishes . . . cleaning the house . . . driving the kids to school, and . . . preparing for the responsibilities I have at church.' When she began to put this idea into practice, she discovered that she was literally living in the presence of the Lord."

She had found a way to do what I believe the apostle Paul meant when he said, "Pray continually." Of course, he could have meant that there should be no break in our pattern of prayer. In other words, there should never be any period in our lives that is characterized by prayerlessness. This is certainly in keeping with Scripture. I believe Paul also meant that praying should be something like breathing—natural, spontaneous, and continuous. When a problem confronts us, when we're reminded of a friend in distress, or when we're made aware of some other need, we can breathe a prayer to God right on the spot. And we can do this at any time, even when doing something else.

Richard DeHaan

If you are too busy to pray, you are too busy.

Praying for People

Read 2 Chronicles 30:13-22

Hezekiah prayed for them. *2 Chronicles 30:18*

A Sailor told an unusual story about a lighthouse keeper who lived on the coast of southern Maine. He said, "We were fogbound in Penobscot Bay and made harbor at Eagle Island. Just as the sun was setting we went on shore. As we walked toward the lighthouse, we were attracted by the voice of someone in prayer. It was an impressive scene. Before us stretched the broad Atlantic, and the gathering shades of evening deepened the solitude.

"In the light above us was the keeper, where he had just lighted his lamp. His face was turned toward the sea; his long hair and beard were whitened with the snows of many winters. His arms were outstretched and his voice alone broke the silence as he besought the Almighty, in the hollow of whose hands the seas are held, to protect the sailors.

"'Those prayers will go higher than the light,' said our skipper, and all of us felt that we had come into the near presence of God on that lonely island. Who can measure the divine providence that shines out from the lighthouse on Eagle Island because of that praying lighthouse keeper?"

Our prayers can affect the lives of others. Hezekiah prayed for the people, and God listened and healed them (2 Chronicles 30:18–20). We as believers have a great prayer responsibility. So, like that old lighthouse keeper, let's be faithful in praying for people.

Richard DeHaan

The best way to influence people for God
is to intercede with God for people.

Take a Number

Read John 14:15–27

Peace I leave with you; my peace I give you. *John 14:27*

We have an ancient cherry tree in our backyard that looked like it was dying, so I called in an arborist. He checked it out and declared that it was "unduly stressed" and needed immediate attention. "Take a number," my wife, Carolyn, muttered to the tree as she walked away. It had been one of those weeks.

Indeed, we all have anxious weeks—filled with worries over the direction our culture is drifting or concerns for our children, our marriages, our businesses, our finances, our personal health and well-being. Nevertheless, Jesus has assured us that despite disturbing circumstances we can be at peace. He said, "My peace I give to you" (John 14:27 NKJV).

Jesus's days were filled with distress and disorder: He was beleaguered by His enemies and misunderstood by His family and friends. Yet there was no trace of anxiety or fretfulness in His manner. He possessed an inner calm, a quiet tranquility. This is the peace He has given us—freedom from anxiety concerning the past, present, and future. The peace He exhibited; His peace.

In any circumstances, no matter how dire or trivial, we can turn to Jesus in prayer. There in His presence we can make our worries and fears known to Him. Then, Paul assures us, the peace of God will come to "guard [our] hearts and [our] minds in Christ Jesus" (Philippians 4:7). Even if we've had "one of those weeks," we can have His peace.

David Roper

In the midst of troubles, peace can be found in Jesus.

God Can Save Anyone!

Read 1 Timothy 2:1–8

I urge . . . that petitions, prayers, intercession
and thanksgiving be made for all people. *1 Timothy 2:1*

Today, as always, there is an urgent need for us to pray for "all those in authority" (1 Timothy 2:2). But does the word *all* include the most wicked of leaders? Are there ever people in positions of power and influence who are beyond the help of prayer?

The answer to this question can be found by noting the word *therefore* in verse 1, which calls our attention to the immediate context. In 1 Timothy 1:12–17, Paul admitted that he was once a blasphemer, a persecutor, and a violent man (v. 13). He vigorously affirmed that Christ Jesus came into the world to save sinners. Then he added this significant phrase: "of whom I am the worst" (v. 15).

Paul explained that he received God's mercy so that Christ would display His limitless grace in him as a pattern for those who are going to believe on Him in the future (v. 16). In effect, Paul was saying, "If I, the worst of sinners, can be saved, anyone can." Paul therefore exhorted us to pray for all in authority, because God our Savior desires all to be saved and to embrace His truth (2:4).

So let's not only pray that honorable leaders will act wisely, but also that ungodly leaders will be saved. Yes, God can save anyone.

Joanie Yoder

To influence leaders for God, intercede with God for leaders.

Talking to God

Read Psalm 142

I cry to you, LORD; I say, "You are my refuge,
my portion in the land of the living." *Psalm 142:5*

Little Judy was telling her mother about the previous evening when she had been cared for by a new babysitter. "She was very nice to me," the youngster said, "but she didn't want to hear me say my prayers to her like I do to you. So," Judy continued with a smile of satisfaction, "I just said them to God."

That child's comment reminds us that when we pray we are to remember that we are talking to God and not to other people. That truth is so obvious, and yet it is something we often fail to grasp and appreciate the way we should. When we pray, we are heard by the all-powerful, all-knowing, everywhere-present One—the eternal God himself. He is our heavenly Father. He listens to us and delights in our dependence on Him.

We should also keep in mind that we are addressing the Lord when we pray in public. We are often more concerned about impressing those who are listening to us than we are about communicating with God himself. True, in group prayer, we do endeavor to lead our fellow-believers in such a manner that they can pray with us. When they hear our praise and requests their hearts will respond with a silent or vocal "Amen" of agreement. But, first and foremost, prayer is talking to God.

Richard DeHaan

The Christian who says his prayers to men
should not expect to get answers from God.

Foreign Worship

Read Acts 17:16–31

"[Paul] seems to be advocating foreign gods."
They said this because Paul was preaching
the good news about Jesus. Acts 17:8

During a trip to the Far East, I visited an unusual shrine made up of hundreds of statues. According to our guide, worshipers would pick the statue that looked the most like an ancestor and pray to it.

A few years ago, I read about a student named Le Thai. An ancestor worshiper, he found great comfort in praying to his deceased grandmother. Because he was praying to someone he knew and loved, he found this to be personal and intimate.

But when he came from Vietnam to the US to study, Le Thai was introduced to Christianity. It sounded like a fairy tale based on American thinking. To him, it was the worship of a foreign God (see Acts 17:18).

Then a Christian friend invited him to visit his home on Christmas. He saw a Christian family in action and heard again the story of Jesus. Le Thai listened. He read John 3 about being "born again" and asked questions. He began to feel the pull of the Holy Spirit. Finally, he realized that Christianity was true. He trusted Jesus as his personal Savior.

When a friend sees Christianity as foreign worship, we need to respect his or her heritage while sharing the gospel graciously and giving them time to explore Christianity. And then trust the Spirit to do His work.

Dave Branon

God is the only true God.

Listening to Your Brother

Read Matthew 18:15–20

Whoever turns a sinner from the error of their way will save them
from death and cover over a multitude of sins. *James 5:20*

"You need to listen to me, I'm your brother!" The plea came from a
concerned older brother in my neighborhood and was directed to a
younger sibling who was moving farther away from him than the
older child was comfortable with. Clearly the older child was better
able to judge what was best in the situation.

How many of us have resisted the wise counsel of a brother or
sister? If you've had to face the consequences of resisting the good
advice of someone more mature, you're not alone.

One of the greatest resources we can have as believers in Jesus is
a family—those who are spiritually related because of a common
faith in Him. This family includes mature men and women who
love God and each other. Like the little brother in my neighborhood, we sometimes need a word of caution or correction to get us
back on track. This is particularly true when we offend someone or
someone offends us. Doing what's right can be difficult. Yet Jesus's
words in Matthew 18:15–20 show us what to do when offenses happen within our spiritual family.

Thankfully, our gracious heavenly Father places in our lives people who are prepared to help us honor Him and others. And when
we listen, things go better in the family (v. 15).

Arthur Jackson

Wisdom grows when we listen to the words of mature believers.

Keep on Praying!

Read Matthew 7:7–11

Ask and it will be given to you; seek and you will find;
knock and the door will be opened to you. *Matthew 7:7*

Do we sometimes give up on our prayers too soon? Perhaps we present our needs or desires to the Lord once or twice, and if the answer doesn't come immediately, we don't ask again. Or we conclude that we are asking too much, forgetting that God is a generous God who has great power. Yet Jesus told us to ask, to seek, to knock—to be determined and persistent in our praying.

On the subject of perseverance in prayer, Andrew Murray wrote, "Think of the wonderful instances among the Old Testament saints: Abraham, who renewed his prayer for Sodom six times, and apologized with the words, 'Let not the Lord be angry.' Abraham wouldn't stop until God granted his petition. And for his sake, Lot was spared.

"Think of Jacob when he feared to meet Esau. The angel of the Lord met him in the dark and wrestled with him. When the angel saw that he could not prevail, he said, 'Let me go.' And Jacob replied, 'I will not let you go.' That boldness forced from the reluctant angel the blessing."

God is not reluctant to respond, but in His infinite wisdom He knows the best answer and the best timing. So let's keep on asking. Then, when the provision comes, we'll know the value of persistent praying.

David Egner

Delay is not denial—pray on!

It's Not about the Fish

Read Jonah 3:10–4:4

When God saw what they did and how they
turned from their evil ways, he relented. *Jonah 3:10*

Sighted numerous times off the coast of Australia's South Queensland, Migaloo is the first albino humpback whale ever documented. The splendid creature, estimated at more than forty feet long, is so rare that Australia passed a law specifically to protect him.

The Bible tells us about a "huge fish" so rare that God had provided it especially to swallow a runaway prophet (Jonah 1:17). Most know the story. God told Jonah to take a message of judgment to Nineveh. But Jonah wanted nothing to do with the Ninevites, who had a reputation for cruelty to just about everyone—including the Hebrews. So he fled. Things went badly. From inside the fish, Jonah repented. Eventually he preached to the Ninevites, and they repented too (3:5–10).

Great story, right? Except it doesn't end there. While Nineveh repented, Jonah pouted. "Isn't this what I said, LORD?" he prayed. "I knew that you are a gracious and compassionate God, slow to anger and abounding in love" (4:2). Having been rescued from certain death, Jonah's sinful anger grew until even his prayer became suicidal (v. 3).

The story of Jonah isn't about the fish. It's about our human nature and the nature of the God who pursues us. "[The Lord] is patient with you," wrote the apostle Peter, "not wanting anyone to perish, but everyone to come to repentance" (2 Peter 3:9). God offers His love to brutal Ninevites, pouting prophets, and you and me.

Tim Gustafson

Our love has limits; God's love is limitless.

Praise the Lord, Everybody

Read Psalm 148

Young men and women, old men and children. Let them
praise the name of the Lord, for his name alone is exalted;
his splendor is above the earth and the heavens. *Psalm 148:12–13*

The writer of Psalm 148 summons the whole created universe to give glory to God. But that's not all. Those who love God are also invited to praise Him, including "young men and women, old men and children." All should sing praises to Him.

During a Sunday evening church service, a group of young people sang a special arrangement of "Jesus Loves Me." Listening intently was a little girl who clearly had entered into the spirit of the song and was expressing her love for Christ through her smile and her excitement. Near her was a middle-aged widow who had known many trials. Her countenance also reflected deep joy. I also noticed an elderly man whose body bore the marks of physical infirmity. He too was smiling, although tears moistened his eyes. Touched by Jesus's love, these people were praising God!

We all have reason to glorify Him! The aged, having tasted life's joys and sorrows, can adore Him for His mercy in the past and His promises for the future. Little children, on the other hand, who have not experienced many trials and pains, can say, "Thank you, Father, for the tender love of my parents and for Jesus who died for me!"

Yes, in His goodness God made us, in His mercy He provided salvation in Christ, and in His grace He'll bring us safely to heaven. Let everyone praise the Lord!

Herb Vander Lugt

Praise is the melody that flows from a heart in tune with God.

The Lord's Prayer

Read Luke 11:1–4

He said to them, "When you pray, say: 'Father, hallowed be
your name, your kingdom come.'" *Luke 11:2*

On one occasion after the disciples saw Jesus praying, they said,
"Lord, teach us to pray" (Luke 11:1). In response, He gave them a
pattern for their own petitions.

James Francis has given a concise explanation of the Lord's
Prayer recorded in Matthew 6:9–13 (NKJV). He notes that it begins
with worship and ends with intercession: "When we are told to pray,
'Our Father in heaven,' we are admonished to come simply as a child
addressing his Father. When we exclaim, 'Hallowed be Your name,'
it is as a worshiper addressing his God. 'Your kingdom come' reminds us that we petition the throne as a citizen who approaches his
King. 'Your will be done on earth as it is in heaven' emphasizes that
we come as a servant speaking to his Master. 'Give us this day our
daily bread' pictures us as a beggar approaching his Benefactor. 'And
forgive us our sins, as we forgive everyone who is indebted to us' is
the plea of a sinner seeking pardon from his Savior. 'And do not lead
us into temptation' depicts a pilgrim beseeching his Guide for safe,
providential direction. 'But deliver us from the evil one' is the cry of
one . . . who seeks help from his great Defender."

As we meditate on the deep significance of our Lord's instructions about prayer, our own prayers will become more effective.

Henry Bosch

Many Christians who pray "Our Father" on Sunday
act like orphans the rest of the week.

Time to Pray

Read Psalm 70

Hasten, O God, to save me. *Psalm 70:1*

One morning, when I was a young child, I was sitting in the kitchen, watching my mother prepare breakfast. Unexpectedly, the grease in the skillet in which she was frying bacon caught fire. Flames shot into the air and my mother ran to the pantry for some baking soda to throw on the blaze.

"Help!" I shouted. And then I added, "Oh, I wish it was time to pray!"

"It's time to pray" must have been a frequent household expression, and I took it quite literally to mean we could pray only at certain times.

The time to pray, of course, is any time—especially when we're in crisis. Fear, worry, anxiety, and care are the most common occasions for prayer. It is when we are desolate, forsaken, and stripped of every human resource that we naturally resort to prayer. We cry out with the words of David, "Hasten, O God, to save me" (Psalm 70:1).

John Cassian, a fifth-century Christian, wrote of this verse: "This is the terrified cry of someone who sees the snares of the enemy, the cry of someone besieged day and night and exclaiming that he cannot escape unless his Protector comes to the rescue."

May this be our simple prayer in every crisis and all day long: "Help, Lord!"

David Roper

There is no place or time we cannot pray.

Prayer and Alms

Read James 2:14–20

*Your prayers and gifts to the poor have come up
as a memorial offering before God. Acts 10:4*

Works without prayer can often be unspiritual; prayer without works is frequently hypocritical. The right formula is prayer *and* works. When in line with the will of God, they become a mighty dynamo of power that gets results and establishes in His presence a lasting "memorial."

A group of Christians once gathered to pray for a family that had suffered a severe financial setback. While one of the men was offering a fervent petition on their behalf, a loud knock was heard at the door. The visitor proved to be the sturdy young son of one of the local farmers. "What do you want?" they inquired. "Well, Pa says he can't join you at this time, but he asked me to bring his prayers in the wagon!" "What do you mean?" asked the leader of the group. "If you'll come out and help me bring in what he wanted me to deliver, you'll soon understand," replied the teenager. When they reached the wagon, they saw that "Pa's prayers" consisted of potatoes, flour, beef, oatmeal, turnips, apples, jars of jelly and fruit, and a bundle of clothing. With new understanding in their hearts, the others decided to take the hint and do likewise. Each pledged a generous amount from his own abundant supplies, and the meeting quickly adjourned on a note of praise.

When nothing else can be done, prayer has a right to stand alone. Otherwise, faith and works, prayer and alms should go together!

Henry Bosch

Prayer that is not accompanied by suitable good works
is often pious presumption.

A Bouquet of Praise

Read 1 Peter 4:7–11

... that in all things God may be praised
through Jesus Christ. *1 Peter 4:11*

Corrie ten Boom (1892–1983) was a World War II concentration camp survivor and Christian who became a popular speaker around the world. Thousands attended her meetings as she talked about how she had learned to forgive her captors just as Christ had forgiven her sins.

After each meeting, people surrounded her and heaped accolades on her for her godly qualities and thanked her for encouraging them in their walk with the Lord. Corrie said she would then return to her hotel room, get down on her knees, and present those compliments in thanks to God. She called it giving God "a bouquet of praise."

The Lord has given each of us gifts to use to minister to one another (1 Peter 4:10) so that "in all things God may be praised through Jesus Christ. To him be the glory and the power for ever and ever" (v. 11). We have nothing to offer others that we have not first received from the Lord (1 Corinthians 4:7), so the glory does belong to Him.

To learn humility, perhaps we could follow Corrie's example. If we receive a compliment for something we've said or done, let's privately give a bouquet of praise to God for the glory He alone deserves.

Anne Cetas

Praise is the fairest blossom that springs from the soul.

A Singing Heart

Read Psalm 98:1–6

*Speaking to one another with psalms, hymns,
and songs from the Spirit. Sing and make music
from your heart to the Lord. Ephesians 5:19*

From my earliest memories I recall that my parents were always singing. There were no radios or TVs in those days, and we could not afford a phonograph, so our lives revolved around the Lord, the Bible, and our big upright mahogany piano. We loved to gather in the parlor, as it was then called, to lift our voices in praise and adoration. Those old hymns—so full of meaning—still thrill my soul. In fact, almost every morning when I awaken, one of those dear sacred songs begins ringing in my soul. What comfort and inspiration they bring—in spite of the trials that often cross my pathway.

I suppose the hymns touch me so deeply because many of the great ones were born out of real-life situations. One day, the words of the gospel song "He's a Wonderful Savior to Me" began running through my mind. It was penned by my friend Virgil P. Brock after hearing a former alcoholic repeat that phrase over and over during a testimony meeting. The man had known the dreadful pangs of being lost—separated from God by his sin.

Then he met Jesus.

No wonder he exclaimed as peace and victory flooded his soul, "He's a wonderful Savior to me!" As I hummed that tune, I thrilled again with the joy of the Lord that only a redeemed sinner can know. What a joy it is to be a rejoicing, singing Christian!

Henry Bosch

The truest expression of Christianity is not a sigh, but a song!

The Day I Couldn't Pray

Read Romans 8:22–26

We do not know what we ought to pray for, but the Spirit himself intercedes for us through wordless groans. *Romans 8:26*

In November 2015, I learned I needed open-heart surgery. Surprised and shaken, I was naturally drawn to think about the possibility of death. Were there relationships I needed to mend or financial matters I needed to attend to for my family? Even if the surgery was successful, it would be months before I could work. Was there work that could be done ahead of time? And what about work that couldn't wait; who should I hand that off to? It was a time to both act and pray.

Except I couldn't do either.

When I tried to pray, my thoughts would drift to the discomfort, or the shallow breathing caused by the damaged heart made me fall asleep. I couldn't work and I couldn't even ask God to let me live so I could spend more time with my family!

But the Creator knew this was happening to me. I would eventually recall He made two preparations for such occurrences in our lives: the prayer of the Holy Spirit for us when we can't pray (Romans 8:26) and the prayer of others on our behalf (James 5:16; Galatians 6:2).

What a comfort it was to know that the Holy Spirit was even then raising my concerns before the Father—and to hear from friends and family as they prayed for me.

What a gift it is in a time of uncertainty to be reminded that God hears our heart even when we think we can't call out to Him.

Randy Kilgore

God never leaves the voices of His children unheard.

"I Talked with God"

Read Luke 11:1–13

He said to them, "When you pray, say: 'Father,
hallowed be your name, your kingdom come.'" *Luke 11:2*

A comment by Robert A. Cook, at the time the president of The King's College in New York, renewed my appreciation for the privilege of prayer. Speaking at Moody Bible Institute, Cook said that the day before, he had been at a gathering in Washington and had talked with the vice president of the United States. Two hours later, he said, he spoke briefly with the president. Then smiling broadly, Cook said to us, "But that's nothing! Today I talked with God!"

Prayer takes on new power and fervency when we become conscious of how great and glorious God is. Think of how the saints of past ages responded when they caught a glimpse of the Almighty. They were awestruck! Job, who had complained bitterly about his misfortune and had made some self-righteous statements, finally met the Lord and cried out, "My ears had heard of you but now my eyes have seen you. Therefore I despise myself and repent in dust and ashes" (Job 42:5, 6). Isaiah saw a vision of God and exclaimed, "Woe to me . . . I am ruined!" (Isaiah 6:5). Ezekiel observed the glory of the Lord and declared, "When I saw it, I fell facedown" (Ezekiel 1:28).

For each of these, the vision of God's greatness and glory brought about an overwhelming sense of their weakness and depravity. Yet God invites us to talk to Him, and He actually wants us to address Him as "Our Father." What a privilege!

Herb Vander Lugt

The highest privilege of man is to talk to God.

Sweet Praise

Read Colossians 3:12–17

Let the message of Christ dwell among you richly . . .
singing to God with gratitude in your hearts. *Colossians 3:16*

Several years ago, my husband helped lead a work crew of high school students on a short-term mission trip to a Christian school in an urban community. Unfortunately, Tom had broken his foot shortly before the trip and was supervising the work from a wheelchair. He was discouraged because he wasn't able to get around as he had hoped.

While he was working on the ground floor, a few of the girls were painting on the third floor. He could hear them singing praise choruses in harmony as their voices echoed down the wide-open staircases. Song after song ministered to him. "It was the most beautiful sound I'd ever heard," he told me later. "And it lifted my spirits."

Colossians 3 reminds us, "Let the message of Christ dwell among you richly as you teach and admonish one another with all wisdom through psalms, hymns, and songs from the spirit, singing to God with gratitude in your hearts" (v. 16). Not only were those teenage girls giving sweet praise to God, they were ministering to a coworker.

Whatever you're doing today, cultivate an attitude of praise. Whether it is through song or conversation, let your joy in the Lord reverberate to others. You never know who you might encourage.

Cindy Hess Kasper

Hope can be ignited by a spark of encouragement.

Serving God with Prayers

Read 1 Kings 18:41–45

*The prayer of a righteous person
is powerful and effective. James 5:16*

God often chooses to move through our prayers to accomplish His work. We see this when God told the prophet Elijah, "I will send rain on the land," promising to end a drought in Israel that had lasted three and a half years (James 5:17). Even though God had promised rain, a short time later "Elijah climbed to the top of Carmel, bent down to the ground and put his face between his knees"—praying intently for the rain to come (1 Kings 18:42). Then, while he continued to pray, Elijah sent his servant to go and look out over the ocean "seven times," scanning the horizon for any sign of rain (v. 43).

Elijah understood that God wants us to join in His work through humble, persistent prayer. Regardless of our human limitations, God may choose to move through our praying in amazing ways. That's why the letter of James tells us that "the prayer of a righteous person is powerful and effective," all the while reminding us that "Elijah was a human being, even as we are" (James 5:16–17).

When we make it our aim to serve God through praying faithfully as Elijah did, we're taking part in a beautiful privilege—where at any moment we may be given a front-row seat to a miracle!

James Banks

Great expectation on our part honors God.

Amazing Jesus

Read Mark 10:23–31

*The disciples were amazed at his words.
But Jesus said again, "Children, how hard
it is to enter the kingdom of God!"* Mark 10:24

Are you amazed by the extraordinary? Astonished by the unusual? Like the rabbit-from-a-hat trick by a sleight-of-hand artist? Like the incredible athletic moves of a Steph Curry? Like the awe-inspiring virtuoso performance of an Itzhak Perlman?

Like the miracles and words of Jesus?

Sometimes in our familiarity with the God-man Jesus Christ, we fail to respond with amazement as the first-century eyewitnesses did.

They marveled at His miraculous power: "This amazed everyone and they praised God" (Mark 2:12).

They were awestruck by His presence: "As soon as all the people saw Jesus, they were overwhelmed with wonder and ran to greet him" (Mark 9:15).

They were astounded by His extraordinary knowledge: "They were amazed. 'Where did this man get this wisdom and these miraculous powers?' they asked" (Matthew 13:54). Some who were astonished by Jesus's words and works later became offended by His teachings and turned away in unbelief. But for others, their amazement led to faith and new life and worship.

How long has it been since we were amazed by the love of Jesus, by the thought of His sacrifice, or by the evidence of His care?

Let's praise and worship this amazing Jesus.

Dave Branon

Ponder the wonder of Jesus.

A Plea for Prayer

Read 2 Thessalonians 3:1–5

Brothers and sisters, pray for us. *2 Thessalonians 3:1*

A missionary recently visited the Bible study I was attending. She described what it had been like to pack up her household, part with friends, and relocate to a distant country. When she and her family arrived, they were greeted with a flourishing drug-trade and hazardous roadways. The language barrier brought on bouts of loneliness. They contracted four different stomach viruses. And her oldest daughter narrowly escaped death after falling through a railing on an unsafe stairwell. They needed prayer.

The apostle Paul experienced danger and hardship as a missionary. He was imprisoned, shipwrecked, and beaten. It's no surprise that his letters contained pleas for prayer. He asked the believers in Thessalonica to pray for success in spreading the gospel—that "the message of the Lord may spread rapidly and be honored" (2 Thessalonians 3:1) and that God would deliver him from "wicked and evil people" (v. 2). Paul knew he would need to "fearlessly make known" the gospel (Ephesians 6:19), which was yet another prayer request.

Do you know people who need supernatural help as they spread the good news of Christ? Remember Paul's appeal, "Brothers and sisters, pray for us" (2 Thessalonians 3:1), and intercede for them before the throne of our powerful God.

Jennifer Benson Schuldt

Intercede for others in prayer; God's throne is always accessible.

Keep on Asking

Read Luke 11:1–3

I say to you: Ask and it will be given to you. Luke 11:9

I heard a woman say that she never prayed more than once for anything. She didn't want to weary God with her repeated requests.

The Lord's teaching on prayer in Luke 11 contradicts this notion. He told a parable about a man who went to his friend's house at midnight and asked for some bread to feed his unexpected visitors. At first the friend refused, for he and his family were in bed. Finally, he got up and gave him the bread—not out of friendship but because the caller was so persistent (vv. 5–10).

Jesus used this parable to contrast this reluctant friend with our generous heavenly Father. If an irritated neighbor will give in to his friend's persistence and grant his request, how much more readily will our heavenly Father give us all we need!

It's true that God, in His great wisdom, may sometimes delay His answers to prayer. It's also true that we must pray in harmony with the Scriptures and God's will. But Jesus moved beyond those facts to urge us to persist in prayer. He told us to ask, seek, and knock until the answer comes (v. 9).

So don't worry about wearying God. He will never tire of your persistent prayer!

Joanie Yoder

God never tires of our asking.

"I'm a Church"

Read 2 Corinthians 6:14–18

We are the temple of the living God. *2 Corinthians 6:16*

When Johnny was saved at a young age, his mother explained that now his body was actually a temple where Jesus lived. She said it was therefore important how he used and cared for it.

One day at Johnny's school, the teacher was called out of the room—and bedlam broke loose. Rubber-band fights. Paper wad wars. Spitball attacks.

When the teacher returned, she looked in through the door and noticed that Johnny was the only one sitting quietly at his desk. When order was finally restored, she called him up front. "I'm proud of you, Johnny," she said, "and I was glad to see that you behaved yourself. I was wondering why you were not acting like the rest of the children?" Remembering what his mother had told him about being a temple where Jesus lived, he replied, "I behaved myself because I'm a church!" The practical aspects of what his mother had taught him could plainly be seen. Because of his consciousness of who was dwelling within, it made all the difference in the world what he did.

A day-by-day realization of the indwelling presence of the Holy Spirit should make a significant change in the life of a believer. When we are tempted to use our bodies wrongfully, we should remember Johnny's words, "I'm a church!"

Because our body is the temple of the living God, let's make sure it is used only for the praise and glory of His name.

Richard DeHaan

The only sermon that never wearies us is that of an eloquent life!

When It's Hard to Pray

Read Romans 8:26–27

Before a word is on my tongue, you, LORD,
know it completely. *Psalm 139:4*

The Bible tells us that God knows our every thought and every word on our tongue (Psalm 139:1–4). And when we don't know what to pray for, the Holy Spirit "intercedes for us through wordless groanings" (Romans 8:26).

These biblical truths assure us that we can have communication with God even without a word being spoken, because He knows the intentions and desires of our heart. What a comfort when we are perplexed or in deep distress! We don't have to worry if we can't find the words to express our thoughts and feelings. We don't have to feel embarrassed if sometimes our sentences break off half-finished. God knows what we were going to say. We don't have to feel guilty if our thoughts wander and we have to struggle to keep our minds focused on the Lord.

And for that matter, we don't have to worry about a proper posture in prayer. If we are elderly or arthritic and can't kneel, that's okay. What God cares about is the posture of our heart.

What a wonderful God! No matter how much you falter and stumble in your praying, He hears you. His heart of infinite love responds to the needs and emotions of your own inarticulate heart. So keep on praying!

Vernon Grounds

Prayer does not require eloquence but earnestness.

Tears and Laughter

Read Ezra 3:7–13

No one could distinguish the sound of the shouts of joy
from the sound of weeping. Ezra 3:13

Last year at a retreat I reconnected with some friends I hadn't seen in a long time. I laughed with them as we enjoyed the reunion, but I also cried because I knew how much I had missed them.

On the last day of our time together we celebrated the Lord's Supper. More smiles and tears! I rejoiced over the grace of God, who had given me eternal life and these beautiful days with my friends. But again I cried as I was sobered by what it had cost Jesus to deliver me from my sin.

I thought about Ezra and that wonderful day in Jerusalem. The exiles had returned from captivity and had just completed rebuilding the foundation of the Lord's temple. The people sang for joy, but some of the older priests cried (Ezra 3:10–12). They were likely remembering Solomon's temple and its former glory. Or were they grieving over their sins that had led to the captivity in the first place?

Sometimes when we see God at work we experience a wide range of emotions, including joy when we see God's wonders and sorrow as we remember our sins and the need for His sacrifice.

The Israelites were singing and weeping, the noise was heard far away (v. 13). May our emotions be expressions of our love and worship to our Lord, and may they touch those around us.

Keila Ochoa

Both tears and smiles bring God praise.

Daddy!

Read 2 Kings 19:10–19

Give ear, LORD, and hear;
open your eyes, LORD, and see. *2 Kings 19:16*

Twenty-month-old James was leading his family confidently through the hallways of their large church. His daddy kept an eye on him the whole time as James toddled his way through the crowd of "giants." Suddenly the little boy panicked because he could not see his dad. He stopped, looked around, and started to cry, "Daddy, Daddy!" His dad quickly caught up with him, and little James reached up his hand, which Daddy strongly clasped. Immediately James was at peace.

Second Kings tells the story of King Hezekiah, who reached up to God for help (19:15). Sennacherib, the king of Assyria, had made threats against Hezekiah and the people of Judah, saying, "Do not let the god you depend on deceive you. . . . You have heard what the kings of Assyria have done to all the countries, destroying them completely. And will you be delivered?" (vv. 10–11). King Hezekiah went to the Lord and prayed for deliverance so "that all the kingdoms of the earth may know that you alone, LORD, are God" (vv.14–19). In answer to his prayer, the angel of the Lord struck down the enemy, and Sennacherib withdrew (vv. 20–36).

If you're in a situation where you need God's help, reach up your hand to Him in prayer. He has promised His comfort and help (2 Corinthians 1:3–4; Hebrews 4:16).

Anne Cetas

God's dawn of deliverance often comes
when the hour of trial is darkest.

Love and Prayer

Read Psalm 92

They will still bear fruit in old age;
they will stay fresh and green. *Psalm 92:14*

In a popular children's book, Winnie the Pooh watches Kanga bound away. *I wish I could jump like that,* he thinks. *Some can and some can't. That's how it is.*

We see younger or more able men and women doing extraordinary things that we cannot do. They can; we can't. That's how it is. It's easy to feel useless when we can't do the things we were once capable of doing.

It's true that we may not be able to "jump" like we once did, but we can love and we can pray. These are the works that time and experience have prepared us to do well.

Love is the very best gift we have to give to God and to others. It is no small matter, for love is the means by which we fulfill our whole duty to God and our neighbor. Our love for one person may seem to be a small action, but love is the greatest gift of all (1 Corinthians 13:13).

And we can pray. Paul encouraged the Colossians to "devote yourselves prayer, being watchful and thankful" (Colossians 4:2). Our prayers are a powerful force in the universe!

Love and prayer are mighty works indeed, the mightiest works for any of us. Why? Because our God, who wants to use us, is an all-loving and all-powerful God.

David Roper

God pours His love into our hearts
that it might flow out to others.

The Value of Waiting

Read Luke 2:22–38

Blessed are all who wait for him! *Isaiah 30:18*

Autumn is hunting season in Michigan. For a few weeks every year, licensed hunters are allowed to go out into the woods and hunt for various species of wildlife. Some hunters build elaborate tree stands high above the ground where they sit quietly for hours waiting for a deer to wander within rifle range.

When I think of hunters who are so patient when it comes to waiting for deer, I think of how impatient we can be when we have to wait for God. We often equate "wait" with "waste." If we're waiting for something (or someone), we think we are doing nothing, which, in an accomplishment-crazed culture, seems like a waste of time.

But waiting serves many purposes. In particular, it proves our faith. Those whose faith is weak are often the first to give up waiting, while those with the strongest faith are willing to wait indefinitely.

When we read the Christmas story in Luke 2, we learn of two people who proved their faith by their willingness to wait. Simeon and Anna waited long, but their time wasn't wasted; it put them in a place where they could witness the coming of Messiah (vv. 22–38).

Not receiving an immediate answer to prayer is no reason to give up faith.

Julie Ackerman Link

Waiting for God is never a waste of time.

Let's Sing

Read Psalm 33:1–11

Sing joyfully to the LORD, you righteous; it is fitting
for the upright to praise him.... Sing to him a new song;
play skillfully, and shout for joy. *Psalm 33: 1, 3*

Singing has always played a vital role in the worship of God. The psalms were sung in the temple, often in the form of beautiful antiphons; that is, responses between a soloist and the choir, then between the choir and the worshipers. Jesus and His disciples sang a hymn after He had instituted the Lord's supper (Matthew 26:30). Paul encouraged believers to address one another with "psalms, hymns, and songs from the Spirit" (Ephesians 5:19).

Why should God's people sing? Is it only to prepare worshipers for the sermon? To say this would imply that singing is just a gimmick. Paul would have frowned upon such an idea because he was convinced that the gospel alone, truthfully proclaimed, is "the power of God that brings salvation" (Romans 1:16). We sing because it is an effective way to express our adoration, our supplication, or our testimony. Through song we praise our God and edify one another.

The writer of Psalm 33 called upon the worshiping Israelites to sing praise to God for His powerful word, His unfailing counsels, and His continual concern for His people.

Let's honor our Lord by joining enthusiastically with others in praising Him through song. Or when we are all alone and our heart is full, let's sing! The Lord is pleased with any melody of praise that comes from the heart.

Herb Vander Lugt

Singing to the Lord is like riding an elevator—you get a real lift.

When We're Weary

Read Galatians 6:1–10

Let us not become weary in doing good. *Galatians 6:9*

Sometimes trying to do the right thing can be exhausting. We may wonder, *Do my well-intentioned words and actions make any difference at all?* I wondered this recently when I sent a prayerfully thought-out email meant to encourage a friend, only to have it met with an angry response. My immediate reaction was a mixture of hurt and anger. How could I be so misunderstood?

Before I responded out of anger, I remembered that we won't always see the results (or the results we desire) when we tell someone about how Jesus loves them. When we do good things for others hoping to draw them to Him, they may spurn us. Our gentle efforts to prompt someone to right action may be ignored.

Galatians 6 is a good place to turn when we're discouraged by someone's response to our sincere efforts. Here the apostle Paul encourages us to consider our motives—to "test our actions"—for what we say and do (vv. 1–4). When we have done so, he encourages us to persevere: "Let us not become weary in doing good, for at the proper time we will reap a harvest if we do not give up. Therefore, as we have opportunity, let us do good to all people" (vv. 9–10).

God wants us to continue living for Him, which includes praying for and telling others about Him—"doing good." He will see to the results.

Alyson Kieda

We can leave the results of our lives in God's hands.

The Daily Prayer

Read Ephesians 6:18–19

Pray in the Spirit on all occasions with all kinds
of prayers and requests. *Ephesians 6:18*

Singer/songwriter Robert Hamlet wrote "Lady Who Prays for Me" as a tribute to his mother, who made a point of praying for her boys each morning before they went to the bus stop. After a young mom heard Hamlet sing his song, she committed to praying with her own little boy. The result was heartwarming! Just before her son went out the door, his mother prayed for him. Five minutes later he returned—bringing kids from the bus stop with him! His mom asked what was going on. The boy responded, "Their moms didn't pray with them."

In the book of Ephesians, Paul urges us to pray "on all occasions with all kinds of prayers" (6:18). Demonstrating our daily dependence on God is essential in a family since many children first learn to trust God as they observe genuine faith in the people closest to them (2 Timothy 1:5). There is no better way to teach the utmost importance of prayer than by praying for and with our children. It is one of the ways they begin to sense a compelling need to reach out personally to God in faith.

When we "start children off" by modeling a "sincere faith" in God (Proverbs 22:6; 2 Timothy 1:5), we give them a special gift, an assurance that God is an ever-present part of our lives—continually loving, guiding, and protecting us.

Cindy Hess Kasper

Daily prayers lessen daily worries.

Sledding and Prayer

Read Mark 14:32–42

*One of those days Jesus went out to a mountainside to pray,
and spent the night praying to God. Luke 6:12*

When the snow flies in Michigan, I like to get my grandkids, grab our plastic sleds, and go slipping and sliding down our backyard. We zoom down the hill for about ten seconds, and then climb back up for more.

When I travel to Alaska with a bunch of teenagers, we also go sledding. We are hauled by bus nearly to the top of a mountain. We jump on our sleds and, for the next ten to twenty minutes (depending on levels of bravery), we slide at breakneck speeds down the mountain, holding on for dear life.

Ten seconds in my backyard or ten minutes down an Alaskan mountain. They're both called sledding, but there is clearly a difference.

I've been thinking about this in regard to prayer. Sometimes we do the "ten seconds in the backyard" kind of praying—a quick, spur-of-the-moment prayer or a short thanks before eating. At other times, we're drawn to "down the mountain" praying—extended, intense times that require concentration and passion in our relationship with Him. Both have their place and are vital to our lives.

Jesus prayed often, and sometimes for a long time (Luke 6:12; Mark 14:32–42). Either way, let us bring the desires of our heart to the God of the backyards and the mountains of our lives.

Dave Branon

The heart of prayer is prayer from the heart.

Chameleon Crawl

Read Acts 2:42–47

Every day they continued to meet together. Acts 2:46

When we think of the chameleon, we probably think of its ability to change color according to its surroundings. But this lizard has another interesting characteristic. On several occasions I've watched a chameleon walk along a pathway and wondered how it ever reached its destination. Reluctantly, the chameleon stretches out one leg, seems to change its mind, attempts again, and then carefully plants a hesitant foot, as if afraid the ground will collapse under it. That was why I couldn't help laughing when I heard someone say, "Do not be a chameleon church member who says, 'Let me go to church today; no, let me go next week; no, let me wait for a while!'"

"The house of the Lord" at Jerusalem was King David's place of worship, and he was far from being a "chameleon" worshiper. Rather, he rejoiced with those who said, "Let us go to the house of the Lord" (Psalm 122:1). The same was true for believers in the early church. "They devoted themselves to the apostles' teaching and to fellowship, to the breaking of bread and to prayer. . . . Every day they continued to meet together in the temple courts" (Acts 2:42, 46).

What a joy it is to join with others in worship and fellowship! Praying and worshiping together, studying the Scriptures together, and caring for one another are essential for our spiritual growth and unity as believers.

Lawrence Darmani

Worshiping together brings strength and joy.

Worrier or Warrior?

Read Ephesians 3:14–21

[God] is able to do immeasurably more
than all we ask or imagine. *Ephesians 3:20*

A missionary wrote a newsletter to thank his supporters for being "prayer warriors." Because of a typing error, though, he called them "prayer worriers." For some of us, that might be a good description.

In his book *Growing Your Soul*, Neil Wiseman writes, "Prayer must be more than a kind of restatement of fretting worries or a mulling over of problems. Our petitions must move beyond gloomy desperation, which deals mostly with calamity and despair."

During an anxious time in my life, I became a "prayer worrier." I would beg, "Lord, please keep my neighbor from causing me problems tomorrow." Or, "Father, don't let that ornery person spread gossip about me."

But then the Lord taught me to pray for people, rather than against them. I began to say, "Lord, bless and encourage my neighbor, and help him to sense your love." Then I watched to see what God would do. The Lord's amazing answers not only helped others but also helped to cure my own anxiety!

Paul was no "prayer worrier." He prayed for God's people that they might know the strength, love, and fullness of God, who is able to do far more than we can ask or even think (Ephesians 3:14–21). Such confidence made Paul a true "prayer warrior." Are our prayers like that?

Joanie Yoder

Fervent prayer dispels anxious care.

Attending to Our Words

Read Psalm 66:10–20

God has surely listened and has heard my prayer. *Psalm 66:19*

A week after C. S. Lewis died in November 1963, colleagues and friends gathered in the chapel of Magdalen College, Oxford, England, to pay tribute to the man whose writings had fanned the flames of faith and imagination in children and scholars alike.

During the memorial service, Lewis's close friend Austin Farrer noted that Lewis always sent a handwritten personal reply to every letter he received from readers all over the world. "His characteristic attitude to people in general was one of consideration and respect," Farrer said. "He paid you the compliment of attending to your words."

In that way, Lewis mirrored God's remarkable attention to what we say to Him in prayer. During a time of great difficulty, the writer of Psalm 66 cried out to God (vv. 10–14). Later, he praised the Lord for His help, saying, "God has surely listened and has heard my prayer" (v. 19).

When we pray, the Lord hears our words and knows our hearts. Truly we can say with the psalmist, "Blessed be God, who has not turned away my prayer, nor His mercy from me!" (v. 20 NKJV). Our prayers become the avenue to a deeper relationship with Him. At all times, even in our hours of deepest need, He attends to our words.

David McCasland

We always have God's attention.

"Lord, Teach Us to Pray"

Read Matthew 6:1–13

"Lord, teach us to pray, just as John taught his disciples." Luke 11:1

Personal prayer is a personal thing; it is the most intimate exercise of communion between the Father and His children. Prayer is more than repeating words and phrases. You may say, "I don't know how to pray!" Then why don't you follow the example of the disciples and go to Jesus and ask Him, "Lord, teach me to pray." You can even pray without using words. Mother used to say, "Gebed is soms maar en zucht," which translated from the Dutch language is: "Prayer can sometimes be only a sigh!" A baby can't tell in words when it is hungry, but it can cry, and mother understands. You too may find it difficult to utter a formal prayer, but you can cry, "O Lord, I'm hungry!"

Prayer cannot be measured by the length of time spent in audible petition. When a person feels a definite, urgent need, it won't take him long to express it. The publican's prayer in the temple took just three seconds (Luke 18:13). Peter's prayer when he was sinking took just two seconds. He didn't have time for a longer one. When we are really in earnest, we will have no trouble praying. God pity the man or woman who has not learned to "talk to the Father," but needs to be taught a little speech to recite to the Lord.

Why not start right now and ask God to teach you to pray? He is your best Teacher.

Henry Bosch

If you want something bad enough,
you won't find it hard to ask for it in prayer.

Thanks Living

Read Psalm 23

*Surely your goodness and love will follow me
all the days of my life. Psalm 23:6*

Wanting to mature in her spiritual life and become more thankful, Sue started what she called a Thanks-Living jar. Each evening she wrote on a small piece of paper one thing she thanked God for and dropped it in the jar. Some days she had many praises; other difficult days she struggled to find one. At the end of the year she emptied her jar and read through all of the notes. She found herself thanking God again for everything He had done. He had given simple things like a beautiful sunset or a cool evening for a walk in the park, and other times He had provided grace to handle a difficult situation or had answered a prayer.

Sue's discovery reminded me of what the psalmist David says he experienced (Psalm 23). God refreshed him with "green pastures" and "quiet waters" (vv. 2–3). He gave him guidance, protection, and comfort (vv. 3–4). David concluded: "Surely your goodness and love will follow me all the days of my life" (v. 6).

I decided to make a Thanks-Living jar. Maybe you'd like to as well. I think we'll see we have many reasons to thank God— including His gifts of friends and family and His provisions for our physical, spiritual, and emotional needs. We'll see that the goodness and love of God follows us all the days of our lives.

Anne Cetas

When you think of all that's good, give thanks to God.

Prayerful Thinking

Read Psalm 8

What is man that You are mindful of him? Psalm 8:4 *(NKJV)*

Augustine was one of the most brilliant Christian thinkers of all time. Interestingly, he did some of his most effective and intimate praying while engaged in deep thought. He was what might be called a "prayerful thinker." Often Augustine began a line of reasoning, then concluded it with a prayer. Here is a sample from Confessions, one of his works on theology:

"Too late came I to love You, O Beauty both ancient and ever new; too late came I to love You. . . . You called to me; yes, You even broke open my deafness. Your beams shined unto me and cast away my blindness."

These are not the dry musings of some pseudo-theologian or armchair philosopher. They are the thoughts of someone with a passionate prayer life.

Prayerful thinking is not unique to Augustine. David pondered the beauty of creation and felt compelled to worship his Creator: "When I consider Your heavens, the work of Your fingers, the moon and the stars, which You have ordained, what is man that You are mindful of him?" (Psalm 8:3–4 NKJV).

As we walk life's journey, our deep thoughts and feelings and our praying can be interwoven. Seeing the beauty of nature, or even solving a problem, can be opportunities for prayerful thinking.

Dennis Fisher

Prayerful thinking leads to purposeful thanking.

Open at the Top

Read Hebrews 4:14–16

We have a great high priest who has ascended into heaven, Jesus the Son of God. Hebrews 4:14

A preacher was delivering a sermon before a large congregation. He pointed out that believers aren't exempt from trouble. In fact, some Christians are surrounded by trouble—trouble to the right, trouble to the left, trouble in front, and trouble behind. At this, a man who had served the Lord for many years, shouted, "Glory to God, it's always open at the top!"

This man's confidence in God is fully supported by Hebrews 4. Because our great High Priest, Jesus the Son of God, has ascended to heaven and is interceding there for us, we have good grounds for trusting Him in the midst of trouble (v. 14). Jesus is able to sympathize with our weaknesses, for when He lived on earth He was tempted in every way that we are, yet He never sinned (v. 15). His throne is completely approachable and is called "God's throne of grace" (v. 16).

In Hebrews we're urged to look up from our trials and to approach that throne boldly by faith. Through humble prayer, we will receive mercy for our failures and grace to help us in our time of need (v. 16).

Are life's trials and temptations hemming you in? Has the tempter told you there's nowhere to go? Take heart. Keep looking up—it's always open at the top!

Joanie Yoder

To improve your outlook, try the uplook.

Pressuring God

Read Matthew 26:36–36

My Father, if it is not possible for this cup to be taken away unless I drink it, may your will be done. Matthew 26:46

Under General George Patton's command in World War II, the Third Army had been driving back the Nazis until fog and rain forced the troops to stop. Patton telephoned a chaplain to ask, "Do you have a good prayer for weather?" Immediately the chaplain complied with the general's request. He wrote a prayer, which Patton ordered to be printed and distributed to the 250,000 soldiers under his command, directing them to pray for clear weather.

The Scriptures teach us that God wants us to bring our requests to Him, and we can be confident that He cares and will answer (Philippians 4:6; 1 John 5:14–15). But He is never obligated to answer in the way we want or just because many people are praying.

When the Son of God was agonizing in Gethsemane, He made His request in humble submission to His Father by saying, "Your will be done" (Matthew 26:42). That Gethsemane principle ought to govern all our praying.

The Father's will is always infused with infinite love and wisdom. So instead of trying to pressure God because we think He's obligated to us, we as trustful children gladly commit to Him our desires. Whatever He grants will prove in the end to be the best of blessings.

Vernon Grounds

Instead of trying to twist God's arm, put yourself in His hands.

Still Say, "Hallelujah!"

Read Psalm 34:1–10, 19

I will bless the Lord at all times;
his praise shall continually be in my mouth. *Psalm 34:1 (KJV)*

A missionary named Mary D. Kimbrough told the following story about her family during America's Great Depression in the 1930s. Winter was upon them and her family was in great distress. Mary's father, who had been employed in a local bakery, was injured and was unable to work. Their money was soon gone and their large flour bin empty.

Mary's devout mother never lost faith, however, that God would supply their needs. She had determined with the Psalmist to "bless the LORD at all times," (Psalm 34:1 KJV), so she said, "How many of you still have faith to say 'hallelujah' even though we have an empty flour bin?" Without exception, each of the family members praised the Lord and said, "Hallelujah!"

A few minutes later the phone rang. It was the baker calling, "A batch of bread was burned. Could you folks use some?" "Could we!" Mary and her two little sisters were dancing about with joy when the bread man arrived and began piling golden brown loaves of bread, buns, and cookies on their kitchen table. Recalling the scene, Mary said, "They weren't burned—just a bit too brown to sell—but they were delicious to our family who had fully trusted God for our daily bread."

Henry Bosch

To trust God is to praise Him.

Creation: NT Style

Read Ephesians 1:3–6

He chose us in him before the creation of the world. Ephesians 1:4

When we think about the marvel of creation—how God spoke the universe into existence and formed the earth and everything in it—we think most often of Old Testament accounts.

But it is encouraging to examine the New Testament to see how that part of the Bible refers to creation. Here is a look at some key passages:

"I will utter things hidden since the creation of the world" (Matthew 13:35). God reveals things to us that He had kept secret since before He spoke the universe into existence.

"Come, you who are blessed by my Father; take your inheritance, the kingdom prepared for you since the creation of the world" (Matthew 25:34). Before the earth was created, God knew each of us—and He knew our future.

"He chose us in him before the creation of the world" (Ephesians 1:4). Before the work of creation even began, God was aware of each of His eventual children.

These New Testament verses comfort us with the truth that God's knowledge of us and His eternal mysteries about us point toward His special creation of mankind as described in Genesis. We can do nothing but bow in awe before One whose knowledge and creative ability are eternal in nature and boundless in power. Creation: New Testament style—still another reason to give God praise!

Dave Branon

Each person is a unique expression of God's loving design.

The Answer Is on the Way

Read Isaiah 65:18–24

Before they call I will answer;
while they are still speaking I will hear. *Isaiah 65:24*

A widow, her young son, and her disabled daughter moved to a poor part of London. They had formerly lived in comfort, but because of the death of the woman's husband they had to move. While living in London, the lady and her son went to a gospel meeting, and they received the Savior. Friends in the church would have gladly helped them financially, but the family did not make their needs known.

The day came when their resources were exhausted, and their meager income would stretch no further. That evening, while the mother and her son knelt in prayer beside the bed of the girl, this dear woman committed her need to God. The very next morning the mailman delivered a letter. In the envelope was the equivalent of a week's wages. It had come from New Zealand and was sent by a total stranger. The benefactor had heard of the husband's death and had been moved to help the woman and her children. The letter went first to the village where they had lived, then it finally reached London. Five months after leaving New Zealand, it arrived the morning after the family prayer.

Although God is fully aware of our need, He still delights to hear our voice. His answer often predates our call and is on the way before our prayer ascends.

Paul Van Gorder

The same God who prompts the asking provides the answer.

Heart Music

Read Psalm 98

*Let the message of Christ dwell among you richly
as you teach and admonish one another with all wisdom
through psalms, hymns, and songs from the Spirit,
singing to God with gratitude in your hearts.* Colossians 3:16

Scripture encourages us to sing. Whether we sing hymns of worship or praise songs, singing should emanate from our hearts. Here are a couple of questions to ask yourself the next time you have an opportunity to sing along with your fellow believers at church: Do I really mean what I'm singing? Is this coming from my heart? Am I going through the motions?

Sometimes we sing "Tis the Blessed Hour of Prayer" and then allow our thoughts to wander aimlessly while others talk to God. We mouth the words to, "For the Beauty of the Earth" and then litter it with garbage and debris. We raise our voices to ask, "Is It the Crowning Day?" and then live as though we had never heard of our Savior's return. We love the hymn "Holy Bible, Book Divine" but spend most of our time reading anything but God's Word. We sing, "It Is Well with My Soul" and worry about every little thing that happens!

This is not singing from our hearts. Someone has observed that "when the heart moves devoutly with the voice, true heart-singing results." I would add that it is whenever "the heart and hand move devoutly with the voice." The sincerity of our devotion is demonstrated by what we sing and do. When our songs are matched by our deeds—this is heart music!

Richard DeHaan

A song coupled with service
will usually outlive a sermon in the memory.

Make a Joyful Shout

Read Psalm 100

Shout for joy to the LORD, all the earth. *Psalm 100:1*

Duke University's basketball fans are known as "Cameron Crazies." When Duke plays archrival North Carolina, the Crazies are given these instructions: "This is the game you've been waiting for. No excuses. Give everything you've got. Cameron [Indoor Stadium] should never be less than painfully loud tonight." Clearly, Duke fans take allegiance seriously.

The songwriter of Psalm 100 took his allegiance to the Lord seriously and wanted others to do the same. "Make a joyful shout to the Lord!" he exclaimed (v. 1 NKJV). His people were to freely express their praise to Him because He was the covenant God of Israel, the God over all other so-called gods. They were called to focus all their energies on Him and His goodness.

God's goodness and grace should motivate us to freely express our love and allegiance to Him with shouts of joy. This may mean that those who are more reserved must push back the boundaries of restraint and learn what it means to be expressive in their praise to God. Those who are so expressive that they miss the beauty of silence may need to learn from those whose style is more reflective.

Worship is a time to focus on our Creator, Redeemer, and Shepherd, and celebrate what He has done.

Marvin Williams

Our thoughts about God should lead us to joyful praise.

Prayers God Cannot Answer

Read Matthew 20:20–28

Who can count the dust of Jacob
or number even a fourth of Israel? *Numbers 23:10*

Perhaps you've heard the story of the little girl who rushed home from her geography examination, looked at the map, and then dropped to her knees. Earnestly she prayed, "Dear God, please make Boston the capital of Vermont!" Now, I don't think the Lord was offended by that childish appeal. But I know He didn't do what she asked. Boston is not in Vermont, and never was. Her test answer was wrong because she hadn't been prepared, and the Lord couldn't conspire with her to make it right—any more than He could make 2 times 2 equal 5.

In Numbers 23, we read that Balaam asked the Lord to let him die like righteous people and go to the same place they go. But the prophet remained unrepentant, and to grant his request would have violated God's integrity. It would be like answering the prayer of someone who asks for success in a dishonest business deal. We see a similar problem in today's Scripture. If Jesus had made James and John His No. 1 and No. 2 men in the kingdom, as their mother had asked, He would have been showing partiality. And this He cannot do.

God never violates His holy character in answering our prayers. Omnipotence does not include the power to do wrong. Therefore, let's come to Him with pure motives and an earnest desire to obey Him. This will keep us from making requests that He cannot answer.

Herb Vander Lugt

When praying, don't give God instructions—report for duty!

Praying Friends

Read 1 Thessalonians 3:6–13

Brethren, pray for us. *1 Thessalonians 5:2 (NKJV)*

I met my friend Angie for lunch after having not seen her for several months. At the end of our time together, she pulled out a piece of paper with notes from our previous get-together. It was a list of my prayer requests she had been praying for since then. She went through each one and asked if God had answered yet or if there were any updates. And then we talked about her prayer requests. How encouraging to have a praying friend!

The apostle Paul had a praying relationship with the churches he served, including the one at Thessalonica. He thanked God for the faith, love, and hope of the people (1 Thessalonians 1:2–3). He longed to see them, and he asked God "night and day" that he might be able to visit them again (3:10–11). He requested that the Lord would help them "increase and abound in love to one another and to all" (v. 12 NKJV). He also prayed that their hearts would be blameless before God (v. 13). They must have been encouraged as they read about Paul's concern and prayers for them. Paul knew too his own need for God's presence and power and pleaded, "Brothers and sisters, pray for us" (5:25).

Loving Father, thank you for wanting us to talk with you. Teach us all to be praying friends.

Anne Cetas

The best kind of friend is a praying friend.

Thanks for Being You

Read Psalm 100

Enter his gates with thanksgiving. Psalm 100:4

When I served as my mom's live-in caregiver at a cancer center, I got to know Lori, another caregiver who lived down the hallway from us with her husband, Frank. I would chat, laugh, vent, cry, and pray with Lori in the shared living areas. We enjoyed supporting each other as we cared for our loved ones.

One day, I missed the free shuttle that took residents to buy groceries. Lori offered to drive me to the store later that evening. With grateful tears, I accepted her offer. "Thanks for being you," I said. I truly appreciated her for who she was as a person, not just for what she did for me as a friend.

Psalm 100 demonstrates an appreciation of God for who He is, not simply for all He does. The psalmist invites "all the earth" (v. 1) to "worship the Lord with gladness" (v. 2), being confident in knowing "the Lord is God" (v. 3). Our Maker invites us into His presence to "give thanks to him and praise his name" (v. 4). Yes, the Lord remains worthy of our ongoing thankfulness because He "is good," His "love endures forever," and His "faithfulness continues through all generations" (v. 5).

God will always be the Creator and Sustainer of the universe and our intimately loving Father. He deserves our genuine joy-filled gratitude.

Xochitl Dixon

Who can you share God's love with today?

The Mighty Power of Prayer

Read James 5:11–18

*Elijah was a human being, even as we are. He prayed
earnestly that it would not rain, and it did not rain
on the land for three and a half years. James 5:17*

A friend once gave me this commentary on prayer: "Prayer is the mightiest power upon which men can lay hold in time of need. Moses prayed and Amalek was beaten. Hannah prayed and Samuel was born some months later in answer to her petition. Hezekiah prayed and the angel of the Lord slew 185,000 of the enemies of Israel. Daniel prayed and the mouths of ferocious, hungry lions were stopped. Elijah prayed and a great drought followed. The early church assembled together and prayed and Peter was released from his jail cell by an angel. Paul and Silas prayed and the doors of the dungeon where they were imprisoned were shaken open.

"Prayer has divided seas, has stemmed the tide of flowing rivers has put to naught the power of fire, has made harmless the deadly venom of serpents, and stopped the course of the sun and moon. Through it God's children have overcome demons and the most dreaded of foes. Prayer has quelled the wild powers of evil men, and whole armies of proud, boasting unbelievers have been put to flight. What hath not prayer wrought?"

Seeing the mighty power that is displayed when God bares His arm on behalf of His beseeching and needy children, one is impelled to cry with the disciples of old "Lord, teach us to pray!"

Henry Bosch

Elijah was a man of like passions as we are, but alas,
we are not men of like prayer as he was!

Crying Out to God

Read Psalm 142

By prayer and petition . . .
present your requests to God. *Philippians 4:6*

After all these years, I still don't fully understand prayer. It's something of a mystery to me. But one thing I know: When we're in desperate need, prayer springs naturally from our lips and from the deepest level of our hearts.

When we're frightened out of our wits, when we're pushed beyond our limits, when we're pulled out of our comfort zones, when our well-being is challenged and endangered, we reflexively and involuntarily resort to prayer. "Help, Lord!" is our natural cry.

Author Eugene Peterson wrote: "The language of prayer is forged in the crucible of trouble. When we can't help ourselves and call for help, when we don't like where we are and want out, when we don't like who we are and want a change, we use primal language, and this language becomes the root language of prayer."

Prayer begins in trouble, and it continues because we're always in trouble at some level. It requires no special preparation, no precise vocabulary, no appropriate posture. It springs from us in the face of necessity and, in time, becomes our habitual response to every issue—good and bad—we face in this life (Philippians 4:6). What a privilege it is to carry everything to God in prayer!

David Roper

God's help is only a prayer away.

The Sensuous Christian

Read Exodus 37:1–9

Every good and perfect gift is from above. James 1:17

The gratification of our senses has gotten a bad reputation, perhaps because we live in a world obsessed with pleasure. But God approves of the proper experience of pleasure through our five senses.

First, God created our senses—sight, hearing, smell, taste, touch—and all that He created is good.

Second, God made sensuousness a part of worship. Consider God's first formal worship setting: the tabernacle. It housed an ornate, gold-covered ark to hold the stone tablets God gave to Moses on Mount Sinai. *God approves of beauty.* The tabernacle had an altar of incense where priests burned a blend of fragrant spices made by a perfumer. *God approves of pleasant aromas.* It had an elaborate table with plates and pitchers. *God approves of a tasteful dining experience.* Around the tabernacle were curtains made from colorful yarn and finely twisted linen. *God approves of beautiful colors and textures.* Music was also a component of worship, as we learn from reading 2 Chronicles 29:28. *God approves of pleasing sounds.*

Yes, God values things that look, sound, smell, taste, and feel good. But He doesn't want us to worship them; He wants our enjoyment and gratitude to prompt us to worship Him, the Creator and giver of all good things.

Julie Ackerman Link

It makes sense to use our senses to glorify God.

Limited or Advantageous?

Read 2 Corinthians 12:1-10

He said to me, "My grace is sufficient for you,
for my power is made perfect in weakness." 2 Corinthians 12:9

We've been taught that when we ask God for something through prayer, His answer may be yes, no, or wait. We're told that even no is an answer, though obviously not the one we may want. It certainly wasn't the answer Paul wanted when he begged God three times to remove what he called his "thorn in my flesh" (2 Corinthians 12:7–8).

Whatever Paul's thorn was, it weakened him. Because he wanted to be strong in his ministry, Paul asked God for deliverance. Although God didn't grant his request, He answered his prayer! He said to Paul, "My grace is sufficient for you, for my power is made perfect in weakness" (v. 9). The all-sufficient strength of Christ became Paul's new boast.

Author J. Oswald Sanders summarized Paul's attitude about his thorn like this: "At first he viewed it as a limiting handicap, but later he came to regard it as a heavenly advantage." Paul could therefore testify, "I delight in weaknesses, in insults, in hardships, in persecutions, in difficulties. For when I am weak, then I am strong" (v. 10).

Have you prayed for deliverance from something that weakens you, but deliverance hasn't come? Remember, God's grace is sufficient for you. He can transform your limitation into your "heavenly advantage."

Joanie Yoder

Our weakness is a blessing when we lean on God's strength.

Walking with God

Read Daniel 6:1–10

*Three times a day [Daniel] got down on
his knees and prayed. Daniel 6:10*

Have you ever stopped to wonder what it would be like to go through life without giving God a thought? I'm sure we all know people who get up in the morning, go to work or school, come home in the afternoon, and spend their evening without even once thinking about their creator. That is sad.

Let this reality be a reminder to us who are children of God through faith in the Lord Jesus Christ that we can experience a deep, settled peace as we enjoy daily communion with Him. From our first waking moment in the morning to our last conscious breath at night, we can find blessed comfort and assurance as we walk and talk with God. Someone has summarized these thoughts as follows:

BEGIN THE DAY WITH GOD. Kneel down to Him in prayer; lift up your heart to Him. And seek His love to share.

OPEN THE BOOK OF GOD. Read a portion there, that it may clarify all your thoughts and sweeten all your care.

GO THROUGH THE DAY WITH GOD. Even though you may not see Him, wherever you are He is near.

CONVERSE IN YOUR MIND WITH GOD. Raise your spirit heavenward; acknowledge every good He provides, and offer grateful praise.

CONCLUDE YOUR DAY WITH GOD. Confess your sins to Him; trust in the Lord's atoning blood, and plead His righteousness.

Richard DeHaan

The Christian on his knees sees more
than the philosopher on tiptoe.

In Partnership with God

Read Matthew 6:5–15

Your Father knows what you need before you ask him. *Matthew 6:8*

A man had transformed an overgrown plot of ground into a beautiful garden and was showing a friend what he had accomplished. Pointing to a bed of flowers, he said, "Look at what I did here." His companion corrected him, "You mean, 'Look at what God and I did here.'" The gardener replied, "I guess you're right. But you should have seen the shape this plot was in when He was taking care of it by himself."

We chuckle at the man's reply, but it expresses a wonderful spiritual truth—we are coworkers with God. This applies to every area of life, including prayer. It answers a question that naturally comes to mind when we reflect on Jesus's statements in Matthew 6. He said we don't need to pray on and on with vain repetitions like the pagans, because our Father knows what we need before we ask (Matthew 6:7–8).

The question is, then, why pray? The answer is simple and comforting. God has graciously chosen to give us the privilege of being His partners in both the physical and spiritual areas of life. Through prayer we work with Him in defeating the powers of evil and in bringing about the fulfillment of His loving purposes in the world. Partners with God—what a privilege! What an incentive to pray!

Herb Vander Lugt

God's work is done by those who pray.

One Mysterious God

Read Isaiah 46:1–11

I am God, and there is no other. *Isaiah 46:9*

My wife and I don't always understand each other. For instance, it's a great mystery to her how I can watch an entire baseball game between two teams that have no chance of making the playoffs. And I surely don't understand her love of shopping.

To love someone intensely doesn't mean you have to understand him or her completely. That's good news, because there's no way we can begin to grasp the deep mysteries of the God we love.

With our finite minds and our self-centered views, we can't deduce why God does what He does. Yet some people look at tragedies, for instance, and turn their backs on God—assuming that their finite knowledge about the situation is better than His infinite wisdom.

Indeed, if we could figure God out—if He were no more than a glorified human with no greater knowledge than that of the smartest person—where would be the awe and the majesty of the Almighty? One reason we know God to be so great is that we cannot reduce His thinking to ours.

The apostle Paul asked, "Who has known the mind of the Lord so as to instruct him?" (1 Corinthians 2:16). Clearly, the answer is no one. Praise God that even when we don't understand Him, we know we can trust Him.

Dave Branon

To fully understand God is impossible;
to worship Him is imperative.

When Do You Pray?

Read Genesis 32:1–12

We may approach God with freedom and confidence. *Ephesians 3:12*

In Genesis 32 Jacob is headed homeward. Although twenty years have passed, his conscience is still actively accusing him about his treatment of his brother. When he hears that Esau is on the way with 400 men, Jacob is filled with fear. Then he prays!

We hear of Jacob turning to God in prayer only at the beginning and end of that twenty years. Both times he is afraid. Here he is, trembling between the past and the future. How like many of us. An uneasy conscience about the failures of the past and an uncertainty about what lies ahead cause some Christians to be petrified with apprehension.

Jacob's prayer was brief yet impressive. Most assuredly he did the right thing in the time of trouble—he turned to God. As he speaks, four things are evident in his petition: a recognition of the covenant-keeping God (v. 9); a confession of personal unworthiness (v. 10); a plea for deliverance (v. 11); an appeal for blessing based on the promises (v. 12). Each of us should follow the same pattern as we approach the "God of all grace."

When we are trembling between the mistakes of the past and the anticipated troubles of the future, we should take it to the Lord in prayer. He delights to hear our voice lifted in frequent and fervent petition.

Paul Van Gorder

To remind God of His promise is one of the privileges of prayer.
–Tucker

I Am Not Forgotten

Read Psalm 13

We wait in hope for the LORD;
he is our help and our shield. *Psalm 33:20*

Waiting is hard at any time; but when days, weeks, or even months pass and our prayers seem to go unanswered, it's easy to feel God has forgotten us. Perhaps we can struggle through the day with its distractions, but at night it's doubly difficult to deal with our anxious thoughts. Worries loom large, and the dark hours seem endless. Utter weariness makes it look impossible to face the new day.

The psalmist grew weary as he waited (Psalm 13:1). He felt abandoned—as if his enemies were gaining the upper hand (v. 2). When we're waiting for God to resolve a difficult situation or to answer often-repeated prayers, it's easy to get discouraged.

Satan whispers that God has forgotten us, and that things will never change. We may be tempted to give in to despair. Why bother to read the Bible or to pray? Why make the effort to worship with fellow believers in Christ? But we need our spiritual lifelines most when we're waiting. They help to hold us steady in the flow of God's love and to become sensitive to His Spirit.

The psalmist had a remedy. He focused on all that he knew of God's love, reminding himself of past blessings and deliberately praising God, who would not forget him. So can we.

Marion Stroud

God is worth waiting for; His time is always best.

God Had Other Plans

Read 1 Peter 1:1–9

In their hearts humans plan their course,
but the LORD establishes their steps. *Proverbs 16:9*

My friend Linda grew up planning to become a medical missionary. She loves the Lord and wanted to serve Him as a doctor by taking the gospel to sick people in parts of the world where medical care is hard to find. But God had other plans. Linda has indeed become a medical missionary, but not the way she expected.

At age fourteen, Linda developed a chronic health problem that required her to be hospitalized for major surgery several times a year. She survived bacterial meningitis that left her in a coma for two weeks and blind for six months. She once celebrated two birthdays in a row in the hospital—without going home in between. She has had several experiences when she was not expected to live. But yet Linda is the most vibrant, grateful, and cheerful person you will ever meet. She once told me that her mission field, as she hoped and planned, is the hospital. But instead of serving God as a doctor, she serves Him as a patient. No matter how sick she is, the light of the Lord radiates from her.

Linda exemplifies the teaching of the apostle Peter. Despite her trials, she rejoices, and the genuineness of her faith brings "praise, glory and honor" to Jesus Christ (1 Peter 1:6–7).

Julie Ackerman Link

Write your plans in pencil and remember that God has the eraser.

A Christmas Letter

Read John 1:1–14

The Word became flesh and made his dwelling among us. We have seen his glory, the glory of the one and only Son, who came from the Father. John 1:14

Every Christmas, a friend of mine writes a long letter to his wife, reviewing the events of the year and dreaming about the future. He always tells her how much he loves her, and why. He also writes a letter to each of his daughters. His words of love make an unforgettable Christmas present.

We could say that the original Christmas love letter was Jesus, the Word made flesh. John highlights this truth in his gospel: "In the beginning was the Word, and the Word was with God, and the Word was God" (John 1:1). In ancient philosophy, the Greek for "Word," logos, suggested a divine mind or order that unites reality, but John expands the definition to reveal the Word as a person: Jesus, the Son of God who was "with God in the beginning" (v. 2). This Word, the Father's "one and only Son," "became flesh and made his dwelling among us" (v. 14). Through Jesus the Word, God reveals himself perfectly.

Theologians have grappled with this beautiful mystery for centuries. However much we may not understand, we can be certain that Jesus as the Word gives light to our dark world (v. 9). If we believe in Him, we can experience the gift of being God's beloved children (v. 12).

Jesus, God's love letter to us, has come and made His home among us. Now, that's an amazing Christmas gift!

Amy Boucher Pye

Jesus—the greatest Christmas gift of all.

Musings on a Winter's Day

Read Psalm 147

He provides food for the cattle
and for the young ravens when they call. *Psalm 147:9*

One bitterly cold morning I looked out the back window and saw almost twenty feathered friends around our birdfeeder. Some were busily eating seed while others were pecking away at a piece of suet fastened to a tree. When I stepped out the front door, I saw our German Shepherd romping in the snow with two canine friends who come to visit her almost every day. I don't know if dogs can smile, but all three surely looked happy. On my way to the office, I drove past a field where four American bison were lying on the ground, a picture of contentment and comfort. They were obviously well-fed, and like the birds and dogs, they seemed oblivious to the cold.

As I reflected upon all of this, Psalm 147 came to my mind. The inspired writer of this beautiful Hebrew song extols the goodness and greatness of God. After declaring His mercy to Israel, he pictures the Almighty directing those mysterious processes by which rain is provided for the earth. He portrays the grass springing up on the hillsides, and says that beasts of burden, domesticated cattle, and even wild creatures like ravens receive their food from the hand of their Creator. He speaks, and all nature obeys. The psalmist closes with the words, "Praise the LORD." I thought, how wonderful He is! And as I parked my car, I said, "Hallelujah!"

Herb Vander Lugt

Nature is but a name for an effect whose cause is God. —Cowper

We Need Hope

Read Colossians 1:3–14

Blessed is the one who trusts in the LORD,
whose confidence is in him. Jeremiah 17:7

Adam and Eve didn't need hope because they didn't lack anything they needed. And they had every reason to think that life would go on as pleasantly as it started—with every good thing that God had given them to enjoy. But they put it all at risk for the one thing the serpent said that God had withheld: the knowledge of good and evil (Genesis 2:17; 3:5). So when the serpent came with his offer, Eve was quick to indulge, and Adam was quick to follow (3:6). They got what they wanted: knowledge. But they lost what they had: innocence. With the loss of innocence came the need for hope—hope that their guilt and shame could be removed and goodness restored.

Christmas is the season of hope. Children hope for the latest popular toy or game. Families hope that everyone can make it home for the holidays. But the hope that Christmas commemorates is much bigger than our holiday desires. Jesus, the "Desire of All Nations" (Haggai 2:7 NKJV), has come! He has "rescued us from the dominion of darkness," bought our redemption, and forgiven our sins (Colossians 1:13–14). He even made it possible for us to be wise about what is good and innocent about what is evil (Romans 16:19). Christ in us gives us the hope of glory.

Praise God for the hope of Christmas!

Julie Ackerman Link

Hope for the Christian is a certainty—because its basis is Christ.

God's Helpers

Read Psalm 103:19-22

Bless the LORD, you his angels. *Psalm 103:20 (NKJV)*

I was having a conversation with some children about God and super-heroes when Tobias asked a question. An imaginative, curious five-year-old, he asked anyone listening: "Does God have a sidekick like Hercules does?" His wiser, older brother, age seven, quickly responded: "Yes, He has thousands of them—they're His angels."

Angels are a popular topic of discussion, and people believe a number of myths about them. For instance, some people pray to angels, thinking they are on the same level as God himself. And some believe that people become angels when they die. But here's what the Bible, our authority, teaches:

- God created angels (Colossians 1:15–17).
- Angels worship God (Nehemiah 9:6) and are known by these terms: archangels (Jude 1:9), cherubim (2 Kings 19:15), and seraphim (Isaiah 6:1–3).
- They minister to God's people (Hebrews 1:13–14) by guarding and protecting them (Psalm 91:9–12).
- They are given special assignments by God (Matthew 1:20; Luke 1:26).
- God's angels rejoice when we repent of sin and turn to Christ for salvation (Luke 15:7, 10).

Only God deserves our worship. So let's join the angels in singing His praises!

Anne Cetas

Angels are God's special helpers.

Job Opening

Read Romans 12:9–12

Be joyful in hope, . . . faithful in prayer. *Romans 12:12*

Several years ago, a job became available in the church my wife and I attended at the time. Just over a week before Christmas, my mother-in-law, Lenore Tuttle, died at the age of eighty-five. When she went home to be with Jesus, she left a void not only in our family but also in our church. The church had lost one of its most faithful prayer warriors.

At Mother Tuttle's funeral, the presiding pastor showed the congregation her prayer box. It contained dozens of prayer cards on which she had written the names of people she prayed for every day, including one that mentioned that pastor's gall bladder surgery. On top of that prayer box was this verse: "Without faith it is impossible to please God, because anyone who comes to him must believe that he exists and that He rewards those who earnestly seek him" (Hebrews 11:6). She was a true prayer warrior who diligently sought the Lord.

Each day, many older saints, who have continued steadfastly in prayer (Romans 12:12), leave this earth through death and move on to heaven. This creates a "job opening" for people who will commit themselves to praying faithfully. Many of these positions remain unfilled. Will you fill one of them?

Dave Branon

Wanted: Prayer Warriors.

Let Us Adore Him!

Read Luke 2:8–20

The shepherds returned, glorifying and praising God
for all the things they had heard and seen,
which were just as they had been told. Luke 2:20

In his portrayal of the nativity scene, *The Adoration of the Shepherds*, the great Dutch artist Rembrandt (1606–1669) focused attention entirely on the Babe in the manger. He did this by depicting a shaft of light that fell exclusively on the Christ-child. All other figures were shrouded in shadows. Rembrandt wanted the viewer to make Christ the sole object of his adoration.

Luke's gospel gives us a similar picture. We are introduced to various people, but the Savior is the focus of their attention. He alone fills their hearts with praise. The Virgin Mary magnified the Lord because through the coming of the Messiah His mercy is extended to "those who fear him" (Luke 1:46–50). Zachariah the priest blessed God, declaring, "He has come to his people and redeemed them" (Luke 1:68). The shepherds, who were the first to hear the joyful message that the Savior had been born, came and looked upon the baby Jesus, then returned "glorifying and praising God" (Luke 2:20). The devout Simeon, taking the infant into his arms, was zealous in his gratitude and referred to Him as a "light for revelation to the Gentiles, and the glory of . . . Israel" (Luke 2:32).

Let's join in that magnificent chorus of praise that began on that holy night. Come, let us adore Him, proclaiming joyfully with the angelic host, "Glory to God in the highest, and on earth peace, good will toward men" (Luke 2:14 KJV).

Henry Bosch

God's highest Gift awakens man's deepest gratitude.

Someone to Celebrate

Read Matthew 2:1–12

Come, let us bow down in worship,
let us kneel before the LORD our Maker. *Psalm 95:6*

Many manger scenes depict the wise men, or magi, visiting Jesus in Bethlehem at the same time as the shepherds. But according to the gospel of Matthew, the only place in Scripture where their story is found, the magi showed up later. Jesus was no longer in the manger in a stable at the inn, but in a house. Matthew 2:11 tells us, "On coming to the house, they saw the child with his mother Mary, and they bowed down and worshiped him. Then they opened their treasures and presented him with gifts of gold, frankincense and myrrh."

Realizing that the magi's visit happened later than we may think provides a helpful reminder as we begin a new year. Jesus is always worthy of worship. When the holidays are past and we head back to life's everyday routines, we still have Someone to celebrate.

Jesus Christ is Immanuel, "God with us" (Matthew 1:23), in every season. He has promised to be with us "always" (28:20). Because He is always with us, we can worship Him in our hearts every day and trust that He will show himself faithful in the years to come. Just as the magi sought Him, may we seek Him too and worship Him wherever we are.

James Banks

When we find Christ we offer our worship.

Isn't He Beautiful!

Read Isaiah 9:1–7

To us a child is born, to us a son is given. *Isaiah 9:6*

A group of children from our city were in a worship service, and we started to sing. Ariel, age seven, leaned close to me and softly said, "I love this song; it makes me cry."

The music and words about Jesus, her Savior, touched her heart: "Isn't He beautiful? Beautiful, isn't He? Prince of peace, Son of God, isn't He?"

Yes, the Lord Jesus is beautiful. We don't find a specific reference in the Bible describing Him that way, but His personal character is strong yet gentle, holy yet forgiving, majestic yet humble—all combined. Simply beautiful!

In his prophecy, Isaiah described Jesus and His coming in this way: "To us a child is born, to us a son is given; and the government will be on his shoulders. And he will be called Wonderful Counselor, Mighty God, Everlasting Father, Prince of Peace" (Isaiah 9:6).

Jesus is the Wonderful Counselor—giving us comfort and wisdom. The Mighty God—acting with power and authority. The Everlasting Father—providing for all our needs and protecting us. And the Prince of Peace—offering reconciliation with God and others.

Isn't Jesus beautiful! Worship Him.

Anne Cetas

Jesus is the image of the invisible God. Colossians 1:15

Now Is the Time

Read Luke 2:8–20

Glory to God in the highest heaven, and on earth peace to those on whom his favor rests! Luke 2:14

During our church's Christmas celebration, I watched the choir members assemble in front of the congregation while the music director rifled through papers on a slim black stand. The instruments began, and the singers launched into a well-known song that started with these words: "Come, now is the time to worship."

Although I expected to hear a time-honored Christmas carol, I smiled at the appropriate choice of music. Earlier that week I had been reading Luke's account of Jesus's birth, and I noticed that the first Christmas lacked our modern-day parties, gifts, and feasting—but it did include worship.

After the angel announced Jesus's birth to some wide-eyed shepherds, a chorus of angels began "praising God and saying: 'Glory to God in the highest!'" (Luke 2:13–14). The shepherds responded by running to Bethlehem where they found the newborn King lying in a barnyard bassinet. They returned to their fields "glorifying and praising God for all the things they had heard and seen" (v. 20). Coming face to face with the Son inspired the shepherds to worship the Father.

Today, consider your response to Jesus's arrival on earth. Is there room for worship in your heart on this day that celebrates His birth?

Jennifer Benson Schuldt

Heaven's choir came down to sing
when heaven's King came down to save.

One Silent Night

Read Luke 2:1–14

*I bring you good news that will cause great joy
for all the people. Luke 2:10*

Simon had emigrated from the Netherlands to the United States. His wife, Kay, and all three of their children had been born in the US. Then Jenny married Roberto from Panama. Bill married Vania from Portugal. And Lucas married Bora from South Korea.

On Christmas Eve, as the family gathered for a celebration, they began singing "Silent Night" in their native tongues—a sweet sound indeed for the Lord of the earth to hear as they celebrated the birth of His Son.

Two thousand years ago, the silence of a quiet night ended abruptly when an angel told the shepherds a baby had been born: "I bring you good news that will cause great joy for all the people" (Luke 2:10). Then a multitude of angels began praising God, saying, "Glory to God in the highest heaven, and on earth peace to those on whom his favor rests!" (v. 14). Christ the Lord, the Savior of the world, was born!

God's gracious gift, His Son, which was announced on that long-ago silent night, is still available to everyone—"every tribe and language and people and nation" (Revelation 5:9–10). "For God so loved the world that he gave one and only Son, that whoever believes in him shall not perish but have eternal life" (John 3:16).

Cindy Kasper

God broke into human history through Jesus
to break the power of sin.

Beginning Again

Read Ezra 1:1–11

Everyone whose heart God had moved—prepared to go up and build the house of the LORD in Jerusalem. *Ezra 1:5*

After Christmas festivities conclude at the end of December, my thoughts often turn to the coming year. While my children are out of school and our daily rhythms are slow, I reflect on where the last year has brought me and where I hope the next will take me. Those reflections sometimes come with pain and regret over the mistakes I've made. Yet the prospect of starting a new year fills me with hope and expectancy. I feel I have the opportunity to begin again with a fresh start, no matter what the last year held.

My anticipation of a fresh start pales in comparison to the sense of hope the Israelites must have felt when Cyrus, the king of Persia, released them to return to their homeland in Judah after seventy long years of captivity in Babylon. The previous king, Nebuchadnezzar, had deported the Israelites from their homeland. But the Lord prompted Cyrus to send the captives home to Jerusalem to rebuild God's temple (Ezra 1:2–3). Cyrus also returned to them treasures that had been taken from the temple. Their lives as God's chosen people, in the land God had appointed to them, began afresh after a long season of hardship in Babylon as a consequence for their sin.

No matter what lies in our past, when we confess our sin, God forgives us and gives us a fresh start. What great cause for hope!

Kristen Holmberg

God's grace offers us fresh starts.

Crowned with Glory

Read Psalm 8

What is man that You are mindful of him? Psalm 8:4 (NKJV)

The Voyager 1 Spacecraft, which was launched in 1977, is on the outer edge of our solar system more than fourteen billion miles away from Earth. In February 1990, when Voyager 1 was almost four billion miles from us, scientists turned its camera toward Earth and took some pictures that revealed our planet as an almost imperceptible blue dot on a vast sea of empty space.

In the immense reaches of our universe, Earth is just a minuscule speck. On this seemingly insignificant pebble in the ocean of galactic objects live more than seven billion people.

If this makes you feel insignificant, God has some good news. Tucked into one of David's psalms is a rhetorical question that can allow you to step out into the night air, look up at the sky, and rejoice. Psalm 8:3–5 tells us that we are superstars in God's eyes: "When I consider Your heavens, the work of Your fingers, . . . what is man that You are mindful of him? . . . You have crowned him with glory and honor" (NKJV). Soak that in! God—who spoke into existence a universe so vast that the Hubble telescope hasn't found the end of it—created you, and He cares deeply for you. He cared enough to ask Jesus to leave heaven to die for you.

Look up in wonder at God's creation and praise Him that He crowned you with glory through His Son Jesus.

Dave Branon

We see the power of God's creation;
we feel the power of His love.

Equal Access

Read Psalm 145:14–21

*Let us then approach God's throne of grace with
confidence, so that we may receive mercy and find grace
to help us in our time of need.* Hebrews 4:16

Pastor Stuart Silvester told me of a conversation he had with an acquaintance who frequently flew his small private plane in and out of Toronto Pearson International Airport. He asked the pilot if he ever encountered problems taking off and landing a small craft at an airport that was dominated by so many large jets. His friend responded, "My plane may be small, but I have the same rights, the same privileges, and the same access to that airport as anyone else—even the jumbo jets!"

Pastor Silvester then made this spiritual application: "It's the same with prayer, with the believer's approach to the throne of grace. No matter who we are or how small we are in comparison with others or how low our station in life, we take a back seat to no one. No one is given priority treatment."

In a world that offers preferential treatment to the wealthy, the famous, and the influential, it's encouraging to know that every child of God has equal access to the Father in heaven. The psalmist said, "The LORD is near to all who call on him, to all who call on him in truth" (Psalm 145:18).

With that assurance, we can "approach God's throne of grace with confidence" in prayer, knowing that our loving God will never turn us away.

Richard DeHaan

Prayer is an open line to heaven.

Increase Our Faith

Read Matthew 11:1–13

The apostles said to the Lord, "Increase our faith!" *Luke 17:5*

Faith is the Christian's life principle. It is a personal, unwavering confidence in God and His Word. To the believer, faith is a shield and a breastplate (Ephesians 6:16; 1 Thessalonians 5:8), enabling us to engage successfully in the "good fight of faith" (1 Timothy 6:12), and sustaining us in our hour of greatest need.

Of all the "fiery darts" of the evil one that fly into the mind of a child of God, the most stinging and damaging is the arrow of doubt. When Adam and Eve questioned the word of the Lord, they lost their place in paradise, and every man and woman since then have suffered because of their unbelief. Although doubt still creates mountains, praise God, faith is able to remove them!

A small boy appeared at a woman's home with a huge basket of soap. When she answered the doorbell, he pleaded, "Please, will you buy some? I am raising $5,000 for our new church."

"But certainly you are not doing it alone, are you?" she inquired.

"Oh, no! God is helping us, and Jerry, my friend, is also taking the other side of the street!" Pleased to see the boy's great faith, the woman smiled and bought several bars.

Exercise the faith you have if you want it to grow; then, resting completely on God's certain word, make the apostle's prayer your daily petition, "Lord, increase [my] faith!"

Henry Bosch

Faith is the only channel through which Divine power can enter
into man and work through him! —Wilson

What's the Best Gift?

Read 2 Chronicles 2:1–10

*The temple I am going to build will be great,
because our God is greater than all other gods.* 2 Chronicles 2:5

My husband recently celebrated a milestone birthday, the kind that ends in a zero. I thought hard about the best way to honor him on this important occasion. I discussed my many ideas with our children to help me home in on the best one. I wanted our celebration to reflect the significance of a new decade and how precious he is to our family. I wanted our gift to be in keeping with the importance of this milestone in his life.

King Solomon wanted to give to God a much greater gift than a "big birthday" would merit. He wished for the temple he built to be worthy of God's presence in it. To secure raw materials, he messaged the king of Tyre. In his letter, he remarked that the temple would be great "because our God is greater than all other gods" (2 Chronicles 2:5). He acknowledged that God's vastness and goodness far exceeded what could ever be built with human hands, yet set about the task anyway out of love and worship.

Our God is indeed greater than all other gods. He has done wondrous things in our lives, prompting our hearts to bring Him a loving and precious offering, regardless of its external value. Solomon knew his gift wouldn't match God's worth, yet joyfully set his offering before Him; we can too.

Kristen Holmberg

The most treasured gift we can give to God is our love.

Times of Completion

Read Acts 14:21–28

They sailed back to Antioch, where they had been committed to the grace of God for the work they had now completed. Acts 14:26

At the end of the year, the burden of uncompleted tasks can weigh us down. Responsibilities at home and work may seem never-ending, and those unfinished today roll into tomorrow. But there are times in our journey of faith when we should pause and celebrate God's faithfulness and the tasks completed.

After the first missionary journey of Paul and Barnabas, "they sailed back to Antioch, where they had been committed to the grace of God for the work they had now completed" (Acts 14:26). While much work remained in sharing the message of Jesus with others, they took time to give thanks for what had been done. "They gathered the church together and reported all that God had done through them and how he had opened a door of faith to the Gentiles" (v. 27).

What has God done through you during the past year? How has He opened the door of faith for someone you know and love? In ways we can't imagine, He is at work through us in tasks that may seem insignificant or incomplete.

When we feel painfully aware of our unfinished tasks in serving the Lord, let's not forget to give thanks for the ways He has worked through us. Rejoicing over what God has done by His grace sets the stage for what is to come!

David McCasland

God is always at work in and through us.

OUR DAILY BREAD WRITERS

JAMES BANKS
Pastor of Peace Church in Durham, North Carolina, Dr. James Banks has written several books for Our Daily Bread Publishing, including *Praying Together* and *Prayers for Prodigals*. His most recent book, co-written with his son Geoff, is titled *Hope Lies Ahead*. James and Cari Banks have two grown children.

JOHN BLASE
An editor for Multnomah Publishers, John has written several books, including *Touching Wonder: Recapturing the Awe of Christmas* and *All Is Grace: A Ragamuffin Memoir*. John's articles first appeared in *Our Daily Bread* in early 2019. He and his wife have three children.

HENRY G. BOSCH (1914–1995)
Henry G. Bosch was the first managing editor of *Our Daily Bread* and one of its first writers. Throughout his life, he battled illness but turned his weaknesses into spiritual encouragement for others through his devotional writing.

DAVE BRANON
An editor with Our Daily Bread Publishing (ODBP), Dave has been writing for *Our Daily Bread* since the 1980s. He earned his master of arts degree in English from Western Michigan University. Dave has written nearly twenty books, including *Beyond the Valley* and *Living the Psalms Life*, both ODBP releases.

ANNE CETAS
After becoming a Christian in her late teens, Anne was introduced to *Our Daily Bread* right away and began reading it. Now she reads it for a living as senior content editor of *Our Daily Bread*. Anne began writing articles for the devotional booklet in 2004. She and her husband, Carl, live in Grand Rapids.

POH FANG CHIA

Like Anne Cetas, Poh Fang trusted Jesus Christ as Savior as a teenager. She is an editor and a part of the Chinese editorial review committee serving in the Our Daily Bread Ministries Singapore office.

BILL CROWDER

A former pastor who is now vice president of ministry content for Our Daily Bread Ministries, Bill travels extensively as a Bible conference teacher, sharing God's truths with fellow believers in Malaysia and Singapore and other places where ODB Ministries has international offices. His Our Daily Bread Publishing books include *Windows on Easter* and *For This He Came*.

LAWRENCE DARMANI

A noted novelist and publisher in Ghana, Lawrence is editor of *Step* magazine and CEO of Step Publishers. He and his family live in Accra, Ghana. His book, *Grief Child*, earned him the Commonwealth Writers' Prize as best first book by a writer in Africa.

DENNIS DEHAAN (1932–2014)

When Henry Bosch retired, Dennis became the second managing editor of *Our Daily Bread*. A former pastor, he loved preaching and teaching the Word of God. Dennis went to be with the Lord in 2014.

MART DEHAAN

The former president of Our Daily Bread Ministries, Mart followed in the footsteps of his grandfather, M. R., and his dad, Richard, in that capacity. Mart, who has long been associated with the TV program *Day of Discovery* as its host and teacher from Israel, is now senior content advisor for Our Daily Bread Ministries.

M. R. DEHAAN (1891–1965)

Dr. M. R. DeHaan founded this ministry in 1938 when his radio program went out over the air in Detroit, Michigan, and eventually Radio Bible Class was begun. He was president of the ministry in 1956 when *Our Daily Bread* was first published.

RICHARD DEHAAN (1923–2002)

Son of the founder of Our Daily Bread Ministries (formerly Radio Bible Class) Dr. M. R. DeHaan, Richard was responsible for the ministry's entrance into television. Under his leadership, *Day of Discovery* television made its debut in 1968. It was on the air continuously until 2015.

XOCHITL DIXON

Xochitl (soh-cheel) equips and encourages readers to embrace God's grace and grow deeper in their personal relationships with Christ and others. Serving as an author, speaker, and blogger at xedixon.com, she enjoys singing, reading, motherhood, and being married to her best friend Dr. W. Alan Dixon Sr., who is a college professor in Wisconsin.

DAVID EGNER

A retired Our Daily Bread Ministries editor and longtime *Our Daily Bread* writer, David was also a college professor during his working career. In fact, he was a writing instructor for both Anne Cetas and Julie Ackerman Link at Cornerstone University.

DENNIS FISHER

For many years, Dennis was senior research editor at Our Daily Bread Ministries—using his theological training to guarantee biblical accuracy. He is also an expert in C. S. Lewis studies. He and his wife, Jan, a former university professor, have retired to Northern California.

VERNON GROUNDS (1914–2010)

A longtime college president (Denver Seminary) and board member for Our Daily Bread Ministries, Vernon's life story was told in the Our Daily Bread Publishing book *Transformed by Love*. Dr. Grounds died in 2010 at the age of 96.

TIM GUSTAFSON

Tim writes for Our Daily Bread and serves as an editor for Discovery Series. As the son of missionaries to Ghana, Tim has an unusual perspective on life in the West. He and his wife, Leisa, are the parents of one daughter and seven sons.

KIRSTEN HOLMBERG

Kirsten has been a part of the *Our Daily Bread* writing team since March 2017. She lives in the northwest part of the United States, and in addition to her writing, she has a ministry of speaking to various church, business, and community groups. She is the author of *Advent with the Word: Approaching Christmas through the Inspired Language of God.*

ARTHUR JACKSON

Having grown up in Kansas City, Arthur returned home after spending nearly three decades in pastoral ministry in Chicago. He began writing for *Our Daily Bread* in 2017. He serves as director of two ministries—one that cares for pastors and one that seeks to plant churches worldwide. He and his wife Shirley have five grandsons.

CINDY HESS KASPER

An editor for the Our Daily Bread Ministries publication *Our Daily Journey* until her retirement in 2018, Cindy began writing for *Our Daily Bread* in 2006. She and her husband, Tom, have three children and seven grandchildren.

ALYSON KIEDA

Most of Alyson's professional career has been wrapped up in editing. She has been an editor at Our Daily Bread Ministries for more than ten years. Her first article in *Our Daily Bread* was published in 2014.

RANDY KILGORE

Randy spent most of his twenty-plus years in business as a senior human resource manager before returning to seminary. Since finishing his master of divinity in 2000, he has served as a writer and workplace chaplain. A collection of those devotionals appears in his Our Daily Bread Publishing book, *Made to Matter: Devotions for Working Christians.* Randy and his wife, Cheryl, and their two children live in Massachusetts.

JULIE ACKERMAN LINK (1950–2015)

A book editor by profession, Julie began writing for *Our Daily Bread* in 2000. Her books *Above All, Love* and *A Heart for God* are available through Our Daily Bread Publishing. Julie lost her long battle with cancer in April 2015.

DAVID MCCASLAND

Living in Colorado, David enjoys the beauty of God's grandeur as displayed in the Rocky Mountains. An accomplished biographer, David has written several books, including the award-winning *Oswald Chambers: Abandoned to God*, and *Eric Liddell: Pure Gold*.

ELISA MORGAN

Elisa has authored over fifteen books on mothering, spiritual formation, and evangelism, including the *NIV Mom's Devotional Bible* and *Hello, Beauty Full: Seeing Yourself as God Sees You*. Her most recent book, *The Prayer Coin*, is available through Our Daily Bread Publishing. For twenty years, Elisa served as CEO of MOPS International. Elisa is married to Evan (long-time senior vice president of global ministry efforts for Our Daily Bread Ministries), and they live in Denver, Colorado.

KEILA OCHOA

In addition to her work with *Our Daily Bread*, Keila assists with Media Associates International, a group that trains writers around the world to write about faith. She and her husband have two children.

REMI OYEDELE

Originally from Nigeria, Remi lives in Central Florida with her husband David. She enjoys writing that appeals to children, and in fact has a master's degree in Writing for Children. Her blog can be found at wordzpread.com.

AMY BOUCHER PYE

Amy is a writer, editor, and speaker. The author of *Finding Myself in Britain: Our Search for Faith, Home, and True Identity*, she runs the Woman Alive book club in the UK and enjoys life with her family in their English vicarage.

PATRICIA RAYBON

A former editor at *The Denver Post*, Patricia has written two award-winning books: *My First White Friend* and *I Told the Mountain to Move*. Patricia still lives in Colorado, and she can be located online at patriciaraybon.com. She and her husband, Dan, have two children and five grandchildren.

DAVID ROPER

David Roper lives in Idaho, where he takes advantage of the natural beauty of his state. He has been writing for *Our Daily Bread* since 2000, and he has published several successful books with Our Daily Bread Publishing, including *Out of the Ordinary* and *Teach Us to Number Our Days*.

JENNIFER BENSON SCHULDT

Chicagoan Jennifer Schuldt writes from the perspective of a mom of a growing family. She has written for *Our Daily Bread* since 2010.

JOE STOWELL

As president of Cornerstone University, Joe has stayed connected to today's young adults in a leadership role. A popular speaker and a former pastor, Joe has written a number of books over the years, including *Strength for the Journey* and *Jesus Nation*.

MARION STROUD (1940–2015)

After a battle with cancer, Marion went to be with her Savior in August 2015. Marion began writing devotional articles for *Our Daily Bread* in 2014. Two of her popular books of prayers, *Dear God, It's Me and It's Urgent* and *It's Just You and Me, Lord* were published by Our Daily Bread Publishing.

HERB VANDER LUGT (1920–2006)

For many years, Herb was senior research editor at Our Daily Bread Ministries, responsible for checking the biblical accuracy of the booklets the ministry published. A World War II veteran, Herb spent several years as a pastor before his ODB tenure began. Herb went to be with his Lord and Savior in 2006.

PAUL VAN GORDER (1921–2009)

A writer for *Our Daily Bread* in the 1980s and 1990s, Paul was a noted pastor and Bible teacher—both in the Atlanta area where he lived and through the *Day of Discovery* TV program. Paul's earthly journey ended in 2009.

SHERIDAN VOYSEY

Sheridan is a writer, speaker, and broadcaster based in Oxford, England. He hosts a radio program in the UK, and his wife Merryn, is a researcher in the Department of Paediatrics in the Medical Sciences Division of the University of Oxford. Sheridan has authored several books including *Resurrection Year*, *Unseen Footprints*, and *Resilient*.

LINDA WASHINGTON

Linda received a BA in English/Writing from Northwestern University in Evanston, Illinois, and an MFA from Vermont College of Fine Arts in Montpelier, Vermont. She has authored or co-authored fiction and nonfiction books for kids, teens, and adults, including *God and Me* and *The Soul of C. S. Lewis*.

MARVIN WILLIAMS

Marvin's first foray into Our Daily Bread Ministries came as a writer for *Our Daily Journey*. In 2007, he penned his first *Our Daily Bread* article. Marvin is senior teaching pastor at a church in Lansing, Michigan. A book of his devotionals, *Radical Generosity*, is available from Our Daily Bread Publishing.

MIKE WITTMER

Mike has a doctorate in systematic theology from Calvin Theological Seminary, and he has been a professor for many years at Grand Rapids Theological Seminary. Among his many books are *Heaven Is a Place on Earth* and *Don't Stop Believing*. He and his wife Julie live in Grand Rapids, Michigan, and are the parents of three.

JOANIE YODER (1934–2004)

For ten years, until her death in 2004, Joanie wrote for *Our Daily Bread*. In addition, she published the book *God Alone* with Our Daily Bread Publishing.

Help us get the word out!

Our Daily Bread Publishing exists to feed the soul with the Word of God.

If you appreciated this book, please let others know.

- Pick up another copy to give as a gift.
- Share a link to the book or mention it on social media.
- Write a review on your blog, on a bookseller's website, or at our own site (odb.org/store).
- Recommend this book for your church, book club, or small group.

Connect with us:

 @ourdailybread

@ourdailybread

 @ourdailybread

Our Daily Bread Publishing
PO Box 3566
Grand Rapids, Michigan 49501 USA

 books@odb.org